XRX BOOKS

BOOK 2: THE PURL STITCH

becoming intuitive

Sally Melville

Contents

Welcome back!

Isn't it a great time to be a knitter! And aren't we having fun?

I started this series 5 years ago, when few were learning to knit and yarn shops were closing. I was pretty lucky that I had a publisher with enough faith to allow me to write something—a learn-to-knit series—that the world didn't seem terribly interested in.

But—oh my goodness—what happened?! Somehow in the last 2 years, knitting became the new yoga, the new black, the new lip gloss, the new pantyhose! We could not have planned or anticipated better timing for *Book 1: The Knit Stitch*. You were learning to knit, and you bought that book in great numbers! (You did in fact and with one great intake of breath, draw the first printing out of stores before we knew what was happening!) I am entirely grateful to you all.

At the same time, I know that the moment of greatest weakness comes right after success. So I knew that expectations would be high for this book and that I needed to be vigilant to not disappoint you.

How to make this book meet your expectations? By continuing to offer what you seem to want: detailed skills, as you need them; pattern for garments you really want to make and wear; meditations on what knitting brings to our lives.

In addition, how to deal with the series became an issue. We didn't want to penalize those who bought *The Knit Stitch* by repeating its skills here. On the other hand, you will need some of those skills to execute the patterns of this book, and we don't expect you to carry both books for every project. What to do? The result is the Skills At-a-Glance section (page 172)—an abbreviated reference to the skills of *The Knit Stitch*. There may be skills you'll have to review at the source, but we hope that most will only require this refresher.

So, how to proceed? By not wasting another moment! Read the next page, and *Go purl, girl!*

In the meantime, if you'd like an understanding of why knitting satisfies, see *The Flow Experience* (page 5). And if you'd like an explanation of why these basic stitches—knit and purl—were divided into two volumes, see page 7. And if you are a guy, please excuse the *Go purl, girl!* reference, but do read *Why Don't More Guys Get This?* (page 89) then get back to me.

How to learn to purl

If you have some experience of knitting, then proceed through the steps that follow.

If you do not know how to knit, I would suggest you *not* learn to purl quite yet. Use *The Knit Stitch,* or some wonderful and willing person, to learn the basics of knitting. You don't necessarily have to have made a garment: you just need some experience of knitting before proceeding through the steps that follow.

1 Look at the photos on the next few pages. These are some of the pieces in this book. Then look through the rest of the book for more. Find something you're excited about making. Check out its difficulty level (in the pattern, under the word EXPERIENCE). If you are just learning to purl, you'll probably want to start with something 'very easy' or 'easy.'

2 Before beginning the piece you want to make, spend some time practicing More Basics (page 10). For this, use an inexpensive, smooth, medium-weight yarn (which will show a suggested gauge of 16–20 sts/4" on the label) and a size 4.5 to 5.5mm/US 7 to 9 circular needle (20–24" long).

3 When you feel reasonably competent, take your pattern to the yarn shop for supplies.

4 If you need it, Ready to Start a Project (page 28) will guide you through this book, your pattern, and your choice of size, yarn, and needles.

5 Each pattern gives a page reference whenever a new skill is required. If a page reference is not given, then the skill is found in either More Basics (page 10) or was taught in *The Knit Stitch* and is shown, by quick reference, in the Skills At-a-Glance section (page 172).

6 If you need it, the Oops! chapter (page 163) offers solutions to the most common mistakes.

40

92

98, 122

72

134

144

94, 98

70

82, 120

70, 116, 124

82

144

78, 92

62, 136

136

82

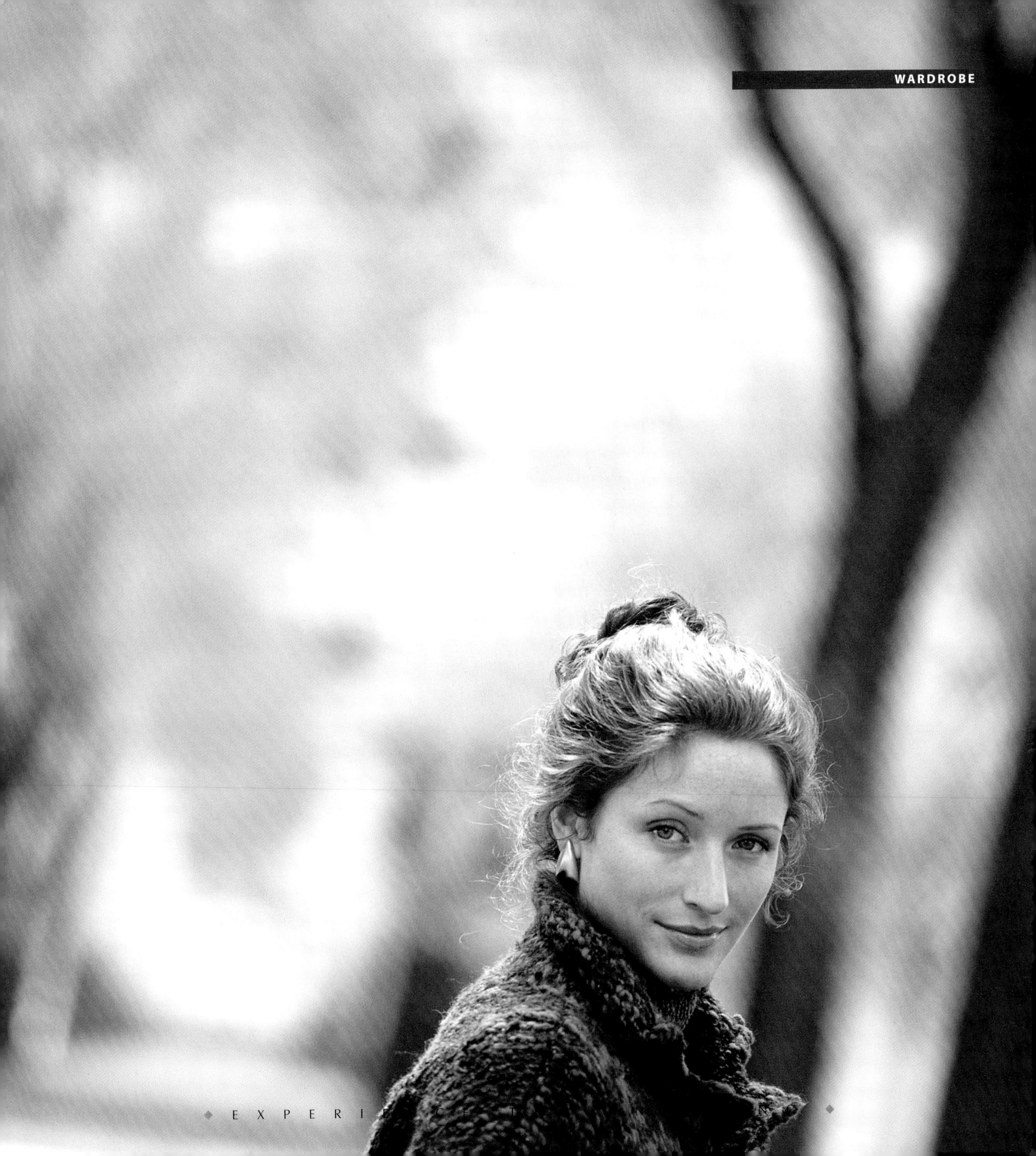

THE FLOW EXPERIENCE

Here's a summary of some amazing work done by a Hungarian-born American psychologist, Mihaly Csikszentmihalyi. It's relevant to how these books were written, to why knitting satisfies, to how we feel about life (both work and play).

Csikszentmihalyi wondered about the quality of experience in everyday life, so he asked people to rate their level of satisfaction with their lives. Most talked about dissatisfaction with their jobs and a wish for more free time to do the things they really wanted to do.

To learn more, he paged his study participants at different times of the week and asked them to rate their level of happiness at that particular time and place. And what would we expect was the lowest point of the week? Monday morning? That's what we'd assume: these people had already said they didn't love their jobs, so we would expect them to be in a less-than-happy state when beginning yet another work week.

But this was not the result he found. In fact, the lowest point in the week was found to be 10 a.m. Sunday morning! Why? Because these people had spent all week looking forward to the weekend, had spent Saturday running errands to allow for a free Sunday, and then on Sunday, had no idea how to use the free time they'd spent all week waiting for!

Csikszentmihalyi's conclusion was that people are satisfied with their lives when they are challenged and when they have skills that meet the challenge. The people he studied were actually more satisfied at work, where they had a job and a skill set with which to do it, than they were at home on Sunday morning.

Their problem with Sunday morning is that they had skills but no idea how to use them, and this caused boredom. At the other extreme were people whose job challenged them beyond their skill set, causing anxiety. But apparently human beings are more unhappy when bored than when anxious.

When are we happiest? Csikszentmihalyi used the word *flow* to describe optimal experience— where skills match challenge. In a low state of flow, with low challenge and low skills, we're happy enough. In a higher state of flow, with high challenge and high skills, we're very, very happy and satisfied with our lives.

How does this translate to knitting? Well, if everyone learned to knit, might we not eradicate Sunday-morning boredom? (I've actually wondered if Csikszentmihalyi had questioned any knitters in his study. Certainly one of the joys of knitting is that we need never be bored.)

How else do his results translate? My purpose is to teach knitting through flow experiences: patterns to knit (challenges) with techniques (skills) to match. It's my plan that over a series of five books, we will all approach a high state of flow. How we doin' so far?

As you work your way through the next chapter and learn how to purl, you'll wonder what the big deal is! There is nothing inherently more difficult about purling, and as Anna Zilboorg says, "It seems to me that purling is nowhere near as hard as trying to avoid it." How, then, did *The Knit Stitch* become a separate volume from *The Purl Stitch*?

What happened 3 years ago is that my original learn-to-knit-*and*-purl book became too large, too cumbersome, too expensive. The natural place to divide was between knit and purl. And once I made that decision, I found the following reasons to support it.

- Garter stitch (the fabric in which most of the pieces in *The Knit Stitch* are made) is a forgiving fabric. Its texture hides the idiosyncrasies that are inevitable in a beginner's work. This is not true of many of the fabrics of this book. Why rush offering less-than-forgiving fabrics?
- The nature of garter stitch—the way it hangs and the ratio of stitches to rows—offers so many design possibilities that before I knew it, I had a whole book devoted to it: to projects knit up from the bottom, down from the top, across from side to side, and in any combination of the above.
- A large part of my mandate was that the projects be things new knitters would really want to knit *and* be proud to wear. This pride would come from attention to detail—choices for casting on or increasing or decreasing, attention to seaming and working in tails. These skills take page space.
- The basic fabric one produces with knit and purl—stockinette stitch—curls at the edges. This demands a whole other set of skills from flat-lying garter stitch—different seams and the addition of an edging to counteract the curl.
- The fabrics one produces with knit and purl require an ability to 'read' your knitting in a way that garter stitch does not: you'll find yourself needing to decide whether to knit or purl the next row or stitch. This will demand that you become a more intuitive knitter, and so the bar for *The Purl Stitch* is set higher, right from the get-go.

I don't expect you to be intimidated by purling. But I do expect that you'll be pretty confident and accomplished and intuitive by the time you've worked through this volume. It's to this that *The Purl Stitch* is dedicated.

More Basic Skills

Knit and purl

The fabrics of knit (and purl) are what we mean when we speak of *stitch patterns*.

Here is some information that will help you understand the basic fabrics of knit (and purl).

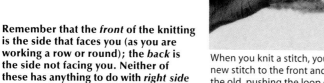 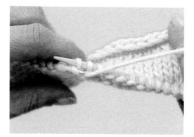

Remember that the *front* of the knitting is the side that faces you (as you are working a row or round); the *back* is the side not facing you. Neither of these has anything to do with *right side* or *wrong side*.

When you knit a stitch, you pull the new stitch to the front and through the old, pushing the loop of the old stitch to the back of the work. This produces a *bump* that sits on the back.

When you purl a stitch, you push the new stitch to the back and through the old, pulling the loop of the old stitch to the front of the work. This brings the bump to the front.

Garter stitch was the predominant fabric of *The Knit Stitch,* and here is what it was about.

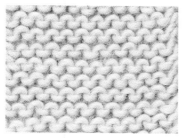

In garter stitch, you knit one row (pushing bumps to the 'wrong side'), then turn and knit another row (pushing bumps to the 'right side'). This produces the evenly textured, ridged fabric of garter stitch.
You could, then, produce garter by purling every row, couldn't you?

The fabrics of *The Purl Stitch* are combinations of knit and purl.

 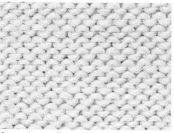  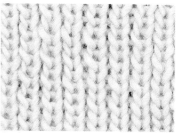

Sometimes all right-side rows are knit and all wrong-side rows are purled, so all bumps are on the wrong side. This is *stockinette stitch*. Its right side is smooth.

Sometimes all wrong-side rows are knit and all right-side rows are purled, so all bumps are on the right side. This is *reverse stockinette stitch*. Its right side is bumpy.

Sometimes rows of knits are combined with rows of purls in other ways. This can produce *the fabric of Chapter 1*.

And sometimes knits and purls are combined in the same row. This could be *ribbing,* introduced in Chapter 4.

Cast-on methods revisited

Here's how I decide which cast-on I prefer.

See Skills At-a-Glance (page 172) for a quick refresher course in these cast-on methods.

I use the *e-wrap cast-on* when a loose cast-on is preferred. I'd use it for a swatch or a scarf or when the cast-on is to be taken into a seam (a rare occurrence).

I use the *cable cast-on* when I want a strong, slightly decorative edge. (I particularly like this cast-on for ribbing, a stitch pattern you will learn in Chapter 4.)

There are many ways to cast on. (Even in *The Knit Stitch*—written for those who have never held yarn and needles—five methods for casting on were shown!) As you become a more experienced knitter, you'll have your own opinions about which cast-on method works best in which situation. So, in this book, you will not be told which cast-on to use unless I think there's a method that is particularly suited to the circumstance.

I use the *crochet cast-on* when I want the cast-on to match the bind-off. (This isn't something I care about very often, mostly just when the garment is knit sideways, and the front edges— one cast-on and one bound-off—are clearly visible together.)

I use the *long-tail cast-on* when working circularly. On the wrong side, it looks like a row of purl bumps. If you turn after the cast-on and immediately work a right-side row, the result will look like this (above). If you turn after the cast-on and work a wrong-side row, the result will look more like a tight version of the *e-wrap*.

Right- and Left-handedness

I think this subject is important enough to repeat what was said in *The Knit Stitch*.
- Knitting is a two-handed activity.
- Either hand may hold the yarn (regardless of handedness), but one hand will do more of the work than the other (depending upon handedness).
- In what follows, stitches move from the left-hand needle onto the right-hand needle.

It is a common mistake to call knitting with the yarn in the left hand 'left-handed' knitting. Holding the yarn in the left hand is a practice that has nothing whatsoever to do with handedness: many lefties knit this way, but so do righties.

Real 'left-handed' knitting is best described as knitting mirror-image (with stitches moving from the right needle to the left) or knitting 'backwards.' I don't recommend starting off one's knitting experience this way, but if, over time, this is how your hands want to move, then let them do so.

It is not uncommon for knitters—beginner or not and regardless of which hand holds the yarn—to purl more loosely than they knit. In a smooth stitch pattern (like stockinette stitch) or a yarn without much elasticity (like cotton), rows of loose purl stitches will produce an uneven fabric. A solution to this uneven fabric is to wrap the yarn more tightly on purl rows. A more limiting solution is to work purl rows on a smaller needle.

The purl stitch *p st*

The *purl stitch* is formed by taking yarn around the right-hand needle and drawing it through a stitch on the left-hand needle, in the manner shown over the next few pages.

THE RIGHT-HAND CARRY

You'll find that purling with the yarn in the right hand is *really* no more difficult than knitting. And while these photos show the over-the-top hold and the yarn threaded around the right pinkie and index, the purl stitch is formed in the same manner and just as easily, no matter how your manage your yarn or hold your needles.

With some number of stitches already cast on,

1 with yarn in front, put right-hand needle through first stitch on left-hand needle so right-hand needle sits in front of left-hand needle.

2 Hold both needles with left hand.

3 With right hand, wrap yarn over top and behind right-hand needle . . .

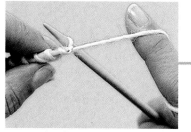

7 Push right-hand needle off end of left-hand needle so new stitch is on right-hand needle only.

8 Repeat Steps 1–7 until all stitches are on right-hand needle.

9 To begin next row, turn work . . . and transfer needle with stitches back into left hand.

Oops, I dropped a stitch. What do I do now? See page 164.

Oops, I knit when I should have purled (or vice versa). What do I do now? See page 166.

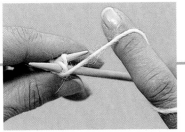

4 ... then snug between two needles.

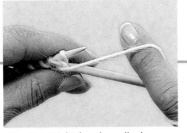

5 Draw right-hand needle down ...

6 ... then take right-hand needle from in front of left-hand needle to behind left-hand needle.

You will find yourself binding off in knit more often than binding off in purl. See Skills At-a-Glance page 175.

This bind-off is shown using right-hand carry, but the maneuvers are the same for left-hand carry.

A bind-off row can often be too tight. To remedy this, bind off using a larger needle.

Oops, I have an ugly loop at the end of my bind-off. What do I do now? See page 165.

Oops, my bind-off row is too loose. What do I do now? See page 175.

Binding off in purl

Patterns will tell you to "bind off in stitch pattern." If you are working in stockinette stitch, and you are on a purl row, you should bind off in purl. Here's how I do it.

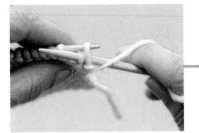

1 Purl 2 stitches as usual. Insert left-hand needle into back of first stitch on right-hand needle.

2 Pass first stitch on right-hand needle over second stitch on right-hand needle.

3 Purl next stitch. Repeat Steps 1–3 to end of row, finishing bind-off by drawing tail through final stitch.

A wrong-side row bound-off in purl looks no different than a right-side row bound-off in knit.

THE LEFT-HAND CARRY

Some find purling with the yarn in the left hand slightly more difficult than knitting with the yarn in the left hand.

I show three common ways to purl for left-hand carry: on these two pages, the yarn is threaded through the pinkie and index finger with Steps 3–6 shown two ways (see 3a–6a or 3b–6b); on the next two pages, the yarn is wrapped around the neck (which isn't exactly left-hand *carry*, but don't tell).

3a With left index finger . . .

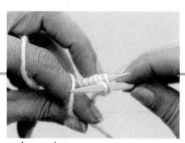
push yarn down . . .

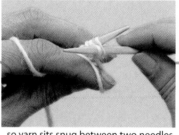
. . . so yarn sits snug between two needles.

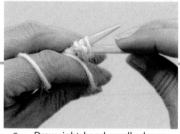
4a Draw right-hand needle down . . .

OR

3b Swing right-hand needle to right, then behind yarn.

For left-hand carry, you may find it easier to wrap the yarn the opposite way—by first taking the yarn under and then over the right-hand needle and then pushing the stitch through. But if you do this, your stitch will be backwards; to straighten it, you must work through the back of it in the next row or your stitch will be twisted (see Orientation of a Stitch, page 164). And then, you need to be able to 'read' your knitting and work decreases so as to not twist your stitches. But, if you can do all this, you'll be a wonderfully intuitive knitter.

Oops, I dropped a stitch. What do I do now? See page 164.

Oops, I knit when I should have purled (or vice versa). What do I do now? See page 166.

PURLING WITH YARN IN LEFT HAND

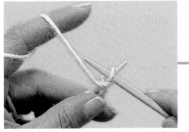

1 With some number of stitches already cast on, with yarn in front, put right-hand needle through first stitch on left-hand needle so right-hand needle sits in front of left-hand needle.

2 With left index finger, lift yarn to front of right-hand needle. Now proceed with either 3a–6a or 3b–6b.

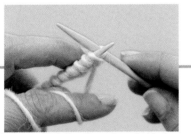

5a . . . then take right-hand needle from in front of left-hand needle to behind left-hand needle.

6a Push right-hand needle off end of left-hand needle so new stitch is on right-hand needle only.

4b Pivot right-hand needle . . .

5b . . . to push stitch towards back . . .

6b . . . and then off left-hand needle.

7 Repeat Steps 1–6a or 1–6b until all stitches are on right-hand needle.

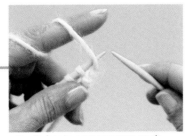

8 To begin next row, turn work . . . and transfer needle with stitches back into left hand.

I first learned the around-the-neck purl from the folks of the Rochester, NY, knitting guild. It was taught to me as the *Portuguese purl*, but since people all over the world (Portugal, Greece, South America, the US, and Canada!) use it, a geographical designation is not the best way to describe it.

This method of purling is so efficient that some use it for circular work, only purling, never knitting. (This would mean that they are working 'inside-out,' wouldn't it?)

You might not prefer it when working flat (when the next row is a knit row and you have to remove the yarn from around your neck) or when combining knits and purls (although I do show—in Chapter 4—how to combine knits and purls in the same row).

PURLING WITH YARN AROUND NECK

This method is a little unusual, so do read the margin note (left) to understand its constraints.

For this to work, the yarn has to sit on the floor and have enough weight that gravity can exert sufficient tension on it. (I tell students to put a foot on their yarn if they need more tension.) And you'll probably want to wear something with a collar, to prevent 'rug burn.'

With some number of stitches cast on,

1 take yarn over left shoulder, behind neck, then down in front of right shoulder. Put remainder of yarn on floor (see photo to right).

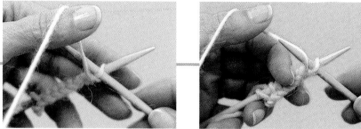

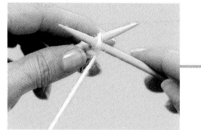

2 Without holding yarn in left hand, put right-hand needle through first stitch on left-hand needle so right-hand needle sits in front of left-hand needle.

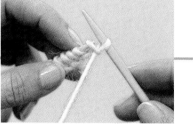

3 With left thumb, lift yarn above and then behind right-hand needle. Pivot right-hand needle (to right and then back) to catch yarn, but do not 'overwork' this by wrapping the yarn with the thumb: just lift it so it will catch behind the right-hand needle.

6 . . . then take right-hand needle from in front of left-hand needle to behind left-hand needle.

7 Push right-hand needle off end of left-hand needle so new stitch is on right-hand needle only.

PURLING WITH YARN AROUND NECK

PHOTO COURTESY OF CYNTHIA LECOUNT SAMAKÉ

Knitters in Chayhuatiri, Peru, make colorful stockinette stitch caps by purling with the yarn tensioned around their necks.

4 Remove left thumb; yarn sits snug between two needles.

5 Draw right-hand needle down . . .

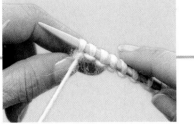

8 Repeat Steps 2–7 until all stitches are on right-hand needle.

9 To begin next row, turn work and transfer needle with stitches back into left hand.

Oops, I knit when I should have purled. What do I do now? See page 166.

Oops, my stockinette stitch garment is too long (or too short). What do I do now? See pages 168–169.

Stockinette stitch *St st*

Stockinette stitch is the smooth fabric we most often associate with knitting. It is produced by knitting all stitches in rounds, or by knitting right-side rows and purling wrong-side rows when working back and forth (also known as working flat).

When you only knew how to knit (in *The Knit Stitch*), your standard fabric was garter stitch. Now that you know how to purl, stockinette stitch becomes your standard fabric. In *The Purl Stitch*, you will measure gauge over stockinette stitch, and we will demonstrate techniques in stockinette stitch.

Measuring gauge

In *The Knit Stitch*, gauge was shown over garter stitches and ridges. But once we start combining knits and purls (as most knitting does), the rules change.

Gauge on a ball band refers to gauge over stockinette stitch. Gauge in a pattern might be over stockinette stitch or over the stitch pattern of the project. (You will be told over what stitch pattern to measure gauge.)

To accurately check your gauge, it's important to be able to recognize stitches and rows in stitch patterns other than garter stitch (especially over the common standard, stockinette stitch).

Here is a garter stitch swatch (produced by knitting all stitches, all rows). The swatch is 12 stitches wide and 12 garter ridges (24 rows) tall.

Here is a swatch in the stitch pattern in Chapter 1 (produced by knitting 5 rows then purling 1 row). This swatch is 12 stitches wide and 18 rows tall.

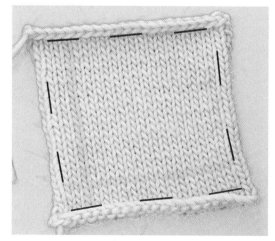

Here is a swatch of stockinette stitch (produced by knitting right-side rows and purling wrong-side rows). The swatch is actually 22 stitches wide and 28 rows tall, but the side edges are obscured because they curl around to the back. To work a gauge swatch in stockinette stitch, always cast on more stitches and knit more rows than suggested by the gauge so you can measure over a flat, non-curling section of the swatch. (It can help to insert a pin at the beginning and end of 4" so you are not trying to hold the tape measure and count at the same time.)
To recognize a stitch, look for a V; to recognize a row, look for a single line of stitches (above). Gauge here is 18 stitches and 24 rows over 4".

Selvedge stitches

The stitches at the side edges of your garment are called *selvedge stitches.* In garter stitch, they were no different from other stitches; but in stockinette stitch, they curl around to the wrong side, they have knots, and they are unattractive—no matter how neat a knitter you are.

We don't want these unattractive selvedge stitches on the right side of our finished pieces. They should be taken into seam allowances. (How to execute these seams follows.)

What is important to know is that, because one stitch is taken from the edge of each piece into a seam allowance, we offer garment measurements as follows:

- the schematics show the measurements as the piece is knit, so they include the selvedge stitches;
- if there is no band shown in a schematic, then that band is not included in that schematic measurement;
- the finished (A, B, C) measurements are after seaming and finishing, so they do not include selvedge stitches (which have been taken into the seam allowances), but they do include any bands.

The edge (selvedge) stitches in stockinette stitch have little knots every two rows. This can help when counting rows; count by twos as you work your way up these little knots.

It may seem surprising, but to make the neatest possible seams, increases and decreases are never worked into these selvedge stitches but always further into the body of the work. (This is called *maintaining the integrity of the selvedge stitch.*)

Cast-on and bind-off edges don't usually demand as much attention as selvedge stitches, but they do follow the same rules. If they are taken into seam allowances, then they are included in schematics but not in final measurements. If they are not taken into seam allowances, then they are included in all measurements.

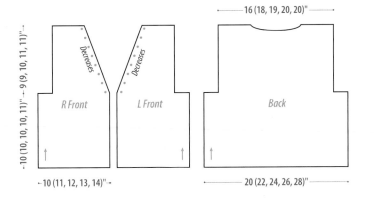

16 (18, 19, 20, 20)"

10 (10, 10, 10, 11)" → 9 (9, 10, 11, 11)"

Decreases

Decreases

R Front

L Front

Back

10 (11, 12, 13, 14)"

20 (22, 24, 26, 28)"

C

B | A

OVERSIZED FIT

S (M, L, 1X, 2X)
A 40 (44, 48, 52, 56)"
B 19 (19, 20, 21, 22)"
C 29 (29½, 30, 30½, 31)"

Working a decrease on a knit row

There are three common ways to decrease on the knit side of stockinette stitch.

If you can't remember how to work a k2tog or SKP, see Skills At-a-Glance, pages 174–175.

KNIT 2 TOGETHER *k2tog*
The first decrease shown in *The Knit Stitch* was knit 2 together (k2tog). It produces a **right-slanting decrease**, visible on the left edge of this stockinette stitch swatch.

SLIP 1, KNIT 1, PASS SLIP STITCH OVER *SKP*
The second decrease shown in *The Knit Stitch* was slip 1, knit 1, pass slip stitch over (SKP). It produces a **left-slanting decrease**, visible on the right edge of this stockinette stitch swatch.

The decreases shown are worked inside the selvedge stitches. To make neat seams, never decrease in them. This is called *maintaining the integrity of the selvedge stitch.*

SLIP 1, SLIP 1, KNIT 2 TOGETHER *SSK*
A third decrease, shown below, also produces a **left-slanting decrease** and can be used instead of SKP.

Here is the result of a series of right-slanting decreases (at left edge of piece) and a series of left-slanting decreases (at right edge of piece).

1 Slip 1 stitch knit-wise from left-hand needle onto right.

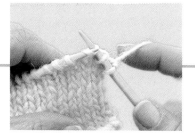

2 Slip the next stitch from left-hand needle onto right, also knit-wise.

3 Put left-hand needle through both slipped stitches in front of right-hand needle.

An SSK, a left-slanting decrease.

4 Knit the 2 stitches together.

HOW DO YOU KNOW HOW LONG AGO YOU WORKED A DECREASE?
Here's how you can look at your work to see when you last worked a decrease.

Presuming you worked your decrease with the right side facing, do all of what follows with the right side facing.

1 Find the single stitch that was formed by working 2 together on the decrease row; call it row 1.

2 Count it and all rows above it, including the row on the needle. This tells you how many rows ago you worked the decrease. Here the count is 4, so the decrease was worked 4 rows ago. If you are to decrease every 6th row, then you have to work 2 more rows before decreasing.

Reverse shaping / in reverse

When a pattern has both a right and left front, you might see full directions for one front but only minimal directions for the second front, with instruction to work the second as the first but with *reverse shaping*. Or you might see full directions for the button band with instruction to work the buttonhole band *in reverse*. Why is this done? To save page space. What does it mean? That requires more explanation.

REVERSE SHAPING OVER A BOUND-OFF EDGE

At the underarm of a garment, we might bind off stitches. For the left front, you are directed to bind off at the beginning of a right-side row. So, reverse shaping would mean that for the right front, you will bind off at the beginning of a wrong-side row.

For round neck shaping, we bind off a succession of stitches. For the left front, you will bind off at the beginnings of wrong-side rows. So, reverse shaping would mean that for the right, front, you will bind off at the beginnings of right-side rows.

And, for shoulder shaping, we also bind off a succession of stitches. For the left front, you will bind off at the beginnings of right-side rows. So, reverse shaping would mean that for the right front, you will bind off at the beginnings of wrong-side rows.

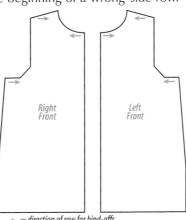

Right Front · Left Front

→ = direction of row for bind-offs

Here are the rules for reversing shaping over a bound-off edge anywhere but the final row of a piece:

- whatever was done on a right-side row should now be done on a wrong-side row;
- whatever was done on a wrong-side row should now be done on a right-side row;
- shaping that was started on a wrong-side row should now be started on a right-side row and continued over right-side rows;
- shaping that was started on a right-side row should now be started on a wrong-side row and continued over wrong-side rows.

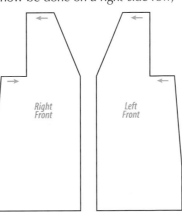

Right Front · Left Front

Here is the one exception where you will not use reverse shaping over a bound-off edge in the final row of a piece:

- if the first piece ended with many stitches bound off on a right-side row (for example, *across an entire unshaped shoulder), then bind off the 2nd piece on a right side row also.*

Directions to work *reverse shaping* have been used in this book so we didn't have to cut patterns that I very much wanted to offer. It truly kept me awake at nights, agonizing over what needed to be cut in order to keep the number of pages—and price—reasonable. The addition of reverse shaping was a solution and a relief.

But there's more to it than that. Once you understand reverse shaping, you'll be a more intuitive knitter . . . which really is the point to this book. Besides, this instruction is how the knitting world presents patterns, so—once you understand it—you'll be able to knit patterns in other wonderful publications and by other talented designers!

It might help you understand this material if you see the following: while you may bind off at the beginnings of rows, you will not bind off at the ends of rows.

It's the getting started that demands attention. Once you get that right, it should be easy enough to see what you are doing and why.

Since almost all decreasing is done with the right side facing, this is how I discuss it here. But decreases are sometimes done on wrong-side rows with purl 2 together (p2tog, a left-slanting decrease, page 110) or with slip 1, slip 1, purl 2 together (SSP, a right-slanting decrease, page 110). If the first piece had wrong-side decreases, then work the second piece with wrong-side decreases.

It's important to understand the concept of right- or left-slanting decreases. Getting this right—something we help you with in the pattern directions—is the kind of attention to detail that will make your finished product something to be proud of.

REVERSE SHAPING OVER SHORT-ROW SHAPING

Short-row shaping requires leaving stitches behind at the end of a row. So, it's the mirror image of shaping over a bound-off edge, and the same rules apply.

REVERSE SHAPING OVER AN EDGE WITH DECREASES

Reverse shaping over decreases is easier than reverse shaping over bind-offs because you will work with the same side of the fabric facing. In other words, if the first piece had decreases worked with the right side facing, then you'll do the second piece with the right side facing. To do this, you need to understand the following.

At the *right edge of a garment piece* (the A-line shaping of the left front, the armhole shaping of the left front, the V-neck shaping of the right front), the decrease will usually involve the following:

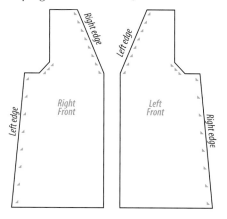

- the selvedge stitch(es), followed by a left-slanting decrease (SSK or SKP), followed by the row worked in stitch pattern.

At the *left edge of a garment piece* (the A-line shaping of the right front, the armhole shaping of the right front, the V-neck shaping of the left front), the decrease will usually involve the following:

- the row worked in stitch pattern to 2 stitches before the selvedge stitch(es), followed by a right-slanting decrease (k2tog), followed by the selvedge stitch(es).

To **reverse shaping over an edge with decreases**, work as follows:

1 determine whether or not your decrease is at the right or left edge of the garment,
2 this will tell you if it should be right-slanting or left-slanting,
3 work the decrease as directed above.

REVERSE SHAPING OVER POCKETS

Pockets are not usually placed in the center of a garment front; they are usually positioned closer to the side seam. To place them appropriately, with the left front in mirror image to the right, work as follows.

To **reverse shaping for pockets**, work the second piece's set-up row as follows:
- first work the number of stitches that was at the end of the row for the previous piece;
- then do what is instructed for the pocket stitches;
- then end with the number of stitches that was at the beginning of the row for the previous piece.

REVERSE SHAPING OVER BANDS

We always want to work the first row of bands with the right side facing. So, a woman's button band will begin at the upper left front (or at the center back neck for a V-neck), and the buttonhole band will begin at the lower right front.

To **work a band in reverse order**, do the following:
- start as you ended the previous band;
- end as you began the previous band.

Right Front   *Left Front*

6 _12_ 12   12 _12_ 6

 # = stitch count

Right Front   *Left Front*

↑ *= direction of pick-up and knit row*

Pockets are almost always set up on right-side rows, so this is how they are discussed here.

In what follows, the seam allowance takes a full stitch from each piece. This is how you should usually work these seams. But sometimes, when the fabric is bulky or the stitch pattern doesn't curl much, you need only take half a stitch into the seam allowance. When I indicate this in a pattern, just work as follows but a half stitch closer to the edge. (This half-stitch seam is shown in rib, page 109.)

Seaming in stockinette stitch

ROWS-TO-ROWS

Unlike the instructions for garter stitch, this stockinette stitch seam will produce a seam allowance. But because stockinette stitch curls to the wrong side along the sides, the selvedge stitches actually *want* to turn into the seam allowance!

Do all of this with right side facing.
1 Take tapestry needle under cast-on edge of first piece.

2 Take tapestry needle under cast-on edge of second piece.

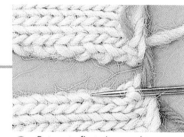

3 Return to first piece and to space you came out of. Take needle down, from front to back, between selvedge stitch and next stitch, then bring needle up, 1 row later (1 bar on needle).

4 Return to second piece and to space you came out of. Take needle down, from front to back, between selvedge stitch and next stitch. Bring needle up 2 rows later (2 bars on needle).

These seams will look virtually invisible as long as you maintain the same vertical between the selvedge stitch and the next stitch. Deviating from this line will ruin your seam.

To close circular knitting at the cast-on edge, work as Steps 1–2. To close circular knitting at the bound-off edge, work as Steps 6–8.

5 Return to opposite piece, take needle down into space you came out of, and come up 2 rows later. Repeat Step 5.

Some rows sewn, before pulling taut.

Some rows sewn, after pulling taut.

In chapter 3, you will seam a reverse stockinette edging before seaming a stockinette stitch piece. Sew the reverse stockinette with the bumpy (right) side facing but otherwise just as shown here in stockinette stitch.

6 At end of piece, close seam by taking needle into final bound-off stitch . . .

7 . . . then under first bound-off stitch of opposite piece . . .

I find it easiest to work all seams from right to left (as shown). If you are left-handed, rotate these pages 180° (upside down), and work from left to right.

Because of the pronounced curl of stockinette stitch, you might choose to block before seaming.

STITCHES-TO-STITCHES

1 Do all of this with right side facing.
On edge of one piece to be seamed, take tapestry needle under first stitch, below bound-off edge.

2 Go across to second piece. Take tapestry needle under first stitch, above bound-off edge.

3 Return to opposite piece. Take tapestry needle into space you came out of and under next stitch (above).
Repeat Step 3 until all stitches are seamed.

4 stitches from each side sewn, before pulling taut.

10 stitches from each side sewn, after pulling taut.

For clarity, seaming demonstrations are shown with contrasting-color yarn. But because seams are not visible from the right side, actual seams may be worked in contrasting-color yarn.

As you seam, pull your sewing yarn taut—just to resistance and not so you pucker your seam—every inch or so. It can help to turn the curl of the bind-off edge into the seam allowance as you go.

8 . . . and back into space you came out of.

Here is the closed seam.

ROWS-TO-STITCHES / THE MATH

In stockinette stitch, this seaming is made more challenging because the ratio of rows to stitches is never the 1-to-1 that was shown for seaming stitches to stitches or rows to rows. (See drawing opposite.)

So, whenever sewing rows to stitches, you will first have to 'do the math.'
- Count the number of rows to be seamed.
- Count the number of stitches to be seamed.
- Divide the smaller number (the stitches) by the larger number (the rows).
- You will get a decimal that represents a fraction, something less than 1. (If the result is greater than 1, you've done something wrong: go back and redo the last step.)
- Go to the Table of Comparative Ratios (page 170, section shown to right), and find the fraction closest to your result. The table gives all the practical information you need for how to sew your rows to stitches.

ROWS-TO-STITCHES / THE SEAMING

After you've done the math, you may do the seaming. (In the example that follows, I assume a ratio of .67 = 2 sts for 3 rows = 1 st / 1 row then 1 st / 2 rows.)

In garter stitch, there is a 1-to-1 relation of stitches to ridges. That's what makes it so much fun to knit in many directions. But that lovely ratio disappears in knitting's more common fabric, stockinette stitch.

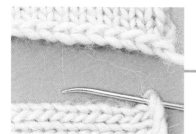

1 Do all of this with right side facing. Take tapestry needle under cast-on edge of first piece.

2 Take tapestry needle under first stitch at edge of second piece.

3 Return to first piece and to space you came out of. Take needle down, from front to back, between selvedge stitch and next stitch.

4 Bring needle up to front, 1 row later (1 bar on needle).

SEAMING ROWS-TO-STITCHES

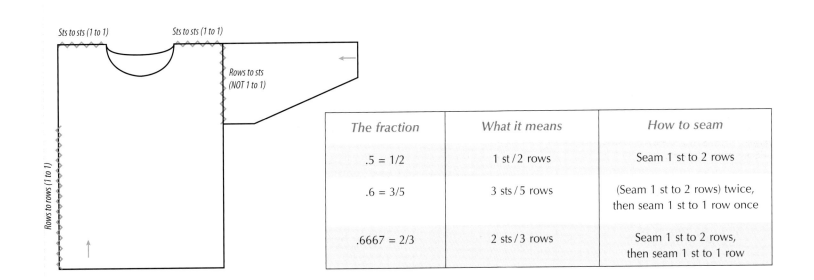

The fraction	What it means	How to seam
.5 = 1/2	1 st / 2 rows	Seam 1 st to 2 rows
.6 = 3/5	3 sts / 5 rows	(Seam 1 st to 2 rows) twice, then seam 1 st to 1 row once
.6667 = 2/3	2 sts / 3 rows	Seam 1 st to 2 rows, then seam 1 st to 1 row

5 Return to second piece and to space you came out of. Take needle down, under next stitch.

6 Return to first piece, and take needle down into space you came out of . . .

7 . . . then come up 2 rows later.

8 Return to second piece and to space you came out of. Take needle down, under next stitch. Repeat Steps 3–8.

9 At end of piece, close seam by taking needle into final bound-off stitch . . .

10 . . . then under first bound-off stitch of opposite piece . . .

11 . . . and back into space you came out of. (See Steps 6-8, pages 22–23.)

Some rows sewn, before pulling taut.

Some rows sewn, after pulling taut.

Sewing a drop shoulder

To prepare for this rows-to-stitches seam, read *Rows-to-stitches / the math* (page 24), and apply the following.

- The number of stitches is half the stitches in the upper sleeve.
- The number of rows to be seamed is found as follows: fold the sleeve in half, and match the fold line to the shoulder seam; lay the sleeve against the side of the garment to find the point to which the sleeve extends down the body of the garment; put a pin at that point on the body; count the number of rows between the shoulder seam and the pin.
- Do the last 3 steps in 'the math' section.

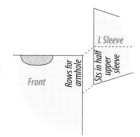

To sew this seam, read *Rows-to-stitches / the seaming,* and work as follows.

- Match the shoulder seam to the mid-point of the sleeve.
- Leaving half the sewing thread behind, seam down one side, in the ratio directed by the Table (page 170).
- Return to the shoulder seam, and sew down the other side, in the same manner.

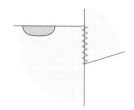

Sewing a modified drop shoulder

This seam is a rows-to-stitches seam that turns a corner at the underarm. To prepare for this seam, read *Rows-to-stitches / the math* (page 24), and apply the following.

- The number of stitches is half the stitches in the upper sleeve.
- The number of rows to be seamed is the number of rows from the underarm bind-off to the shoulder seam.
- Do the last 3 steps in 'the math' section.

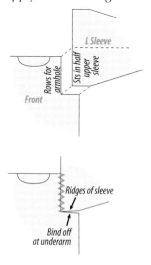

To sew this seam, read *Rows-to-stitches / the seaming,* and work as follows.

- Match the shoulder seam to the mid-point of the sleeve.
- Leaving half the sewing thread behind, seam down one side, in the ratio directed by the Table (page 170).
- Turn the corner, and in the same ratio, seam the bound-off stitches at the underarm to rows of the sleeve. Stop at the end of the bound-off stitches.
- Return to the shoulder seam, and sew down the other side, in the same manner.

Sewing a set-in sleeve

This seam is a combination of stitches-to-stitches, rows-to-rows, then rows-to-stitches. Here's how it's done for the left sleeve and after sewing the front and back together at the shoulder.

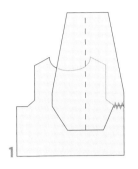

- Begin at the underarm. Sew bound-off stitches of left sleeve to bound-off stitches of left front at underarm (drawing 1).
- Sew rows of left sleeve to rows of left front up to sleeve cap (drawing 2).
- Count number of stitches in half-sleeve cap.
- Count number of rows remaining on left front to shoulder seam (drawing 3).
- Do the last 3 steps in *Rows-to-stitches / the math* (page 24).
- Sew stitches of sleeve cap to remaining rows of left front up to shoulder seam as directed by the Table (drawing 4).
- In same manner, sew remaining stitches of sleeve cap down rows of left back to end of sleeve cap.
- Sew rows of left sleeve to rows of left back from sleeve cap down to bound-off sts.
- Sew bound-off stitches of left sleeve to bound-off stitches of left back at underarm.

1

2

Remaining arm rows / Sts in 1/2 sleeve cap

3

4

Sewing a raglan sleeve

This seam is mostly rows-to-rows; sometimes there are a few bound-off stitches at the underarms, so it might also be stitches-to-stitches. Both are almost always a 1-to-1 ratio, so this is the easiest of all sleeve shapings to sew.

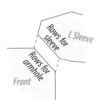

Rows for sleeve
L Sleeve
Rows for armhole
Front

- Begin at underarm and, if there are any, sew bound-off stitches of left sleeve to bound-off stitches of left front.
- Count rows of sleeve, then count rows of left front.
- Usually, these numbers will be the same. If so, sew rows of right sleeve to left front in a 1-to-1 ratio.
- Sometimes there might be just 2–4 more rows in one piece than in the other. If this is the case, sew rows of left sleeve to left front easing in extra rows as you go.
- Return to underarm, and sew left sleeve to back in same manner.

The story about
this pattern

Notes
(to elaborate a point,
to coach you through
a process, to alert you
to an issue)

The vitals
(see facing page)

The pattern instructions

The first time an abbreviation is used in
a pattern, it will appear like this: knit (k).

For a quick reference to terms and
abbreviations, see the Glossary, pages 176.

The first time a new skill is used in
a pattern, it will appear like this:
how to read a chart, page 149

If no page reference is given, the skill
appears in More Basics (pages 6–27) or
in Skills At-a-Glance (pages 172–175).

Additional skills
New skills are
found at the end of
each chapter

Fixing mistakes
Common mistakes are anticipated:
the remedies are in the Oops! chapter,
pages 163–169. As you knit a pattern,
check 'em out.

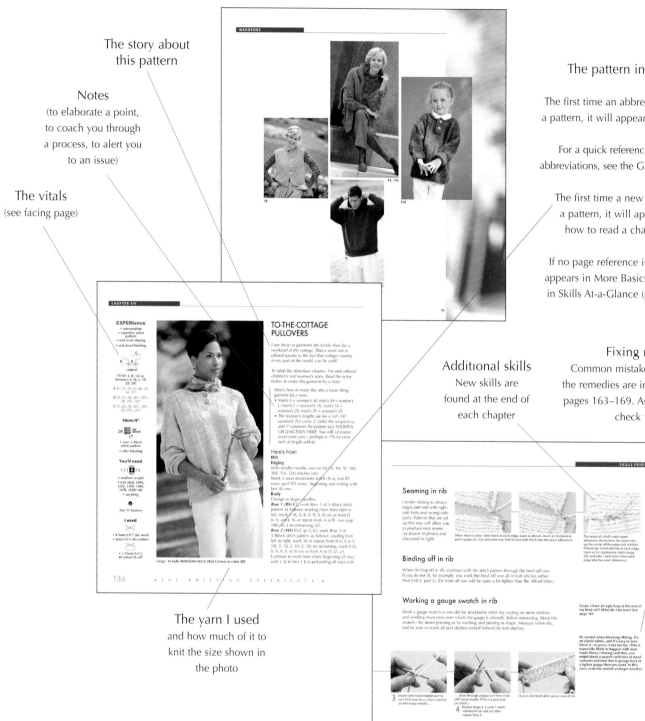

The yarn I used
and how much of it to
knit the size shown in
the photo

You're ready!

On these two pages is what you need to know to work through the patterns that follow.

The vitals column that accompanies every pattern is loaded with information, replacing a whole lot of words that can make knitting patterns look like no-fun text books. I think these icons are more knitter-friendly and more intuitive, and I know that they save page space . . . allowing me to include more patterns. But their most important function may be to make knitting a universal language.

EXPERIence

- *intermediate*
- *repetitive stitch pattern*
- *mid-level shaping*
- *mid-level finishing*

Difficulty rating The more bold letters, the more experienced you should be before you attempt the pattern.

C
B A
LOOSE FIT

Fit How closely the garment will fit your body, see page 159.

Woman's S (M, L, 1X, 2X)
A 39 (42, 46, 50, 54)"
B 28 (28, 28, 29, 29)"
C 28 (28, 28, 29, 29)"

Sizes See page 159.

Measurements of the actual garment as they correspond to the A, B, C lines on the fit icon, see page 159.

10cm/4"

28 **GET GAUGE!**
17

- *over 3-Block stitch pattern*
- *after blocking*

Gauge The number of stitches you should have in 10cm or 4", see pages 156–158.

Stitch pattern The kind of stitches you should use for your gauge swatch and how it should be treated, see pages 156–157.

You'll need

1 2 3 **4** 5 6

- *medium weight*
- *1090 (1220, 1300, 1380, 1470) yds*
- *anything*

Yarn weight See page 154.

Amount of yarn See page 160.

Kind of yarn See page 154.

two ¾" buttons

Buttons

I used

- *4.5mm/US 7*
- *4mm/US 6*

Needles can be straight, circular, or double-pointed, see page 155.

Needle size I used You may use another size based on your gauge swatch, see pages 156–158.

Finally, you learn to purl! Did you know there are knitters who have spent their lives avoiding this skill? I'm not sure what the difficulty is, 'cause there isn't that much to it; it's really just a variation of the knit stitch, accomplished easily enough, don't you think? (As discussed in the description of the around-the-neck purl, there are folks in the world who *prefer* purling and do entire garments in the round and in purl!)

Having said that, you'll have to look at the different purling methods and decide which works best for you. And you can expect that it might take a bit of practice for your gauge to be as even as I am sure your knit gauge is by now.

The stitch pattern of this chapter is a pretty gentle introduction to purling: only one row out of six demands that you purl. (You will work four rows of knit stitches on smaller needles, then one row of knit stitches on larger needles, then one row of purl stitches on larger needles.)

By imbedding your newly learned purl row among all these knit rows, a slightly different gauge in purl will not show. So this stitch pattern offers a good fabric upon which to practice. But it won't take long for you to produce any of these garments. The two rows on larger needles make this stitch pattern work up pretty quickly.

In addition, the two rows on larger needles produces a loose fabric; hence all the garments of this chapter are fairly open and feminine. Sorry guys, nothing for you here.

Chapter One

The Patterns

Additional Skills

Large: 11 balls CASCADE YARNS Pima Tencel in color 2493

TRICIA'S SHAWL

Shawls used to be considered grandmotherly items. There's nothing wrong with this, especially since the image of 'grandmother' may include a globe-trotting, laptop-toting power broker. But more and more younger women are discovering the beauty of shawls. What better item to have when a jacket is not appropriate—when we are more dressed-up, when the climate is more temperate, when we want both the romance and coziness of being wrapped in a length of luscious fabric.

My friend Tricia—a relatively new knitter—knit the lace-edged version of this shawl. When I gave her the pattern for the edging, she was daunted by how difficult it looked and how long she thought it would take. But a few hours later she called to joyously announce that it was 'easy, quick, and addictive!'.

You should knit to gauge and know that these pieces will stretch extensively—especially in width—after knitting and blocking. The measurements on the schematic are after blocking but without the edgings.
The fringe will add 4½" to each edge, and the lace edging will add 2" to each edge.
The yarn amounts include the edgings as shown on the model garments.
You may, of course, make this shawl any size you want. Just work the Triangle as written, ending with row 4, and proceed with the Finishing directions.

STITCH PATTERNS
Shawl stitch
Rows 1 & 3 (right side/RS) With smaller needle, knit (k) 1, yarn over (yo), k to 1 stitch (st) remaining, yo, k1.
Rows 2 & 4 (wrong side/WS) With smaller needle, k all sts.
Row 5 With larger needle, k1, yo, k to 1 st remaining, yo, k1.
Row 6 With larger needle, purl (p) all sts.
To read this stitch pattern, see page 44.

Here's how!

TRIANGLE

Mid-row joins of new balls of yarn will show in this fabric; begin new balls at beginnings of rows only. Tails will be taken into fringe (so be sure to leave them as long as you will want the fringe to be) or will be sewn into small seam allowance between shawl and lace edging.

With smaller needle, e-wrap cast on 4 sts.

K 2 rows.

Beginning with row 1, work stitch pattern to 272 (290) sts, ending with row 4.

Here's where you decide what edging you want. I don't recommend the fringe for the mohair because the yarn is too light; besides, mohair makes a gorgeous lace edging.

While the large, cotton version is shown with a fringe, the lace edging would also suit, but you might need an extra ball or two.

For lace edging, work as follows.

Next row (RS) Continuing on smaller needle, k all sts. Break yarn.

For fringe, work as follows.

Next row (RS) Continuing on smaller needle, *knit 2 together (k2tog), yo, repeat from * across.

Next row (WS) Bind off all sts knit-wise.

FINISHING

Block pieces.

The blocking of an openwork shawl is called 'dressing' the shawl. It's where you spread the piece out, to open up the stitch pattern and to stretch it to its final dimensions.

FRINGE

For 4½" fringe, work as follows.

Find a book with a circumference of approximately 10". (Book circumference = [length of fringe × 2] + 1")

Note that the strands must be a little over double the length of the desired fringe.

Wrap yarn around book and cut, to make pieces of 10" length.

Attach 2 fringe pieces at every yo around entire edge of shawl as follows: holding 2 fringe pieces, fold in half; insert crochet hook, from RS to WS, through yo; draw fold of fringe through to form a loop; pull cut edge of fringe through this loop.

Yo's will be smaller and more difficult to find between rows worked on smaller needles, but you need to attach fringe there, too. Just make sure you attach 3 fringes for every 6 rows of knitting (one full stitch pattern repeat).

Include yarn tails into fringe as you encounter them. Trim fringe to suit.

EXPERience
(with fringe)
- *easy*
- *repetitive stitch pattern*
- *simple shaping*
- *simple finishing*

EXPERience
(with lace edging)
- *easy intermediate*
- *repetitive stitch pattern*
- *simple shaping*
- *mid-level finishing*

It'll fit
M (L)

10cm/4"
30–34
18–20
- *over shawl stitch pattern*
- *after blocking*

You'll need
1 2 **3** 4 5 6
- *light weight*
- *1100 yds for M shawl with lace edging (1200 yds for L shawl with fringe)*
- *something soft*

I used
- *4mm/US 6, 80cm/32"*
- *6mm/US 10, 80cm/32"*
- *4–5mm/US F–H (for fringe)*

68-72 (74-78)"

36 (39)"

Increases   Increases

Measured after blocking but before edging or fringe

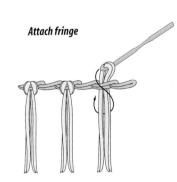

Attach fringe

Medium: 7 balls GGH Soft Kid in color 13

LACE EDGING

Read 'a lengthwise edging' (page 48) to orient yourself through what follows.

1 Top edge

Slip sts to other end of needle (to beginning of final row). With RS facing and with new yarn, e-wrap cast on 6 sts onto left-hand needle.

Work lace edging stitch pattern as follows across long upper edge of shawl triangle.

Lace edging pattern (use smaller needle)

Row 1 (RS) K5, slip 1 (sl1), k1 (from shawl), pass slip stitch over (psso) (joining lace edging to shawl). Turn.

Do you see how you just joined your lace edging to your shawl? That will happen at every 'psso' that follows.

Row 2 (WS) K2, yo, k2tog, yo, k2—edging now has 7 sts.

Row 3 K6, sl1, k1 (from shawl), psso. Turn.

Row 4 K3, yo, k2tog, yo, k2—edging now has 8 sts.

Row 5 K7, sl1, k1 (from shawl), psso. Turn.

Row 6 K4, yo, k2tog, yo, k2—edging now has 9 sts.

Row 7 K8, sl1, k1 (from shawl), psso. Turn.

Row 8 K5, yo, k2tog, yo, k2—edging now has 10 sts.

Row 9 K9, sl1, k1 (from shawl), psso. Turn.

Row 10 K6, yo, k2tog, yo, k2—edging now has 11 sts.

Row 11 K10, sl1, k1 (from shawl), psso. Turn.

Row 12 K7, yo, k2tog, yo, k2—edging now has 12 sts.

Row 13 (RS) Bind off 6 sts at beginning of row (1 st on right-hand needle), k4 (5 sts on right-hand needle), sl1, k1 (from shawl), psso. Turn.

Repeat rows 2–13 across upper edge of shawl.

2 Turn first corner

It does not matter on what row of the lace pattern you are when you reach the corner, just do as follows.

At corner, end with RS row but do not turn work.

To make lace edging turn corner, work 6 extra rows as follows.

A wedge of 6 extra rows of lace edging at the corner is accomplished by working into the same stitch 3 times.

*At end of RS row do not turn. Use left-hand needle to pick up st below last k1. Leave this st on left-hand needle and attach edging to it at end of next RS row. Turn. Work WS row and RS row. Repeat from * twice more.

3 First side edge

Go to lower point of triangle and, using left-hand needle, pick up 1 st for each garter ridge plus 1 st for each row worked on larger needle along entire side edge of shawl.

▌ *You have picked up 4 sts for every 6 rows of shawl.*
Work lace edging pattern down this side to lower point;
end with RS row but do not turn.

4 Turn lower corner

To turn lower point, use left-hand needle to pick up 3 sts
at the lower edge cast-on.
Work 4 extra rows of lace edging in first of these 3 sts
as follows.

▌ *Here, again, wedges are produced at corners by working
into the same stitch more than once.*

Next (RS) row Work lace edging, attaching to first of these
picked-up sts as usual.
*At end of RS row, do not turn. Use left-hand needle to
pick up st below last k1. Leave this st on left-hand needle
and attach edging to it at end of next RS row. Turn. Work
WS row and RS row.* Work from * to * once more.
Work 6 extra rows of lace edging in second of these 3 sts
as follows.

Next (RS) row Work lace edging, attaching to next of these
picked-up sts as usual.
Work from * to * (above) 3 times.
Work 4 extra rows of lace edging in third of these 3 sts
as follows.

Next (RS) row Work lace edging, attaching to next of these
picked-up sts as usual.
Work from * to * (above) 2 times.

Second side edge

Go to upper corner of triangle (where you began the lace
edging) and, using left-hand needle, pick up 1 st for each
garter ridge plus 1 st for each row worked on larger needle
along entire diagonal side edge.

▌ *You have picked up 4 sts for every 6 rows of shawl.*
Work lace edging pattern up this side to point where
you began.

5 Final corner

When lace edgings meet at final corner, bind off sts.

▌ *You will not turn the final corner so there is no need
to work extra rows there. And no matter what you do,
or where your final lace bit ends, the cast-on edge (the
beginning of the lace edge) and the bound-off edge (at
the end of the lace edging) will not match at this corner.
Just do the best you can, and it'll look fine.*

Sew cast-on and bind-off edges of lace together.
Block lace edging.

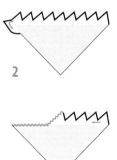

5

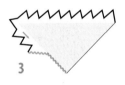

4

3

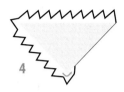

2

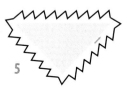

1

Medium: 5 skeins S. R. KERTZER LTD Super 10 Cotton
(or 12 skeins TAHKI Cotton Classic) in color 3995 (Persian Red)

SIMPLE CARDIGAN

The single-yarn, red cardigan was made first, and it surprised me in two ways: the first was how quickly it was made, and the second was how many knitters admired such a simple little thing. (The latter is a discovery I have made over and over through the progress of this series. Am I beginning to sound like a broken record?)

I immediately made the child's two-yarn, pink cardigan next, wanting beginner knitters to see that they can change yarns to wonderful effect.

The final garment for this chapter was the denim version, 'cause we always need something to go with jeans!

*The shape of this piece is short and wide—a style I prefer for warm-weather garments.
The bands are narrow and contribute a negligible amount to the A measurement.*

To make a version with two yarns, do the following:
- *find the yardage that your size demands in a single yarn;*
- *divide this yardage by 3;*
- *you will need this one-third yardage for rows 5–6 (the stockinette stitch rows);*
- *multiple by 2; you will need this two-thirds yardage for rows 1–4 (the garter stitch rows);*
- *now go find these amounts in two fabulous and coordinating yarns!*

STITCH PATTERNS

In one yarn

Rows 1–4 With smaller needles, knit (k) all sts.
Row 5 (right side/RS) With larger needle, k all sts.
Row 6 (wrong side/WS) With larger needles, purl (p) all sts.

To read this stitch pattern, see page 44.

In two yarns

Work as above, with rows 1–4 in one yarn and rows 5–6 in second yarn.

Here's how!

BACK

With smaller needles, cast on 66 (76, 86, 100, 110, 120, 130, 140) sts. Beginning with row 1, work stitch pattern to 5 (6, 7½, 10, 10, 10, 10, 11)" from beginning, ending with WS row.
SHORTEN OR LENGTHEN HERE.

Continue stitch pattern through armhole and neck shaping.

Armhole shaping

Bind off 5 (5, 5, 10, 10, 12, 15, 20) sts at beginning of next 2 rows—56 (66, 76, 80, 90, 96, 100, 100) sts remain.
Work to 4 (5, 6½, 8, 8, 9, 10, 10)" from armhole bind-off, ending with WS row.

Right neck shaping

Row 1 (RS) K19 (21, 24, 25, 30, 33, 35, 35). Put next 18 (24, 28, 30, 30, 30, 30, 30) sts on holder (for neck). Turn work (ready to work WS row), leaving 19 (21, 24, 25, 30, 33, 35, 35) sts behind for left shoulder and shaping right neck as follows.
*Next 2 WS rows Bind off 1 stitch at neck edge, work to end.
Next 2 RS rows Work stitch pattern.
Work one WS row without binding off.
Next RS row Bind off remaining 17 (19, 22, 23, 28, 31, 33, 33) sts.

Left neck shaping

Return to 19 (21, 24, 25, 30, 33, 35, 35) sts left behind for left shoulder, ready to work RS row. Work 1 RS row and 1 WS row, then work as right neck from * to end with reverse shaping (page 19).

LEFT FRONT

With smaller needles, cast on 33 (38, 43, 50, 55, 60, 65, 70) sts.
Beginning with row 1, work stitch pattern to same length as Back to armhole, ending with same WS row of stitch pattern.

Continue stitch pattern through armhole and neck shaping.

Armhole shaping

Bind off 5 (5, 5, 10, 10, 12, 15, 20) sts at beginning of next RS row—28 (33, 38, 40, 45, 48, 50, 50) sts remain.
Work 1 WS row.

V-neck shaping

Next (decrease) row (RS) K to 3 sts remaining, work right-slanting decrease (k2tog), k1.
Work 3 rows without shaping.
Repeat last 4 rows to 17 (19, 22, 23, 28, 31, 33, 33) sts remaining.
Work to same length as Back above armhole bind-off, ending with WS row.
Next row (RS) Bind off all sts.

EXPERience

- *easy*
- *repetitive stitch pattern*
- *simple shaping*
- *simple finishing*

OVERSIZED FIT

Child's 12 mos (2–4, 6–8, Woman's S, M, L, 1X, 2X)

A 26 (30, 34, 40, 44, 48, 52, 56)"

B 10 (12, 15, 19, 19, 20, 21, 22)"

C 12½ (19½, 22, 29, 29½, 30, 30½, 31)"

10cm/4"

34 GET CLOSE
20

- *over stitch pattern*
- *after blocking*

You'll need

1 2 **3** 4 5 6

- *light weight*
- *350 (575, 800, 1225, 1275, 1450, 1585, 1735) yds (in only one yarn)*
- *summery yarn(s)*

- *5/8" buttons*
Four (four, four, five, five, five, five, five)

I used

- *4mm/US 6*
- *5mm/US 8*

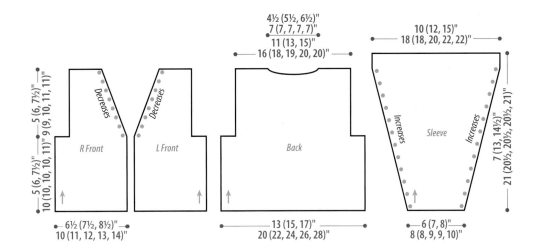

R Front | L Front | Back | Sleeve

5 (6, 7½)" / 9 (9, 10, 11, 11)"
5 (6, 7½)" / 10 (10, 10, 10, 11)"
Decreases
6½ (7½, 8½)" / 10 (11, 12, 13, 14)"

4½ (5½, 6½)"
7 (7, 7, 7, 7)"
11 (13, 15)"
16 (18, 19, 20, 20)"
13 (15, 17)" / 20 (22, 24, 26, 28)"

10 (12, 15)"
18 (18, 20, 22, 22)"
Increases
7 (13, 14½)" / 21 (20½, 20½, 20½, 21)"
6 (7, 8)" / 8 (8, 9, 9, 10)"

Medium: 11 balls ALMEDAHLS Texas in color 40

RIGHT FRONT
Work as Left Front but with reverse shaping.

SLEEVES
With smaller needles, cast on 30 (36, 40, 40, 40, 46, 46, 50) sts. Beginning with row 1, work stitch pattern for 12 rows.

Continue stitch pattern through shaping.

Next (increase) row (RS) K1, knit into front and back of next st (kf&b), k to 2 sts remaining, kf&b, k1.

Work 3 rows without shaping. Repeat last 4 rows to 50 (60, 76, 90, 90, 100, 110, 110) sts.

Work to 7 (13, 14½, 21, 20½, 20½, 20½, 21)" from beginning, ending with WS row.

SHORTEN OR LENGTHEN HERE.

The garment will seam nicely and look best if the sleeve ends with row 4.

Bind off all sts loosely and with smaller needle.

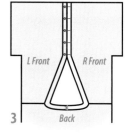

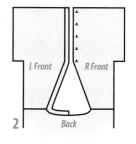

FINISHING
Sew shoulder seams.

If using two yarns, use smoother yarn for bands.

Use smaller needles for all edgings.

Button band
Beginning at lower Left Front edge and with RS facing, pick up (page 48) 1 st in each garter ridge (up entire Left Front edge to shoulder seam) and all sts from holder to center Back neck.

Row 1 (RS) Beginning at center Back neck, work as follows:
- pick up and knit around curve of Back neck (page 46) to shoulder seam,

- k1 in each picked-up st plus pick up and k1 in each row worked on larger needles (from shoulder seam down to point of V),
- k1, yarn over (yo), k1 in st at point of V,
- k1 in each picked-up st plus pick up and k1 in each row worked on larger needles (from point of V down to lower Left Front edge).

1 *Rows 2–4* K all sts.
Row 5 Bind off all sts.

2 **Buttonhole band**
Place markers for 4 (4, 4, 5, 5, 5, 5, 5) buttonholes along Right Front edge, the first at point of V, the last ½" from bottom edge, and the others spaced evenly between. Beginning at center Back neck, pick up as Button band but in reverse order.

3 *Row 1 (RS)* Beginning at lower Right Front edge, work as Row 1 of Button band but in reverse order.
Begin buttonholes: Row 2 (WS) K all sts, making buttonholes where indicated by working k2tog, yo at marker.

End buttonholes
Row 3 (RS) K all sts, working through yo's so as not to twist them (page 49).
Row 4 K all sts.
Row 5 Bind off all sts.
Sew bands together at center Back. Sew buttons onto Button band to correspond to buttonholes.

Sleeves to armholes
When seaming along a row edge, take one-half st into seam allowance. Sew Sleeves into armholes (as for modified drop shoulder, page 26). Sew side and Sleeve seams.

Child's 12 months: 240 yds CHERRY TREE HILL YARN Silk & Merino DK in color Wild Cherry (used for garter stitch rows) + 120 yds CHERRY TREE HILL YARN Ballerina Mini in color Wild Cherry (used for St st rows)

VISION COAT

Design is sometimes about faith. We have a vision of the finished product, and we hold tightly to it while we knit. But it is only a vision: it's not the final garment as we see it, beautifully photographed and modeled.

Sometimes we know that it's working well before we finish. That's fun and makes finishing pretty exciting. But sometimes we don't know until the final moment, when it is seamed and worn. In this situation, finishing can be a difficult time: faith and persistence are all we have to motivate us!

This coat fell into the latter category. I wasn't sure about the yarn, the style, the measurements . . . but I finished it anyway . . . then I tried it on. And I was thrilled by how beautiful it was. Seems I'm not the only one who has had that reaction: there are many knitters waiting for this book because they want to knit this coat!

STITCH PATTERN

Rows 1–4 With smaller needles, knit (k) all sts.

Row 5 (right side/RS) With larger needle, k all sts.

Row 6 (wrong side/WS) With larger needles, purl (p) all sts.

To read this stitch pattern, see page 44.

Medium: 14 balls TRENDSETTER Dune in color 54

Here's how!

BACK

With smaller needles, cast on 110 (116, 124, 130, 136) sts.

Beginning with row 1, work stitch pattern to approximately 11", ending with row 6.

Continue stitch pattern through all side, armhole, and shoulder shaping.

Side shaping

Rows 1 and 5 (decrease) K1, work left-slanting decrease (SKP or SSK, page 18), k to 3 sts remaining, work right-slanting decrease (k2tog), k1.

Rows 2, 3, 4, 6 Work without decreases.

Repeat last 6 rows to 72 (78, 86, 92, 98) sts remaining. Work straight to 23" from beginning, ending with WS row.

SHORTEN OR LENGTHEN HERE.

Armhole shaping

Bind off 3 (3, 4, 6, 8) sts at beginning of next 2 rows—66 (72, 78, 80, 82) sts remain.

Next (decrease) row (RS) K1, SKP (or SSK), k to 3 sts remaining, k2tog, k1.

Work 1 WS row without decreasing.

Repeat last 2 rows to 48 (52, 52, 56, 56) sts.

Work to 8 (9, 9, 10, 10)" above armhole bind-off, ending with WS row.

Shoulder and neck shaping

Bind off 3 (4, 4, 4, 4) sts at beginning of next 2 rows. Bind off 3 (3, 3, 4, 4) sts at beginning of next RS row, then k to 8 (9, 9, 10, 10) sts on right-hand needle. Put next 20 sts on holder (for neck), then turn, ready to work WS row over sts of right shoulder.

*Right neck and shoulder shaping

Next (WS) row Bind off 1 st at neck edge, work to end.

Next (RS) row Bind off 3 (4, 4, 4, 4) sts at shoulder, work to neck edge.

Next (WS) row Bind off 1 st at neck edge, work to end.

Next (RS) row Bind off remaining 3 (3, 3, 4, 4) sts.

Left neck and shoulder shaping

Return to 11 (12, 12, 14, 14) sts of right shoulder, ready to work RS row.

Work 1 RS row.

Next (WS) row Bind off 3 (3, 3, 4, 4) sts, work to end.

Now work as right neck and shoulder shaping from * to end but with reverse shaping (page 19).

LEFT FRONT

With smaller needles, cast on 36 (40, 42, 46, 48) sts. Beginning with row 1, work stitch pattern to approximately 6", ending with row 6.

Continue stitch pattern through all side, armhole, neck, and shoulder shaping.

EXPERIence

- intermediate
- repetitive stitch pattern
- mid-level shaping
- mid-level finishing

OVERSIZED FIT

S (M, L, 1X, 2X)

A (at bust) 43 (47, 51, 55, 59)"

A (at hem) 57 (61, 65, 69, 73)"

B (at front) 27 (28, 28, 29, 29)"

B (at back) 32 (33, 33, 34, 34)"

C 29 (30, 30, 31, 31)"

10cm/4"

21 GET CLOSE

13

- over stitch pattern
- after blocking

You'll need

1 2 3 4 **5** 6

- bulky weight
- 1200 (1260, 1350, 1470, 1550) yds
- mohair or mohair blend

I used

- 5mm/US 8
- 6mm/US 10

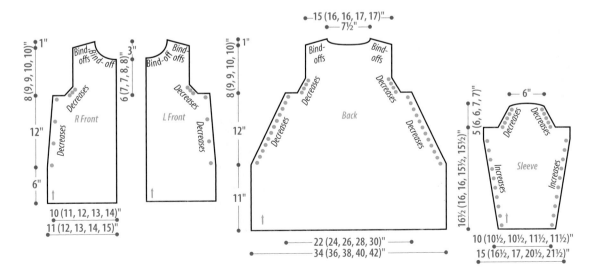

8 (9, 9, 10, 10)" / 1" / Bind-offs / Bind-off / 6 (7, 7, 8, 8)" / 3" / R Front / Decreases / Decreases / 12" / 6" / 10 (11, 12, 13, 14)" / 11 (12, 13, 14, 15)"

Bind-off / Bind-offs / L Front / Decreases / Decreases

8 (9, 9, 10, 10)" / 1" / 15 (16, 16, 17, 17)" / 7½" / Bind-offs / Bind-offs / Decreases / Decreases / Back / Decreases / Decreases / 12" / 11" / 22 (24, 26, 28, 30)" / 34 (36, 38, 40, 42)"

6" / 5 (6, 6, 7, 7)" / Decreases / Decreases / Sleeve / Increases / Increases / 16½ (16, 16, 15½, 15½)" / 10 (10½, 10½, 11½, 11½)" / 15 (16½, 17, 20½, 21½)"

Side shaping

Next row (decrease) K1, SKP (or SSK), k to end.

Work 11 rows without decreases.

Repeat last 12 rows to 32 (36, 38, 42, 44) sts remaining.

Work to approximately 18" from beginning, ending with same WS row as Back at armhole.

SHORTEN OR LENGTHEN HERE.

Armhole shaping

Bind off 3 (3, 4, 6, 8) sts at beginning of next RS row—29 (33, 34, 36, 36) sts remain.

Work 1 WS row.

Next (decrease) row (RS) K1, SKP (or SSK), work to end.

Work 1 WS row without decreasing.

Repeat last 2 rows to 24 (26, 26, 28, 28) sts remaining.

Work to 6 (7, 7, 8, 8)" above armhole bind-off, ending with RS row.

Neck shaping

Work RS rows straight through neck shaping.

Bind off 6 sts at beginning of next WS row, 2 sts at beginning of following WS row, then 1 st at beginning of next 4 WS rows—12 (14, 14, 16, 16) sts remain.

Shoulder shaping

Next (RS) row Bind off 3 (4, 4, 4, 4) sts at shoulder, work to end.

Work 1 WS row.

Next (RS) row Bind off 3 (3, 3, 4, 4) sts at shoulder, work to end.

Work 1 WS row.

Next (RS) row Bind off 3 (4, 4, 4, 4) sts at shoulder, work to end.

Work 1 WS row.

Next (RS) row Bind off remaining 3 (3, 3, 4, 4) sts.

Medium: 14 balls TRENDSETTER Dune in color 6

RIGHT FRONT

Work as Left Front but with reverse shaping.

SLEEVES

With smaller needles, cast on 32 (34, 34, 38, 38) sts. Beginning with row 1, work stitch pattern to approximately 2 (2, 2, 1, 1)", ending with row 6.

Continue stitch pattern through all shaping.

Row 1 (increase) K1, k into front and back of next st (kf&b), k to 2 sts remaining, kf&b, k1.

Work 5 (5, 5, 3, 3) rows without increases.

Repeat last 6 (6, 6, 4, 4) rows to 50 (54, 56, 66, 70) sts.

Work to 16½ (16, 16, 15½, 15½)" from beginning, ending with same WS row as Back at armhole. SHORTEN OR LENGTHEN HERE.

Cap

Bind off 3 (3, 4, 6, 8) sts at beginning of next 2 rows—44 (48, 48, 54, 54) sts remain.

Next (decrease) row (RS) K1, SKP (or SSK), k to 3 sts remaining, k2tog, k1.

Work 1 WS row without decreasing.

Repeat these 2 rows to 20 sts remaining.

Bind off 2 sts at beginning of next 2 rows, then bind off remaining 16 sts.

FINISHING

Sew shoulder seams.

Use smaller needles for all edgings.

Neck edging

With RS facing and beginning at Right Front neck edge, pick up and k around curve (page 46)— approximately 72 sts.

K 5 rows, then bind off all sts.

1 Button band

Beginning at lower Left Front edge, with left-hand needle and with RS facing, pick up (page 44) 1 st in each garter ridge (up entire Left Front edge, including neck edging).

Row 1 (RS) Beginning at Left Front neck, k1 in each picked-up st plus pick up and k1 in each row worked on larger needles.

Rows 2–10 K all sts.

Row 11 Bind off all sts.

Buttonhole band

Place markers for 6 buttonholes along Right Front edge, the first ½" from neck edge, the last at 21" from neck edge, and the rest spaced evenly between. Beginning at Right Front neck edge, pick up as for button band but in reverse order.

Row 1 (RS) Beginning at lower Right Front edge, work as for button band.

Rows 2–4 K all sts.

Begin buttonholes: Row 5 (RS) K all sts, making buttonholes where indicated by markers by working k2tog, yarn over (yo) at each marker.

End buttonholes: Row 6 (RS) K all sts, working through yo's to twist them (page 49).

Rows 7–10 K all sts.

Row 11 Bind off all sts.

Sew buttons onto button band to correspond to buttonholes.

Sleeves to armholes

Sew set-in Sleeves to armholes (page 27).

When sewing Sleeve cap to armhole rows, count as follows: each garter ridge = 1 row, each row worked on larger needles = 1 row.

Therefore each 6 rows of stitch pattern = 4 rows.

2 Lower side edgings

Sew side and Sleeve seams, taking one-half st into seam allowance and leaving unseamed 6" at lower edge of Fronts and 11" unseamed at lower edges of Back. Hold right lower edging so it is a continuous 17" opening.

Beginning at lower Right Front edge, with RS facing and with left-hand needle, pick up 1 st in each garter ridge along side opening (to lower Back edge).

Row 1 With RS facing, work as follows: k1 st in each picked-up st plus pick up and k1 st in each row worked on larger needles—approximately 60 sts.

Rows 2 K all sts.

Row 3 Bind off all sts.

Work Left lower edging in same manner but in reverse order. Fold openings over slightly, and press. Sew fold in place, if needed.

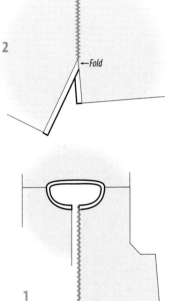

←Fold

Reading the stitch pattern of this chapter

If you leave your knitting, then return to it, you need to know where you are in the stitch pattern. Here's how to sort this out with respect to this chapter's stitch pattern.

Hold your knitting with right side facing. (This would be the smooth side of the large-needle rows.)

Here you need to work a second garter ridge, so you are ready to work row 3 (a right-side row).

Here you need to work the 2nd row on large needles, so you are ready to work row 6 (a wrong-side row).

Here what sits just below your needle are rows 5–6 (2 rows on larger needles), so you are ready to work row 1 (a right-side row).

Pick up/pick up and knit

In most patterns, you may be asked to either pick up or to pick up and knit. In this chapter you are asked to do both: to pick up along an edge, and then to pick up and knit along the same edge and between the picked-up stitches. You'll really understand these concepts once you're done!

Pick up and *pick up and knit* mean very different things. The difference is illustrated and explained in what follows.

PICK UP

To pick up, insert the needle from left to right along an edge. No yarn is involved.

Picking up can produce a stitch that is oriented backwards (see Oops, page 164). If so, work through the back of it.

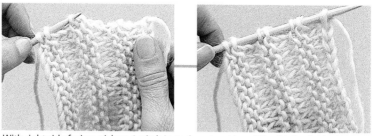

With right side facing, pick up 1 stitch in each garter ridge of the fabric of this chapter.

PICK UP AND KNIT ALONG A STRAIGHT EDGE

To pick up and knit, use needle and yarn to work the first row of an edging. Here, this is shown along an edge of stockinette stitch, and the rather ugly, curling selvedge stitch is turned into the seam allowance.

1 With right side facing, insert right-hand needle into space between first selvedge stitch and next stitch. (You'll see two threads on right-hand needle.)

2 Draw through a loop. (You have picked up and knit 1 stitch for 1 row.)

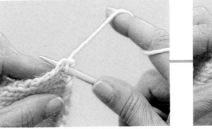

3 Insert right-hand needle into next space, between selvedge stitch and next stitch, and draw through a loop. (You have picked up and knit 2 stitches for 2 rows.)

4 Continue working in this way to the ratio directed by the pattern. For example, many of the patterns that follow direct you to "pick up and knit 3 stitches for every 4 rows." Here are 3 stitches picked up for 3 rows, but now the right-hand needle will skip a space . . .

5 . . . to continue picking up only 3 stitches for every 4 rows.

5 Here is the ratio of 3 stitches for every 4 rows continued across the entire edge.

6 When you work the next row of the edging, the spaces between every 3 stitches disappear.

It helps to see that the curve has 3 parts:

A **a flat edge of live stitches, at the base of the curve;**

B **a curve produced by a succession of bound-off sts;**

C **a straight edge at the top to finish the curve.**

You would normally begin picking up and knitting around a round-neck pullover at a shoulder. But to demonstrate, we begin at the base of the curve.

To prepare to pick up and knit along the curved area, it helps to see the following.

• **There are bound-off sts (indicated by numbers: here 3 sts are bound off, then 2, then 1, then 1, then 1).**

• **There are 2-row jogs between bound-off sts (indicated by arrows: here are 5 of these 2-row jogs).**

PICK UP AND KNIT ALONG A CURVED EDGE WITH BOUND-OFF STITCHES

Picking up and knitting around the curve of round-neck shaping is more complex than picking up along a straight edge. But if you use the principles that follow, the number of stitches you pick up and knit will always be the right number for the curve, and they will be spaced evenly.

A For the flat edge at the base of the curve, work as follows.

1 Knit all live stitches as usual.

2 Before the progression of bound-off stitches, there will be a rather steep step. Pick up and knit 1 in the base of this step.

B For the curve, pick up and knit 1 stitch in every bound-off stitch plus 1 stitch in every 2-row jog between bound-off stitches. Here's how this is done.

1 Look at your 2-row jog. You may see rather large holes. Never pick up in the hole: this will only enlarge it. *Look for a tight spot above the hole (above) . . .

2 . . . and pick up and knit in it.

3 Now you have come to the bound-off stitches. The first stitch will be immediately to the left.

C For the straight edge, work as for Pick up and knit along a straight edge (page 45). For the straight edge at the top of a curve, picking up and knitting 3 stitches for every 4 rows is usually the right proportion.

Here are the results of picking up and knitting around a curve.

Patterns often say "pick up and knit 103 sts evenly around neck" . . . period. With no more instruction than that, knitters, quite justifiably, struggle somewhat.

The approach offered here should give you the tools you need to achieve the right number of stitches spaced evenly around a curve. And attention to the details offered should give you a perfectly executed result. Since this part of the garment frames the face, it's worth the effort, don't you think?

Here are stitches picked up along a curve plus 1 wrong-side knit row.

Here is the same curve, bound off.

4 Put right-hand needle into this stitch, below the bound-off edge, and draw through loop. You will have picked up and knit 2 stitches that are quite close together, which will help close the hole below.

5 Continue to pick up and knit in each bound-off stitch until you come to the next 2-row jog.

6 Repeat from * (in Step 1), knitting in each 2-row jog and each bound-off stitch until you arrive at the straight edge.

When picking up in the 2-row jog, do not pick up at the edge. Pick up 1 stitch in from the edge. This will make this work secure and neat.

When picking up in stitches, it can really help to see a stitch as a V. If you put your needle into a V, it's in a stitch; if you put your needle between Vs, it's between stitches.

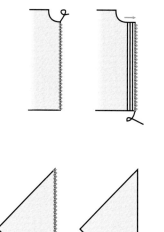

A lengthwise edging

For most of the edgings in this book, you will pick up and knit stitches from a finished edge. You will then work some number of rows across these stitches until the edging is the required depth.

For a *lengthwise edging*, as worked in the lace edging of Tricia's Shawl, you leave live stitches in the final row of the shawl, and then you do something quite different. First you cast on an extra few stitches for the edging (in this case, 6); then you work back and forth across these edging stitches, connecting to the live stitches of the shawl at the end of every right-side row, until the edging has used up all the live stitches from the final row of the shawl.

Yarn over

YARN OVER, IN PURL *yo*
Now that you know how to purl, you might need to know how to work a yarn over in purl. (While this is shown in right-hand carry, the maneuver is the same with the yarn in the left hand.)

Sometimes if you forgot a yarn over, you can insert one in the next row (for example, to make a stitch count add up). Other times if you forgot a yarn over, you must rip back to insert it where it belongs (for example, to make a buttonhole in the right place). As you determine the difference between these two situations, you'll become an intuitive knitter.

1 With yarn in front, take yarn over top of right-hand needle . . .

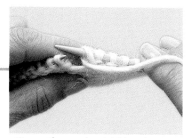

2 . . . then under right-hand needle, returning to front of work. There is now an extra loop on right-hand needle.

YARN OVERS, REVISITED

There is no right or wrong way to make a yarn over. (You could wrap the yarn around the needle differently than I have demonstrated.) But it's important that the following two criteria be met:

- that the yarn is in the place it needs to be (front or back) for the next stitch (purl or knit);
- that the yarn over is oriented on the needle properly for the next row.

When the next stitch is to be a knit, make the yarn over by just bringing yarn to the front and then knitting the next stitch as usual (page 172); when the next stitch is to be a purl, make the yarn over as shown to left. Read on for how to deal with the yarn over on the next row.

TO TWIST OR NOT TO TWIST (A YARN OVER)

On the row after producing a yarn over, you need to consider, 'Do I want to twist or not twist this yarn over?' Twisting it will produce a smaller hole than not twisting it. Here's the very best way to sort this out, however the yarn over was made and in whatever stitch pattern.

1 First look at the yarn over. It should look like this. The part of the loop that sits closest to the tip of the left-hand needle is called the leading edge.

2 If you knit through the leading edge, you will not twist the yarn over.

Your yarn over could look backwards to the yarn over in Step 1. You may remove it and reorient it. Or you could see that the 'leading edge' is now at the back (rather than the front of the needle), and you could still apply Steps 2 and 3. (If the leading edge is on the back, knitting through the back will not twist it; if the leading edge is on the back, knitting through the front will twist it.)

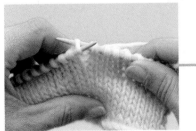

3 If you knit through the non-leading edge, you will twist the yarn over.

Here are the results—a yarn over not twisted (to right) and a yarn over twisted (to left).

For buttonholes, I indicate in the patterns whether or not I think a yarn over should be twisted. However, my result may not be the same as yours, so you should always test your first buttonhole with your button to see if you are doing what you need to do to produce an appropriate buttonhole.

PROCESS VERSUS PRODUCT

Knitting is two things: process (the activity in which we engage) and product (the piece we knit). If I had to say which of the two was more valuable, I'd come down unequivocally on the side of process.

I do know the importance of product—the final garment. As I wrote these books, I knew I had to offer designs you would want to wear, and I knew I had to offer all the skills you would need to do the work well. In addition, I realized the importance of helping you make decisions (with respect to color and yarn and fit) that would make you look good in the products you knit. I also know, all too well, the frenzy as one approaches the finish line! (Those are the times I find myself driving to some take-out joint at 9 p.m. because I've forgotten to eat!)

But product isn't the most valuable part of knitting. Consider the following.

First, we could pay someone else to knit the garment. And why don't we? Because we can't sacrifice that indescribably wonderful moment the first time we get to say, "I made it myself!"

Second, even if the product makes us look much *less* than fabulous—if the piece we knit doesn't turn out as imagined—we keep knitting, totally engaged by the process.

And third, if you ask a knitter what she loves, she often won't even *mention* the finished garment.

What does it mean to say that process is more valuable than product? It means that you shouldn't let one bad result discourage you. It means that you shouldn't feel you must finish one project before starting another. It means that you should always have more than one piece of knitting on needles, in case you're stuck on one or it's too complex to be portable.

We could do the process/product analysis on most anything in life, couldn't we? There's the studying, then there's the degree. There's the getting-to-know-just-the-right-person, then there's the wedding. There's the nurturing, then there—before your eyes and long before you were ready—is your adult child. There's the day-to-day of life, then there's that moment—the one you *never* thought you'd reach—your 60th birthday.

Okay, so in knitting, in relationships, in life, which is more important: process or product? The moments we live on the way to the prize, or the prize itself? When you make these analogies, the answer is a no-brainer, isn't it? As wonderful as the celebration is, earning it is what matters.

But how easy it is to lose sight of this, that it's what we do in the time we pass—whether it's fun or folly or just hard work—that makes up a lifetime. The journey *is* the destination!

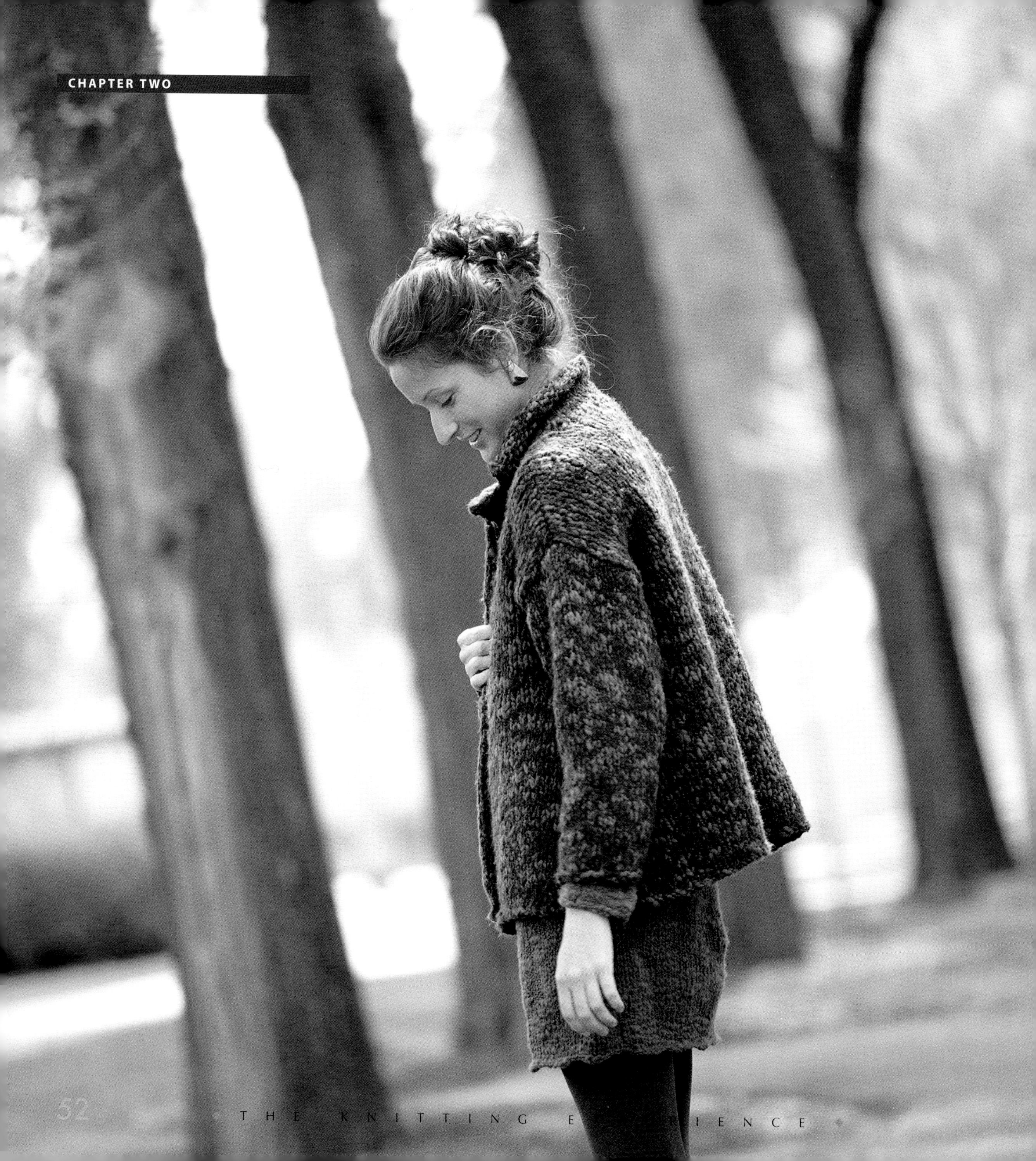

And now, finally, you are introduced to a fabric long associated with knitting: the beautifully plain and simple stockinette stitch.

In this chapter, this stitch pattern stands alone; in the next chapter, it is used with its reverse; in following chapters, we move on to other possibilities. But since so much of knitting is dedicated to this stitch pattern, you might ask why we devote only one chapter to stockinette stitch.

Actually, it is relatively rare to have stockinette stitch stand alone—without some other stitch pattern to hold it from curling at the edges or without some change in color or texture to provide interest. But in this chapter it stands alone, worked in yarns that can be blocked or pressed to hold the edges from curling and in yarns whose texture or color make this plain and simple fabric interesting.

Also, to give this chapter more range, two of the patterns give a choice of yarn weights and gauge. While gauge (and therefore measurement) is important, it's equally important to see that there's more than one way to get there!

But sometimes, the unexpected happens: I pick a yarn, I make a wonderful garment (or two), we take the photos and write the patterns . . . then just before (or after!) we go to press, the yarn is discontinued.

What to do? Rise to the challenge! Make the best of a bad situation! Overcome adversity! (Don't you love all those platitudes?) In fact, we did just that. Go to *Not Your Mother's Suit*, both the *Coat* and *Dress*, and see what we've done to offer you wonderful choices, wonderful substitutions. For more, go to **www.knittinguniverse.com**.

And please understand that this happens *all the time* in knitting. Without some old favorites being discontinued, there'd be no room for exciting new yarns—on the shelves or in your knitting life. One of the advantages of our offering generic yarn descriptions is that you can learn to do this for yourself.

The styles of this chapter are probably the most exciting in the book. While I did have all our new, 25- to 35-year-old knitters in mind when I designed these pieces, it's been cool to see how well women 'of a certain age' (my age or thereabouts) have responded to them.

Apologies to the guys—the pieces of this chapter are all shaped, and not in ways that flatter the male physique. Please skip to the remaining chapters. There's lots for you there.

Chapter Two

The Patterns

Additional Skills

EXPerience

- *very easy*
- *simple shaping*
- *minimal finishing*

STANDARD FIT

XS (S, M, L, 1X, 2X)

A (at hem) 33 (37, 41, 44, 48, 52)"

A (at bust) 32 (36, 39, 43, 47, 50)"

B (not including collar) 20 (20, 20, 21, 21, 22)"

10cm/4"

(for bulky version)

19 | **GET GAUGE!**
13

(for medium version)

26 | **GET GAUGE!**
17½

- *over stockinette stitch*
  - *after blocking or pressing*

You'll need

(for bulky version)

1 2 3 4 **5** 6

- **bulky weight**
- **400 (440, 500, 560, 620, 680) yds**
  - **anything**

(for medium version)

1 2 3 **4** 5 6

- **medium weight**
- **450 (500, 550, 630, 690, 750) yds**
  - **anything**

I used

(for bulky version)
- **5.5mm/US 9, 50cm/20"**

(for medium version)
- **4.5mm/US 8, 50cm/20"**

Medium: 5 balls BERROCO Zen in color 8253 (medium version)

SIMPLE AND SLEEVELESS

I drafted this garment from a fleece piece my daughter loved. The original was pretty casual, so I first knit it in the rust-colored, thick-and-thin wool. But then I thought about making a dressier garment (to wear with the gauntlets of Chapter 5), so I made one in black ribbon.

But is the distinction between casual and dress really that clear-cut? Can't you just see a certain actress wearing the rust wool version with a black taffeta skirt? And can't you imagine someone else wearing the black ribbon version with jeans?

The gauges for the two yarns are different: the rust wool (a bulky weight) is heavier than the black ribbon (a medium weight). But the patterns have been combined and are referenced as bulky or medium. Where there is only one set of numbers or instructions, it applies to both.
For a medium-weight version done in something slinky (like the black ribbon), you might want a closer fit. If you choose one size smaller than your usual size, the fit will be 'close' = bust + 1–2".

STITCH PATTERN

Stockinette stitch (St st)
  Work all pieces in St st, including bind-offs.
Right-side (RS) rows Knit (k) all stitches (sts).
Wrong-side (WS) rows Purl (p) all sts.
  To read this stitch pattern, see page 64.

Here's how!

BACK/FRONT

Back and Front are identical.
Cast on
56 (62, 68, 74, 80, 86) sts in bulky,
76 (84, 92, 98, 108, 116) sts in medium.
Work straight for 3", ending with WS row.

Side shaping

Next (decrease) row (RS) K1, work left-slanting decrease (SKP or SSK, page 18), k to 3 sts remaining, work right-slanting decrease (k2tog), k1.
Work 3 rows straight.

Repeat these last 4 rows to
50 (56, 62, 68, 74, 80) sts remaining in bulky,
66 (74, 82, 90, 100, 108) sts remaining in medium.
Work straight to 7" from beginning, ending with WS row.
SHORTEN OR LENGTHEN HERE.

The length worked straight, after the decreases, should center over the waist.

Next (increase) row (RS) K1, k into st below next st plus k into next st (lifted increase, page 67), k to 2 sts remaining, work lifted increase, k1.
Work 3 rows straight.
Repeat last 4 rows to
54 (60, 66, 72, 78, 84) sts in bulky,
72 (80, 88, 96, 104, 112) sts in medium.
Work straight to 12½ (12½, 12, 12½, 12, 12½)" from beginning, ending with WS row.
SHORTEN OR LENGTHEN HERE.

To determine length, the following armhole bind-off should occur 6½ (6½, 7, 7½, 8, 8½)" from where you wish to start shoulder shaping—at outside edge of shoulder.

Armhole shaping
Bind off at beginning of next 2 rows
2 (3, 5, 6, 7, 8) sts for bulky—50 (54, 56, 60, 64, 68) sts remain,
2 (3, 5, 6, 8, 10) sts for medium—68 (74, 78, 84, 88, 92) sts remain.

Next (decrease) row (RS) K1, SKP (or SSK), k to
3 sts remaining, k2tog, k1.
Work 1 (WS) row without decreasing.
Repeat these last 2 rows to
44 (44, 46, 48, 50, 50) sts remaining in bulky,
60 (60, 62, 66, 68, 68) sts remaining in medium.
Work straight to 6½ (6½, 7, 7½, 8, 8½)" above armhole bind-off, ending with WS row.

Shoulder shaping
Bind off for bulky
3 (3, 3, 3, 4, 4) sts at beginning of next 4 rows, then 2 (2, 3, 4, 3, 3) sts at beginning of next 2 rows—28 sts remain.
Bind off for medium
3 (3, 3, 3, 4, 4) sts at beginning of next 6 rows, then 2 (2, 3, 5, 3, 3) sts at beginning of next 2 rows—38 sts remain.
Put remaining sts on holder (for neck).

FINISHING
Block or press pieces to minimize curl at edges.
Sew shoulder seams.
Sew side seams.

Collar
Put all sts for neck onto a circular needle.
With RS facing, k in rounds to desired height.

There are 2 collars shown: the wool version is 2" tall, and the ribbon version is 5" tall. For the ribbon version, I kept knitting until I ran out of yarn! How will you know if you have enough to bind off? It takes 4 times the neck circumference to bind off.

Bind off loosely.

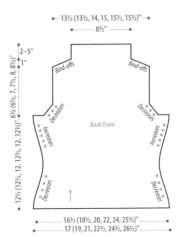

13½ (13½, 14, 15, 15½, 15½)"
8½"
2–5"
1"
Bind-offs
Bind-offs
Decreases
Decreases
Back/Front
Increases
Increases
Decreases
Decreases
6½ (6½, 7, 7½, 8, 8½)"
12½ (12½, 12, 12½, 12, 12½)"
16½ (18½, 20, 22, 24, 25½)"
17 (19, 21, 22½, 24½, 26½)"

Small: 8 balls GARNSTUDIO Ull-Flame in color 16 (bulky version)
Scarf: 6 balls; Shape it! Scarf, *The Knit Stitch*, page 46

NOT YOUR MOTHER'S SUIT COAT

I love this coat! And I have had both versions much admired when I've worn them. They're fun—from the first decision (combining yarns to get the desired color and texture) through the knitting (pretty quick at 7 stitches to 4") to the wearing (pretty fun styling happening here)!

Given how instantly gratifying it is to knit to a gauge of 7 stitches to 4", why don't we do it more often? There are two reasons. One is that big yarn can make us look big: I'm often disappointed in the look of a large-gauge piece, but this one works because it is generously oversized. The second reason is that it isn't easy on the hands to knit with big needles and big yarn: we move more slowly and clumsily. (Good thing the experience doesn't last long!)

By the way, here is the story for the name of this piece (and the one that follows). I originally made it with my daughter in mind, never dreaming that I would be able to wear it. But I do wear it, so there's a tongue-in-cheek each time I borrow it from her, 'cause it was meant to be a 'not your mother's' suit.

The coat is made with two yarns—a super bulky + either a super bulky or a bulky—knit together. The combination gives the same gauge as super bulky alone might have produced, but the doubled fabric is thicker and more appropriate for a coat.

The A measurement and the schematic measurements are very different, and here's why: there is an allowance for overlap at the front (approximately 6" at the hem and 4" at the bust). Also the garment may spread across the shoulders and collar, and this will add to the sleeve length.

Coat, Medium: For best substitute, use 25 balls JAEGER Fur in color 053 (black) + 6 balls JAEGER Natural Fleece in color 524 (grays)
Dress, Small: For best substitute, use 9 balls JAEGER Natural Fleece in color 524 (grays; bulky)

STITCH PATTERN
Stockinette stitch (St st)
▌ *Work all pieces in St st, including bind-offs.*
Right-side (RS) rows Knit (k) all stitches (sts).
Wrong-side (WS) rows Purl (p) all sts
▌ *To read this stitch pattern, see page 64.*

Here's how!
BACK
Cast on 54 (58, 62, 66, 70) sts.
Work straight for 6 rows.
Next (decrease) row (RS) K1, work left-slanting decrease (SKP or SSK, page 18), k to 3 sts remaining, work right-slanting decrease (k2tog), k1.
Work 5 rows straight.
Repeat last 6 rows to 44 (48, 52, 56, 60) sts remaining.
Work straight to 14" from beginning, ending with WS row.
SHORTEN OR LENGTHEN HERE.
Armhole shaping
Bind off 2 (4, 6, 8, 10) sts at beginning of next 2 rows—40 sts remain.
Work straight to 11 (11, 12, 12, 13)" above armhole bind-off, ending with WS row.
▌ *A little taller is better than a little shorter.*
Neck shaping
Next (RS) row K13 (sts of right shoulder). Turn, leaving 27 sts behind.
Next (WS) row P.
Next (RS) row Bind off 13 sts loosely.

Return to remaining sts. Put center 14 sts on holder (for neck).
Next (RS) row K13 (sts of left shoulder).
Next (WS) row P.
Next (RS) row Bind off loosely.

LEFT FRONT
Cast on 31 (33, 35, 37, 39) sts.
Work straight for 6 rows.
Next (decrease) row (RS) K1, work left-slanting decrease (SKP or SSK, page 18), k to end.
Work 5 rows straight.
Repeat last 6 rows to 26 (28, 30, 32, 34) sts remaining.
Work straight to same length as Back to armhole, ending with WS row.
Armhole shaping
Bind off 2 (4, 6, 8, 10) sts at beginning of next row—24 sts remain.
Work straight to 10 (10, 11, 11, 12)" above armhole bind-off, ending with RS row.
▌ *A little taller is better than a little shorter.*
Neck shaping
Bind off 4 sts at beginning of next (WS) row, p to end—20 sts remain.
Short row 1 (RS) K to 6 sts from end, then turn.
Rows 2 & 4 P.
Short row 3 K to 7 sts from end, then turn.
Next (RS) row Bind off 13 sts loosely; put 7 neck sts on hold.

EXPErience
• *easy*
• *simple shaping*
• *simple finishing*

OVERSIZED FIT

S (M, L, 1X, 2X)
A (at hem) 60 (64, 68, 73, 77)"
A (at bust) 50 (54, 59, 63, 67)"
B 26 (26, 27, 27, 28)"
C 28½ (29, 29½, 30, 30½)"

10cm/4"
 GET CLOSE
10
7
• *over stockinette stitch*
• *after blocking*

You'll need
1 2 3 4 **5-6**
• *super bulky weight + bulky weight (used together)*
• *530 (540, 600, 640, 700) yds (of each yarn used)*
• *wool or wool blends*

☺
• *2 large toggles or buttons*

I used

• *9mm/US 13*

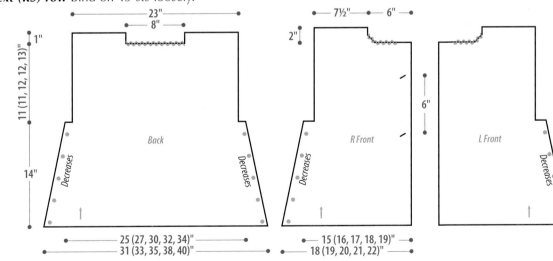

RIGHT FRONT

Work as Left Front, but with reverse shaping (page 19) and working buttonholes as follows.

At 2 (2, 1, 1, 1½)" short of Back length to armhole, end with WS row.

Begin buttonhole, next (RS) row K3, k2tog, yarn over (yo), k to end.

End buttonhole, next (WS) row P all sts, p through yo's so as to twist them (page 49).

At 6" past first buttonhole, end with WS row.

Make buttonhole over next 2 rows as above.

SLEEVES

Cast on 22 sts.

Work straight for 4 rows.

Next (increase) row (RS) K1, increase 1 by k into st below next st plus k into next st (lifted increase, page 67), k to 2 sts remaining, work lifted increase, k1.

Work 1 WS row without increasing.

Repeat these last 2 rows to 30 (30, 34, 34, 36) sts.

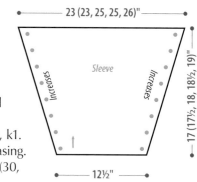

Next (increase) row (RS) Work increase row as above.

Work 3 rows without increasing.

Repeat last 4 rows to 40 (40, 44, 44, 46) sts.

Work straight to 17 (17½, 18, 18½, 19)" from beginning, ending with WS row.

SHORTEN OR LENGTHEN HERE.

Next row Bind off loosely.

FINISHING

Block pieces to minimize curl at edges.

Sew shoulder seams.

Collar

Pick up all live sts and sts on holder around neck.

Row 1 (RS) K all live sts plus pick up and k 1 st in each 2-row jog between live sts plus pick up and k 3 sts in straight edges (across shoulder seams)—36 sts around entire neck.

Work straight to 6".

Next row Bind off loosely.

Sew Sleeves into armholes (as for modified drop shoulder, page 26).

Sew side and Sleeve seams.

Sew buttons to Left Front, matching placement of buttonholes with desired overlap.

Coat, Medium: For best substitute, use 10 balls LION BRAND YARNS Lion Bouclé in color 205 (Sunset) + 6 skeins LION BRAND YARNS Chenille Thick & Quick in color 133 (Eucalyptus)

NOT YOUR MOTHER'S SUIT DRESS

I actually did not imagine this suit as separate pieces: the dress-plus-coat image came as a duo. And I think it works wonderfully that way. But I have been surprised at how much I liked the dress all on its own.

The problem with knit dresses, however, is that we wear them, then stand, and find our butts (pardon the expression!) following us across the room. (Apparently the proper way to say this is that the fabric 'seats.' Other, less-polite expressions are 'going butt-sprung' and getting 'bucket butt.' Nice, eh?)

How to avoid this? See the note that follows with respect to yarn choice, and don't wear the dress two days in a row.

Wool has memory so will resume its original shape. That shape will hold best with yarns that are mostly wool (or mohair) but have a bit of nylon or a 'binder'—a second, thin thread—in them.

Two yarns were used: a bulky-weight, gray thick-and-thin wool and a medium-weight, orange mohair. Both were knit to a looser gauge than usual. When considering a yarn, look for the following gauges on the label: 12–15 sts/4" (bulky) or 16–20 sts/4" (medium). The yarn for the gray dress is noted in the caption, page 56.

While both model garments were knit on the same size needles, the gauges were different. But the patterns have been combined. Throughout the pattern, they are referenced as bulky or medium. Where there is only one set of numbers or instructions, it applies to both.

The yarn for the gray dress has been discontinued. We've found a wonderful substitute: a multi-colored gray, Jaeger Natural Fleece. Go to www.knittinguniverse.com to see a knit sample along with many exciting coat and dress possibilities.

EXPERience

- *easy intermediate*
- *simple shaping*
- *mid-level finishing*

S (M, L, 1X, 2X)

A (at hem) 46 (50, 54, 57, 62)"
A (at bust) 40 (44, 48, 51, 56)"
B (not including collar) 32 (32, 33, 33, 34)"
C 28½ (29, 29¾, 30¼, 31¼)"

10cm/4"

(for bulky version)

17 — GET GAUGE!
10.5

(for medium version)

21 — GET GAUGE!
13

- *over stockinette stitch*
- *after blocking*

You'll need

1 2 3 **4-5** 6

- *medium or bulky weight*
- *830 (900, 1040, 1120, 1250) yds for medium weight*
- *770 (810, 940, 1025, 1140) yds for bulky weight*
  - *mohair or wool, with a little nylon*

I used

- *6mm/US 10, 50cm/20"*

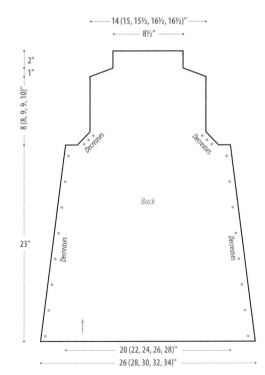

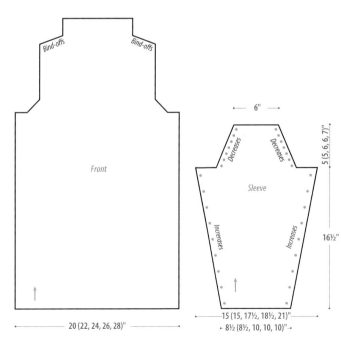

Medium: 10 balls CLASSIC ELITE LaGran Mohair in color 6585 (Pumpkin; medium version)

STITCH PATTERN
Stockinette stitch (St st)
Work all pieces in St st, including bind-offs.
Right side (RS) rows Knit (k) all stitches (sts).
Wrong side (WS) rows Purl (p) all sts.
To read this stitch pattern, see page 64.

Here's how!
BACK
Cast on
69 (73, 79, 85, 89) sts in bulky,
85 (91, 97, 105, 111) sts in medium.
Work straight for 2", ending with WS row.
Side shaping
Next (decrease) row (RS) K1, work left-slanting decrease (SKP or SSK, page 18), k to 3 sts remaining, work right-slanting decrease (k2tog), k1.
Work 11 rows straight.
SHORTEN OR LENGTHEN HERE by working as follows (instead of 11 rows straight between decreases):
working 9 rows without decreasing will make the dress approximately 3½" shorter;
working 13 rows without decreasing will make the dress approximately 3½" longer;
working 15 rows without decreasing will make the dress approximately 7" longer;
working 17 rows without decreasing will make the dress approximately 10½" longer.
If this is not the precise difference you want to make, you will have another opportunity to shorten or lengthen just before the armhole shaping.
Repeat these last 12 rows (or different number of rows as stated to get alternate length) to
53 (57, 63, 69, 73) sts remaining in bulky,
65 (71, 77, 85, 91) sts remaining in medium.
No matter how many rows you worked between decreases, you will still work to this number of sts remaining.
Work straight to 23", or desired length to underarm from beginning, ending with WS row.
SHORTEN OR LENGTHEN HERE.

If you have reached your desired length but have 2 extra sts remaining, don't go to extraordinary measures (like ripping or working an extra decrease) to get rid of these extra sts. Just bind off at armhole as directed, then decrease as directed, getting rid of these extra 2 sts in the armhole shaping. The right number of sts for the shoulder width is essential; the right number of sts for the bust is not.

Armhole shaping
Bind off at beginning of next 2 rows
3 (3, 4, 5, 6) sts for bulky—47 (51, 55, 59, 61) sts remain,
3 (3, 5, 6, 7) sts for medium—59 (65, 67, 73, 77) sts remain.
Next (decrease) row (RS) K1, work left-slanting decrease SKP (or SSK), k to 3 sts remaining, work right-slanting decrease (k2tog), k1.
Work 1 (WS) row without decreasing.
Repeat last 2 rows to
37 (39, 41, 43, 43) sts remaining in bulky,
45 (49, 51, 53, 53) sts remaining in medium.
Work straight to 8 (8, 9, 9, 10)" above armhole bind-off, ending with WS row.

Shoulder shaping
Bind off in bulky
2 (3, 3, 3, 3) sts at beginning of next 4 rows, then
3 (2, 3, 4, 4) sts at beginning of next 2 rows—23 sts remain.
Bind off in medium
3 (4, 4, 4, 4) sts at beginning of next 4 rows, then
3 (3, 4, 5, 5) sts at beginning of next 2 rows—27 sts remain.
Put remaining sts on holder (for neck).

FRONT
Cast on
53 (57, 63, 69, 73) sts in bulky,
65 (71, 77, 85, 91) sts in medium.
Work straight to same length as Back to armhole bind-off, ending with WS row.
Work as Back from Armhole shaping to end.

SLEEVES
Cast on
22 (22, 26, 26, 26) sts in bulky,
28 (28, 32, 32, 32) sts in medium.
Work straight for 1", ending with WS row.

Next (increase) row (RS) K1, increase 1 by k into st below next st plus k into next st (lifted increase, page 67), k to 2 sts remaining, work lifted increase, k1.
Work 3 rows even.
Repeat last 4 rows to
40 (40, 46, 48, 54) sts in bulky,
50 (50, 58, 60, 68) sts in medium.
Work straight to 16½" from beginning, ending with WS row.
SHORTEN OR LENGTHEN HERE.

Cap
Bind off at beginning of next 2 rows,
3 (3, 4, 5, 6) sts in bulky—34 (34, 38, 38, 42) sts remain,
3 (3, 5, 6, 7) sts in medium—44 (44, 48, 48, 54) sts remain.
Next (decrease) row (RS) K1, work left-slanting decrease SKP (or SSK), k to 3 sts remaining, work right-slanting decrease (k2tog), k1.
Work 1 (WS) row without decreasing.
Repeat last 2 rows to
16 sts remaining in bulky,
20 sts remaining in medium.
Work 1 WS row.
Bind off 2 sts at beginning of next 2 rows; then bind off remaining sts.

FINISHING
Block or press pieces to minimize curl at edges.
Sew shoulder seams.
Sew set-in Sleeves to armholes (page 27).
Sew side and Sleeve seams.
Collar
Put all sts for neck onto a circular needle.
With RS facing, k in rounds to 2".
Bind off loosely.

EXPERience

- *easy intermediate*
- *simple shaping*
- *mid-level finishing*

OVERSIZED FIT

S (M, L, 1X, 2X)

A (at hem) 44½ (48, 52½, 56, 60½)"

A (at bust) 41 (45, 49, 53, 57)"

B (not including collar) 21 (21½, 22, 22½, 23)"

C 27½ (28, 29, 29½, 30½)"

10cm/4"

16 **GET GAUGE!**

10

- *over stockinette stitch*
- *after blocking*

You'll need

1 2 3 4 5 **6**

- *super bulky weight*
- *560 (600, 660, 710, 750) yds*
- *wool or wool blend*

I used

- *6mm/US 10, 50cm/20"*

Medium: For best substitute, use 4 skeins MOUNTAIN COLORS Homespun in color Firestorm

BASIC PULLOVER

This pullover started out as another version of the Not Your Mother's Suit Dress, but I shortened it to pullover length. And if you don't like your dress, you can shorten it (page 168) . . . or you can just make a pullover by following this pattern.

A super bulky yarn is knit to a typical super bulky gauge. So while some of the pattern is shared with the dress pattern, the fabric will be denser and the fit will be looser.

STITCH PATTERN

Stockinette stitch (St st)
Work all pieces in St st, including bind-offs.
Right side (RS) rows Knit (k) all stitches (sts).
Wrong side (WS) rows Purl (p) all sts.
To read this stitch pattern, see page 64.

Here's how!
BACK
Cast on 61 (65, 71, 75, 81) sts.
Work straight for 2", ending with WS row.
Side shaping
Next (decrease) row (RS) K1, work left-slanting decrease (SKP or SSK, page 18), k to 3 sts remaining, work right-slanting decrease (k2tog), k1.
Work 7 rows even.
Repeat last 8 rows to 53 (57, 63, 67, 73) sts remaining.
Work straight to 12 (12½, 12, 12½, 12)" from beginning, ending with WS row.
SHORTEN OR LENGTHEN HERE.

Armhole shaping
Bind off 3 (3, 4, 5, 6) sts at beginning of next 2 rows—47 (51, 55, 57, 61) sts remain.
Next (decrease) row (RS) K1, SKP (or SSK), k to 3 sts remaining, k2tog, k1.
Work 1 (WS) row even.
Repeat last 2 rows to 37 (39, 41, 43, 43) sts remaining.
Work straight to 8 (8, 9, 9, 10)" above arm-hole bind-off, ending with WS row.
Shoulder shaping
Bind off 2 (3, 3, 3, 3) sts at beginning of next 4 rows, then 3 (2, 3, 4, 4) sts at beginning of next 2 rows—23 sts remain.
Put remaining 23 sts on holder (for neck).

FRONT
Cast on 53 (57, 63, 67, 73) sts.
Work straight to same length as Back to arm-hole bind-off, ending with WS row.
Follow directions for Back from Armhole shaping to end.

SLEEVES
Work as Not Your Mother's Suit Dress (page 61), following directions for bulky and with Sleeve length to armhole as 15".
SHORTEN OR LENGTHEN HERE.

FINISHING
Work as Not Your Mother's Suit Dress.

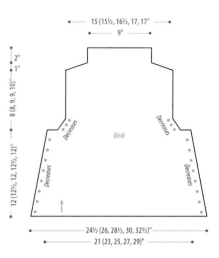

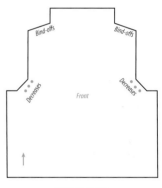

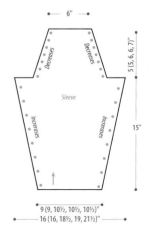

Reading stockinette stitch

Stockinette stitch is the smooth fabric produced by knitting all right-side rows and purling all wrong-side rows. The bumps are thrown to the wrong side.

How do you know where you are when you have left your knitting for a while?

Oops, I knit when I should have purled (or vice versa)! What do I do now? See page 166.

Oops, I dropped a stitch! What do I do now? See page 164.

If you are working (or ready to work) a smooth, right-side row, you will knit.

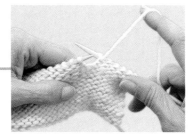

If you are working (or ready to work) a bumpy, wrong-side row, you will purl.

Tails in stockinette stitch

KNITTING IN TAILS, MID ROW

When ending one ball and beginning another, you may knit in tails (as shown below). On some fabrics this will work fine; on others it will be visible, so you'll have to explore the alternatives that follow.

I show what follows on a purl row, but it may also be done on a knit row. Just follow the instructions as written.

1 When you have a 5" tail of the old ball, leave a 1" tail of the new ball on the wrong side . . .

2 . . . then work 4–6 stitches in pattern with the new yarn and the old tail held together. Drop the old tail to the wrong side of work, and continue with only the new yarn. Trim tails to no less than ½."

3 On the next row, you will have stitches with doubled yarn. Work them as single stitches.

SPIT-AND-SPLICE

Here's a rather unrefined way of fusing two tails together to make an invisible join.
It is particularly useful for garments without a right or wrong side: a scarf or a shawl.

1 Lick about 2" of the old and the new tail. (This really does require saliva!) Overlap in palm.

2 Rub tails together, vigorously in the palms of your hands . . .

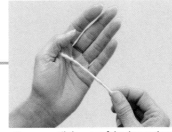

3 . . . until they are felted together. Knit over this join.

Spit-and-splice works best in non-superwash wool and other animal fibers. Will it work if a bit of something else in blended in? Try it and see!

If the yarn is plied (strands twisted together), separate the plies for an inch or so before this maneuver.

SEWING IN TAILS, MID ROW

When you join yarn mid row, you may work one stitch with the old tail and the new yarn together, to secure things. Then you may sew in tails just as you did in garter stitch, along a row of bumps. Here is that process, shown in stockinette stitch.

1 Thread the tail onto a tapestry needle. With wrong side facing, sew in and out of purl bumps for 1½".

2 Turn . . .

3 . . . then work in the opposite direction for 1". (If, in the second direction, you drive the tapestry needle through the tail already sewn, this can help to secure it.) Trim tails to no less than ½".

For clarity, demonstrations are shown with contrasting-color yarn.

Here are two sewn-in tails, in the yarn of the piece, both worked away from a mid-row join.

Here is how it looks, on the right side.

If you prefer to sew the tails into the seam allowance, then you need to know if you have enough yarn remaining to get to the end of the row. Remember that it takes approximately three times the width of a row to work a row.

SEWING IN TAILS, IN SEAM ALLOWANCES

If mid-row joins don't work, you have seam allowances . . . and perfect places to sew in tails.

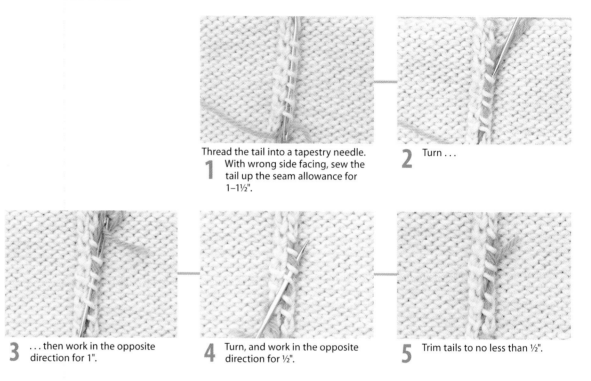

1 Thread the tail into a tapestry needle. With wrong side facing, sew the tail up the seam allowance for 1–1½".

2 Turn . . .

3 . . . then work in the opposite direction for 1".

4 Turn, and work in the opposite direction for ½".

5 Trim tails to no less than ½".

Working an increase in stockinette stitch

The increases of *The Knit Stitch*—the Make 1 (M1) and knitting into the front and back (kf&b) of a stitch—are perfectly okay to continue using. But they are not the most invisible increases in stockinette stitch. What follows is my preference.

INCREASING BY WORKING INTO THE STITCH BELOW *lifted increase*

1 Put right-hand needle through stitch below next stitch on left-hand needle.

2 Knit as usual.

Remember that to make the neatest seams possible, increases are never worked in the selvedge stitch. They are always worked at least one stitch into the body of the piece.

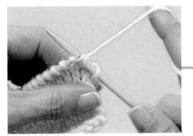

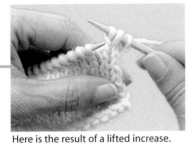

3 Now knit next stitch on left-hand needle.

Here is the result of a lifted increase.

HOW DO YOU KNOW HOW LONG AGO YOU WORKED AN INCREASE?

Patterns may have you increase every 6th row. Here's how you can look at your work to see when you last worked an increase.

If you worked your increase with the right side facing, do all of what follows with the right side facing.

1 Find the stitch that was formed on the increase row; call it row 1.

2 Count it and all rows above it, including the row on the needle. This tells you how many rows ago you worked the increase. Here the count is 4, so the increase was worked 4 rows ago. If you are to work an increase every 6th row, then you have to work 2 more rows before increasing.

Okay, so what's reverse stockinette, and why do we need it?

Reverse stockinette stitch is the name given to the back side of stockinette stitch. (Seems simple enough, but there are knitters with some experience who don't know this, and it's best to take nothing for granted.)

Reverse stockinette is produced in the same way as stockinette stitch except that the right- and wrong-side rows are reversed: all wrong-side rows are knit, and all right-side rows are purled. The result is seen as an evenly 'bumpy' fabric rather than an evenly 'smooth' one. And since it really is just stockinette stitch turned wrong-side out, this fabric has the opposite 'curl' to stockinette stitch. Where stockinette stitch is a somewhat concave fabric that curls up at its lower edge, reverse stockinette is a somewhat convex fabric that curls under.

In this chapter, these two stitch patterns are used in the same garment: the body of each piece is done in stockinette stitch, and the edges are done in reverse stockinette. And why do we use the two in combination? Because the inward curl of reverse stockinette is a neat edge treatment that holds shape, plus the combination is aesthetically pleasing.

Chapter Three

The Patterns

Additional Skills

The pattern for the felted Hat and Mitts is available as a free download on our Web site: www.knittinguniverse.com

EXPerience

- *easy*
- *simple color changes*
- *simple finishing*
- *lots of knitting*

It'll fit

One size fits all

10cm/4"

20 ⊞ GET CLOSE
13½

- *over stockinette stitch*
- *using larger needles*
- *after blocking*

You'll need

1 2 3 4 **5** 6

- *bulky weight*
- *760 yds in C1
  (charcoal)*
- *109 yds each:
  C2 (off-white)
  C3 (purple)
  C4 (eggplant)
  C5 (red)*
- *wool or wool blend*

I used

- *5.5mm/US 9, 60cm/24"*
- *4.5mm/US 7, 60cm/24"*

Lopi (REYNOLDS or ALAFOSS): 7 balls C1 (0052), 1 ball each in colors C2 (0051), C3 (0163), C4 (Reynolds 417; Alafoss 9316), and C5 (Reynolds 389; Alafoss 9389)

BASIC SERAPE

This garment came of the realization that the second volume of The Knitting Experience *needed a dead-easy piece. So, here it is, the most basic of garments—a comfort piece that can be used as a blanket when not being worn as a jacket. Having said that, there is a lot of yardage to be knit. If you just want the product (without all the hours of process), you might befriend someone with a knitting machine—on which the pieces can be produced in short order.*

This garment was designed to be knit in two pieces so you wouldn't have too much knitting in your lap. And it is knit side to side so the stripes are vertical.

> *The color pattern is only meant as a suggestion: choose any colors you like, make the stripes any width, use more colors, vary the repeats. Have fun! But here's a hint: 109 yards will yield 20 rows on each piece.*

STITCH PATTERNS

Stockinette stitch (St st)
Right side (RS) rows Knit (k) all stitches (sts).
Wrong side (WS) rows Purl (p) all stitches (sts).

Reverse stockinette stitch (RSS)
RS rows P all sts.
WS rows K all sts.

> *To read these stitch patterns, see pages 64 and 86.*

Here's how!

FRONT

With larger needle and C1, e-wrap cast on 65 sts.
SHORTEN OR LENGTHEN HERE.

> *To shorten by 1", cast on 3 fewer sts. To lengthen by 1", cast on 3 more sts.*

*With C1, work 26 rows St st (beginning with RS row and ending with WS row). Cut C1.
With C2, then C3, then C4, work 2 rows St st. Do not cut C2–C4.
With C5, work 4 rows St st. Cut C5.
With C4, then C3, then C2, work 2 rows St st. Cut C2–C4.
Repeat from * to 5 repeats—210 rows.

> *To make this garment narrower or wider, work fewer or more repeats than directed.*

With C1, work 26 rows St st. Put sts onto holder or thread. Cut all yarns.

BACK

With larger needle and C1, e-wrap cast on 95 sts.
SHORTEN OR LENGTHEN HERE.

> *To shorten by 1", cast on 3 less sts. To lengthen by 1", cast on 3 more sts.*

Work as Front, but start all colors with WS row and end with RS row.

> *Beginning with WS row will ensure that the ends are at the hem, not the neck.*

FINISHING

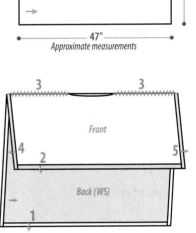

Approximate measurements

1 Back lower edging
Use smaller needle and C1.
With RS facing, pick up and k 3 sts for every 4 rows along entire back edge (page 45).
Work RSS for 5 rows, then bind off all sts in p.
Attach bind-off row of edging to selvedge, knotting and tucking all tails and/or carried colors under edging.

2 Front lower edging
Work as Back lower edging.

3 Neck opening
Sew Front and Back together, up sides without edgings and to within 5" of center (leaving center 10" open for neck). Reinforce corners of neck before cutting sewing yarn.

4 Side edgings
Use smaller needle and C1. With RS facing, pick up and k 3 sts beginning at fold line of Back edging, then 1 st in each cast-on st, then 3 sts along Front edging (ending at fold line).

> *Do not pick up sts in seam allowance.*

Next row *K8, knit 2 together (k2tog), repeat from *, k to end.
Work RSS for 3 rows, then bind off all sts in k.
Attach bind-off row of edging to selvedge. Sew edging closed at both ends.

5 Work edging along other side, beginning at Front and ending at Back and knitting sts from holders.

> *There will be 1 live st in each seam allowance. K2tog on either side of seam to eliminate these extra sts.*

Sew in any remaining tails.

EXPErience
• *easy*
• *simple shaping*
• *simple finishing*

STANDARD FIT

S (*M, L, 1X, 2X*)

A *36 (40, 44, 48, 52)"*
B (shoulder to hem)
20 (20½, 21½, 22, 23)"
C *28½ (30, 30½, 32, 32½)"*

10cm/4"

30 ⊞ GET GAUGE!
21

• *over stockinette stitch*
• *using larger needles*
• *after blocking*

You'll need

1 2 **3-4** 5 6

• *light-medium weight*
• *600 (650, 740, 790, 870) yds in light color*
• *450 (500, 550, 590, 650) yds in dark color*
• *slightly fuzzy wool or wool blend*

I used

• *4mm/US 6*

• *3.5mm/US 4, 40–50cm/16–20"*

Medium: **GARNSTUDIO Karisma Angora-Tweed, 3 skeins in color 01 (medium gray) and 4 skeins in color 02 (light gray); shown on page 74 in color 01 (medium gray) and 08 (rust).**

TWO-TONE TOP

This garment is very easy to both knit and wear. I have a difficult time not choosing to wear it.

It is knit in a yummy yarn, an angora blend whose 'hairiness' might obscure any unevenness in your early attempts to produce the smooth fabric of stockinette stitch.

The back and front of this garment are identical, which means that there is no neck shaping . . . which means that the front is high and straight and might not be attractive on someone with a short neck. This 'straight across' neck is also not flattering if your shoulders slope, but that situation is easily remedied with shoulder pads.

When using circular needles for edgings, work back and forth.

STITCH PATTERNS
Stockinette stitch (St st)
Right side (RS) rows Knit (k) all stitches (sts).
Wrong side (WS) rows Purl (p) all stitches (sts).

Reverse stockinette stitch (RSS)
RS rows P all sts.
WS rows K all sts.

To read these stitch patterns, see pages 64 and 86.

Here's how!
BACK/FRONT
The Back and Front are identical.
You may work this garment in other colors, but you must designate one the dark color (I used medium gray) and the other the light color (I used light gray or rust). The lighter (or brighter) color must go on the upper body, to draw the eye upward.

RSS edging

With smaller needle and dark color, cast on 88 (97, 106, 115, 126) sts. Work RSS for 4 rows, beginning with k (WS) row and ending with p (RS) row.

Next (increase) row (WS) With smaller needle, *k8, k into st below next st plus k into next st (lifted increase, page 67), repeat from * 8 (9, 10, 11, 12) times more, ending k7 (7, 7, 7, 9)—97 (107, 117, 127, 139) sts.

St st body

Change to larger needles and, beginning with k (RS) row, work St st to 11 (11, 10½, 10½, 10½)" from natural fold line of edging, ending with WS row.

SHORTEN OR LENGTHEN HERE.

Continue St st through all shaping and bind-offs that follow.

Armhole shaping

Bind off 5 (5, 7, 9, 11) sts at beginning of next 2 rows—87 (97, 103, 109, 117) sts remain.

Next (decrease) row (RS) Work left-slanting decrease (SKP or SSK, page 18), k to 3 sts remaining, work right-slanting decrease (k2tog), k1.

Next row P.

Repeat last 2 rows to 79 (81, 85, 87, 89) sts remaining.

Work straight (without decreasing) to 3 (3½, 4, 4½, 5)" above armhole bind-off. End dark color and begin light color.

Continue in St st to 7 (7½, 9, 9½, 10½)" above armhole bind-off.

Shoulder shaping

Bind off 2 sts at beginning of next 12 (12, 12, 14, 14) rows.

Bind off 1 (2, 3, 2, 3) sts at beginning of next 2 rows.

Put remaining 53 (53, 55, 55, 55) sts on holder (for neck).

SLEEVES

RSS edging

With smaller needle and light color, cast on 44 (44, 49, 53, 59) sts. Work RSS for 4 rows,

beginning with k (WS) row and ending with p (RS) row.

Next (increase) row (WS) With smaller needle, *k7, work lifted increase in next st, repeat from * 4 (4, 5, 5, 5) times more, ending k4 (4, 1, 5, 11)—49 (49, 55, 59, 65) sts.

St st body

Change to larger needles and, beginning with k (RS) row, work St st for 4 rows.

Continue St st through all shaping and bind-offs that follow.

Next (increase) row (RS) K1, work lifted increase in next st, k to 2 sts remaining, work lifted increase in next st, k1.

Work 7 (7, 5, 3, 3) rows straight.

Repeat last 8 (8, 6, 4, 4) rows to 69 (73, 89, 97, 111) sts.

Work straight to 16 (16½, 15½, 16, 15)" from natural fold line of edging, ending with WS row.

SHORTEN OR LENGTHEN HERE.

Cap

Bind off 5 (5, 7, 9, 11) sts at beginning of next 2 rows—59 (63, 75, 79, 89) sts remain.

Next (decrease) row (RS) K1, SKP (or SSK), k to 3 sts remaining, k2tog, k1.

Next row (WS) P.

Repeat last 2 rows to 21 sts remaining.

Bind off 2 sts at beginning of next 2 rows, then bind off remaining 17 sts.

FINISHING

Sew shoulder seams.

Sew set-in Sleeves to armholes (page 27).

Sew side and Sleeve seams (page 22).

Neck edging

Put all sts for neck onto circular needle.

Round (rnd) 1 With light color and WS facing, *k8, k2tog, repeat from *, ending k6 (6, 10, 10, 10)—96 (96, 100, 100, 100) sts remain.

Continue with WS facing and without decreasing, k 3 more rnds.

Bind off loosely.

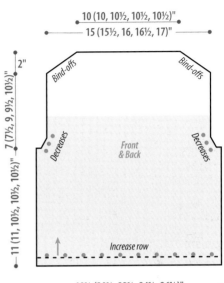

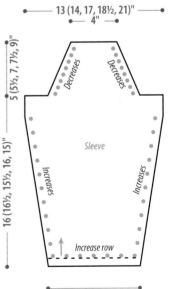

Large: 4 balls NATURALLY Naturelle Double Knit in color 254 (charcoal gray)

BASIC VEST

I love vests, and this one is as basic as they come. The shape and styling are so simple that it works for both men and women. But it is an intermediate pattern because of the level of skill demanded for the finishing and the insertion of pockets. If you want to lower the difficulty level, don't make the pockets.

There is something essential to note about this piece: the model garment has been fulled. (Its fulling factor is 1.25, something you'll understand when you read page 87.) But fulling is optional: the garment could be worn as knit, and the pattern has been written to reflect this. For further information, read the notes below.

If you don't intend to full, choose a medium-weight yarn, knit to gauge and to the measurements of the schematic.
If you do intend to full, choose a lightweight yarn, knit to gauge, treat the swatch to find your fulling factor (page 87), and follow the directions. Your garment will initially be longer than the measurements of the schematic but should match these measurements after fulling. The length changes with fulling; the width stays the same.

This garment is a 'loose' fit on a man but 'oversized' on a woman.

STITCH PATTERNS
Stockinette stitch (St st)
Right side (RS) rows Knit (k) all stitches (sts).
Wrong side (WS) rows Purl (p) all stitches (sts).

Reverse stockinette stitch (RSS)
RS rows P all sts.
WS rows K all sts.

> To read these stitch patterns, see pages 64 and 86. If fulling the garment, make a gauge swatch and treat it as directed on page 87 to find your 'fulling factor.' In the pattern, use this factor as directed.

Here's how!
BACK
RSS edging
With smaller needles, cast on 85 (94, 103, 112, 120) sts. Work RSS for 4 rows, beginning with k (WS) row and ending with p (RS) row.
Next (increase) row (WS) With smaller needle, k3 (4, 5, 6, 3), *k into st below next st plus k into next st (lifted increase, page 67), k6, repeat from * 11 (12, 13, 14, 16) times more, ending k4 (5, 6, 7, 4)—97 (107, 117, 127, 137) sts.

St st body
Change to larger needles and, beginning with k (RS) row, work St st to 12" from fold line of edging, ending with WS row.

> If fulling, work to this length multiplied by your fulling factor.

SHORTEN OR LENGTHEN HERE.
Continue St st through all shaping and bind-offs that follow.

Armhole shaping
Bind off 8 (8, 10, 12, 14) sts at beginning of next 2 rows—81 (91, 97, 103, 109) sts remain.
Next (decrease) row (RS) K1, work left-slanting decrease (SKP or SSK, page 18), k to 3 sts remaining, work right-slanting decrease (k2tog), k1.
P 1 row.
Repeat last 2 rows to 75 (81, 81, 85, 85) sts remaining. Work straight to 11" above armhole bind-off, ending with WS row.

> If fulling, work to this length multiplied by your fulling factor.

Shoulder shaping
Bind off 5 (6, 6, 6, 6) sts at beginning of next 2 rows.
Bind off 4 (5, 5, 6, 6) sts at beginning of next 2 rows—57 (59, 59, 61, 61) sts remain.

Right shoulder and neck shaping
Bind off 4 (5, 5, 6, 6) sts at beginning of next RS row, then k to 10 sts on right-hand needle.
Put next 29 sts on holder (for neck), then turn, ready to work WS row over sts of right shoulder.
*Next (WS) row Bind off 1 st at neck edge, p to end.
Next (RS) row Bind off 4 sts at shoulder, k to neck edge.
Next (WS) row Bind off 1 st at neck edge, p to end.
Next (RS) row Bind off remaining 4 sts.

EXPERience
- *intermediate*
- *simple shaping*
- *mid-level finishing*

LOOSE FIT

S (M, L, 1X, 2X)
A 41 (45, 49, 53, 57)"
B 24"

10cm/4"

26   **GET GAUGE!**
19

- *over stockinette stitch*
- *using larger needles*

You'll need

1 2 **3-4** 5 6

- *light weight (if fulling)*
- *medium weight (if not fulling)*
- *710 (780, 850, 930, 1000) yds*
- *wool (not superwash if fulling)*

- *1 separating zipper (length determined by finished garment)*

I used

- *3.75mm/US 5*
- *4.5mm/US 7*

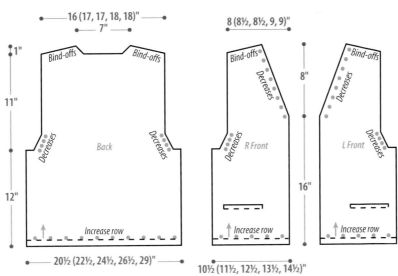

Left shoulder and neck shaping

Return to 14 (15, 15, 16, 16) sts of left shoulder.

K 1 row.

Next (WS) row Bind off 4 (5, 5, 6, 6) sts at shoulder. Work as for right shoulder and neck shaping from * to end but with reverse shaping (page 19).

RIGHT FRONT

RSS edging

With smaller needles, cast on 43 (48, 52, 56, 61) sts. Work RSS for 4 rows, beginning with k (WS) row and ending with p (RS) row.

Next (increase) row (WS) With smaller needle, k3 (6, 4, 3, 5), *work lifted increase in next st, k6, repeat from * 5 (5, 6, 7, 7) times more, ending k4 (6, 5, 3, 6)—49 (54, 59, 64, 69) sts.

St st body

Change to larger needles and, beginning with k (RS) row, work St st to 4½" from fold line of edging, ending with WS row.

> If you don't want pockets, work as Back to Armhole shaping.

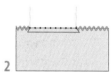

Pocket edging

Continue on larger needles.

Next row (RS) K26 (29, 32, 35, 38), *p7, purl 2 together (p2tog, page 110), repeat from * once more. Turn, leaving 5 (7, 9, 11, 13) sts behind.

Next row (WS) K16. Turn, leaving 26 (29, 32, 35, 38) sts behind.

Work RSS for 1 more row over these 16 sts, then bind off in purl.

Put 26 (29, 32, 35, 38) sts and 5 (7, 9, 11, 13) sts on holders (sts on either side of pocket edging).

Pocket lining

Fold pocket edging down so WS is facing. Slip smaller needle, from left to right, through 18 purl bumps just below pocket edging.

With larger needle, k these 18 sts.

Continue to work these 18 sts in St st for 8", ending with WS row. Break yarn.

Pocket lining to Front

With RS facing, k26 (29, 32, 35, 38) sts from first holder, k18 sts from pocket lining, then k5 (7, 9, 11, 13) sts from second holder.

> As you do this, the pocket lining folds to form a little pouch.

Continue St st to same length as Back to armhole, ending with RS row.

> Continue St st through all shaping and bind-offs that follow.

Armhole shaping

Bind off 8 (8, 10, 12, 14) sts at beginning of next WS row—41 (46, 49, 52, 55) sts remain.

Next (decrease) row (RS) K to 3 sts remaining, k2tog, k1.

P 1 row.

Repeat last 2 rows to 38 (41, 41, 43, 43) sts remaining. Work straight to 16" from fold line of lower edging, ending with WS row.

> If fulling, work to this length multiplied by your fulling factor.

V-neck shaping

Rows 1 & 3 (RS) K1, SKP (or SSK), k to end.

Rows 2 & 4 P.

Row 5 K.

Row 6 P.

Repeat last 6 rows (decreasing at neck 2 of 3 RS rows) until 17 neck decreases have been worked and 21 (24, 24, 26, 26) sts remain.

AT SAME TIME, begin shoulder shaping when piece is same length as Back above armhole bind-off (ending with RS row).

Shoulder shaping

Bind off 5 (6, 6, 6, 6) sts at beginning of next WS row. Bind off 4 (5, 5, 6, 6) sts at beginning of next 2 WS rows.

Bind off 4 sts at beginning of next 2 WS rows.

LEFT FRONT

Work as Right Front but with reverse shaping (page 19). Reverse shaping is required through Pocket edging, Pocket lining to front, Armhole shaping, V-neck shaping, and Shoulder shaping.

FINISHING

Pockets

Sew sides of pocket edgings to garment, allowing them to curl along fold line.

Sew sides of pocket linings closed.

Front edging

Sew shoulder seams.

With RS facing, smaller needle, and beginning at lower Right Front edge, pick up and k (page 45) the following around entire front opening:

- 2 sts along lower edging (beginning at fold line),
- 2 sts for each 3 rows to point of V,
- k1, yarn over (yo), k1 in st at point of V,
- 3 sts for each 4 rows from point of V to shoulder,
- 3 sts around right Back neck shaping,
- (k6, k2tog) 3 times along Back neck sts then k5 remaining Back neck sts,
- 3 sts around left Back neck shaping,
- 3 sts for each 4 rows from shoulder to point of V of Left Front,
- k1, yo, k1 in st at point of V,
- 2 sts for each 3 rows from point of V to lower edging,
- 2 sts along lower Left Front edging (ending at fold line).

Work RSS for 4 rows, beginning with WS row and ending with RS row, then bind off in knit.

Sew bound-off edge of edging to selvedge of garment.

Armhole edgings

With RS facing, smaller needle, and beginning at underarm, pick up and k the following:

- 7 (7, 9, 10, 12) sts for bind-off sts at underarm,
- 2 sts for each 3 rows around armhole edge,
- 7 (7, 9, 10, 12) sts for bind-off sts at underarm.

Work RSS for 4 rows, beginning with WS row and ending with RS row, then bind off in knit.

Sew bound-off edge of edgings to selvedge of garment.

Sew side seams (page 22).

Sew in all tails (page 64).

Full garment if desired (page 87).

Measure garment from point of V to lower edge; purchase separating zipper this length or less.

Position front edgings so they just meet at center front, and stitch zipper in place.

Medium: 6 skeins CLASSIC ELITE Waterspun in color 5088 (Sweet Potato)

CROSS-OVER TOP

What makes a vest a vest, rather than a top? Obviously, it's a vest if it's worn with something underneath. If it can be worn without something underneath, then it's a top. What is the factor that limits this choice? The cut of the armholes. If they are shaped too deeply for you to feel comfortable without another piece of clothing underneath, then it can only be a vest.

This garment is shown both ways: as a top (in a shimmery yarn) with nothing underneath, and as a vest (in wool) with something quite slim underneath. The shape of both garments is the same, with high armholes, so you have choices.

The silver clasps for the shimmery top are made by my friend and well-known Canadian metal artist, Aggie Beynon, of Harbinger Gallery (see Suppliers, page 171).

All measurements are for the garment as knit. It can be worn as knit. But I knit the melon-colored wool version to the length suggested, and then I fulled it by washing and tumbling in a warm dryer until it was the length I wanted (2" shorter). The width did not change. If you want to full AND make it B length (or longer), add length wherever it says SHORTEN OR LENGTHEN HERE.

STITCH PATTERNS

Stockinette stitch (St st)
Right side (RS) rows Knit (k) all stitches (sts).
Wrong side (WS) rows Purl (p) all stitches (sts).

Reverse stockinette stitch (RSS)
RS rows P all sts.
WS rows K all sts.

> To read these stitch patterns, see pages 64 and 86.

Here's how!

BACK

RSS edging

With smaller needles, cast on 90 (100, 108, 118, 128) sts. Work RSS for 4 rows, beginning with k (WS) row and ending with p (RS) row.

Next (increase) row (WS) With smaller needle, k4 (9, 4, 9, 8), *k into st below next st plus k into next st (lifted increase, page 67), k8 (8, 8, 8, 9), repeat from * 8 (8, 10, 10, 10) times more, increase 1, k4 (9, 4, 9, 9)—100 (110, 120, 130, 140) sts.

St st body

Change to larger needles and, beginning with RS row, work St st to 10½ (11, 11½, 12, 12½)" from fold line of edging, ending with WS row.
SHORTEN OR LENGTHEN HERE.

> Continue St st through all shaping and bind-offs that follow.

Armhole shaping

Bind off 5 (7, 9, 11, 13) sts at beginning of next 2 rows—90 (96, 102, 108, 114) sts remain.
Next (decrease) row (RS) K1, work left-slanting decrease (SKP or SSK, page 18), k to 3 sts remaining, work right-slanting decrease (k2tog), k1.
P 1 row.
Repeat last 2 rows to 74 (80, 84, 90, 94) sts remaining.
Work straight to 7 (7½, 7½, 8, 8)" above armhole bind-off, ending with WS row.

Shoulder shaping

Bind off 3 sts at beginning of next 10 rows.
Bind off 2 (3, 3, 4, 5) sts at beginning of next 2 rows.
Bind off 2 (3, 4, 5, 5) sts at beginning of next 2 rows.
Bind off 2 (3, 4, 5, 6) sts at beginning of next 2 rows.
Put remaining 32 sts on holder (for Back neck).

EXPERIence

- *intermediate*
- *mid-level shaping*
- *mid-level finishing*

S (M, L, 1X, 2X)
A (approximately)
39 (44, 47, 51, 56)"
B (if not fulled)
19½ (20½, 21, 22, 22½)"

10cm/4"

30 | GET GAUGE!
20

- *over stockinette stitch*
- *using larger needles*
- *after blocking*

You'll need

1 2 3 **4** 5 6

- *medium weight*
- *700 (800, 900, 1000, 1100) yds*
- *anything (non-superwash wool, if fulling)*

- *Three 2" hook-and-eye clasps OR five ¾" buttons*
- *(optional) Two ¾" snaps*

I used

- *4mm/US 6*
- *3.5mm/US 4*

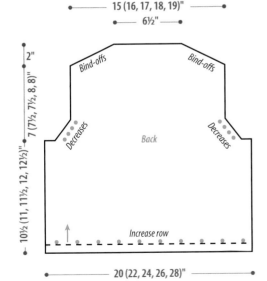

15 (16, 17, 18, 19)"
6½"
2"
7 (7½, 7½, 8, 8)"
10½ (11, 11½, 12, 12½)"
Bind-offs   Bind-offs
Decreases   Decreases
Back
Increase row
20 (22, 24, 26, 28)"

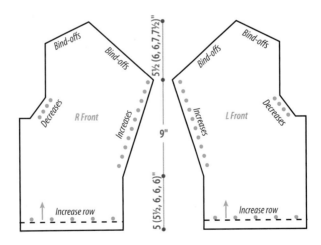

Bind-offs   Bind-offs
5½ (6, 6, 7, 7½)"
Decreases   Increases   Increases   Decreases
R Front   L Front
9"
5 (5½, 6, 6)"
Increase row   Increase row
10 (11½, 12, 13, 14½)"

RIGHT FRONT
RSS edging
With smaller needles, cast on 44 (51, 55, 60, 66) sts. Work RSS for 4 rows, beginning with k (WS) row and ending with p (RS) row.
Next (increase) row (WS) With smaller needle, k3 (6, 4, 7, 5), *work lifted increase in next st, k8 (8, 8, 8, 8), repeat from * 3 (3, 4, 4, 5) times more, increase 1, k4 (8, 5, 7, 6)—49 (56, 61, 66, 73) sts.
St st body
Change to larger needles and, beginning with RS row, work St st to 5 (5½, 6, 6, 6)" from fold line of edging, ending with WS row.
SHORTEN OR LENGTHEN HERE.

> *Continue St st through all shaping and bind-offs that follow. You might have difficulties unless you count (and make note of) neck increases and armhole decreases as you make them.*

Front shaping
Next (increase) row (RS) K1, work lifted increase in next st, k to end.
Work 3 rows straight.
Repeat these last 4 rows to same length as Back to armhole, ending with row 3.
Armhole shaping
Bind off 5 (7, 9, 11, 13) sts at beginning of next WS row.
Next (neck increase and armhole decrease) row (RS) K1, work lifted increase in next st, k to 3 sts remaining, k2tog, k1.
P 1 row.
Next (armhole decrease) row (RS) K to 3 sts remaining, k2tog, k1.
P 1 row.
Repeat last 4 rows until 8 (8, 9, 9, 10) armhole decreases and 17 neck increases have been made—53 (58, 60, 63 67) sts remain.

> *Armhole decreases will be finished before 17 neck increases have been made. Work armhole straight while continuing to make neck increases.*

Neck shaping
P 1 row.
Next row (RS) Bind off 2 sts at beginning of row, work to end (decreasing for armhole at end of row if necessary).
P 1 row.
Repeat last 2 rows until armhole is same length as Back from armhole bind-off to shoulder.
Continue neck shaping (binding off at beginning of RS rows) while shaping shoulder. After 32 (34, 34, 34, 36) neck sts have been bound off, work neck edge straight.

> *It's easy to count bound-off sts at neck edge: each bound-off jog = 2 sts.*

Shoulder shaping
Bind off 3 sts at beginning of next 5 WS rows.

Bind off 2 (3, 3, 4, 5) sts at beginning of next WS row.
Bind off 2 (3, 4, 5, 5) sts at beginning of next WS row.
Bind off 2 (3, 4, 5, 6) sts at beginning of next WS row.

LEFT FRONT
Work as Right Front to Front shaping.
Continue to work as Right Front but with reverse shaping (page 19) and with following hints.

> *Work **RS (increase) row** as follows: K to 2 sts remaining, work lifted increase in next st, k1.*
> *After armhole bind-off, work **RS neck increase and armhole decrease row** as follows: K1, SKP, k to 2 sts remaining, work lifted increase in next st, k1.*
> *At neck shaping and after final neck increases, work 1 WS and then 1 RS row.*
> *Shape shoulder at beginning of RS rows.*

FINISHING
Sew shoulder seams.
Neck edging
With RS facing, smaller needle, and beginning at Right Front neck, pick up and knit around curved edge (page 46).
Work 4 rows RSS, beginning with WS row and ending with RS row.
Next row Bind off.
Sew bound-off edge of edging to selvedge of garment.
Left Front edging
With RS facing, smaller needle, and beginning at neck edging, pick up and k the following (page 45):
  • 3 sts from neck edging (beginning at fold line),
  • 3 sts for every 4 rows (to lower edging),
  • 3 sts from lower edging (ending at fold line).
Work 4 rows RSS, beginning with WS row and ending with RS row.
Next row Bind off.
Sew bound-off edge of edging to selvedge of garment.
Right Front edging
Pick up and knit as Left Front edging but in reverse.
For clasps
Work 4 rows RSS, beginning with WS row and ending with RS row.
Next row Bind off in knit.
Attach hooks On Right Front, place the top clasp 1" from neck edging, the bottom clasp just before this diagonal ends, and the center one spaced evenly between; sew in place.

> *Make sure hook mechanisms begin at outer edge of edging and extend completely past edging.*

Attach eyes Try top on, and find degree of overlap desired; mark placement of eyes to correspond to hooks, then sew eyes in place.

If desired, sew snaps in place (one where Right Front and Left Front meet at neck edge, and the other where they meet below the lowest clasp).

For button loops

After pick-up-and-knit row, k 1 (WS) row. Mark 5 spots for button loops along diagonal edge, with top spot 1½" from neck edging and lowest spot where diagonal edge ends and straight edge begins.

Use cable cast-on through next row.

Next row (RS) P to first marked spot, *turn work, cast on 4 sts, insert needle for 5th st, wrap yarn and make st as usual, but *before putting this st onto left-hand needle* bring yarn to front (between the needles). Now put final cast-on stitch onto left-hand needle. Turn work, p to next marked spot, repeat from * until 5 button loops have been made. With RS facing, p to end.

K 1 (WS) row.

Next row P to first button loop; *look very carefully at work, then bind off the same 5 sts as were cast on, work to next button loop, repeat from * until 5 button loops have been bound off, p to end.

Next row Bind off in knit.

Sew bound-off edge of edging to selvedge of garment.

Sew buttons onto Left Front to correspond to button loops.

Armhole edgings

With RS facing and smaller needle, pick up and k the following:

- 4 (6, 8, 10, 12) sts for bound-off sts at armholes,
- 2 sts for each 3 rows around entire armhole,
- 4 (6, 8, 10, 12) sts for bound-off sts at armholes.

Work RSS for 4 rows, beginning with WS row and ending with RS row, then bind off all sts. Sew side seams (page 22).

Medium: 10 balls BERROCO Cotton Twist in color 8368

EXPERience

- *easy intermediate*
- *simple shaping*
- *mid-level finishing*

LOOSE FIT

*Child's 6-8 (10-12,
Man's S, M, L, 1X, 2X)*

A *29 (33, 39, 43, 47,
51, 55)"*

B *16 (20, 26, 26, 27,
27½, 28)"*

C *22½ (24½, 32, 33, 34,
35, 36)"*

10cm/4"

30 ▦ GET GAUGE!
20

- *over stockinette stitch*
- *using larger needles*
- *after blocking*

You'll need

1 2 3 **4** 5 6

- *medium weight*
- *820 (1170, 1840,
2070, 2250, 2460,
2620) yds*
- *wool or wool blend*

😊

- *2 cord locks
(in coordinating color)*
- *2 (2, 3, 3, 3, 3) yds
1/8" elastic cord
(in coordinating color)*

I used

- *4mm/US 6*
- *3.5mm/US 4*

CLASSIC ELITE Waterspun: Man's Medium, 15 skeins in color 5046 (Blue Spruce); Child's 6-8, 6 skeins in color 5072 (Lt. Teal)

KANGAROO DUO

I was cross-country skiing with a friend (who was wearing a kangaroo sweatshirt, with bird seed for the chickadees in the pouch) when I saw a family go by and thought, "Wouldn't it be nice to produce a family of kangaroo sweaters?" These garments are the result— one for a Mom or Dad, and one for a child.

The adult garment was made for a 5'10" – 6' man. The sleeves and body are, therefore, long on a woman. I wear mine this way (and I'm only 5'4"), so I decided not to write a separate woman's pattern. If you wish, you may shorten where directed: the body may not need shortening, but for a 5'4" woman, the sleeves could be shortened by 4".

STITCH PATTERNS

Stockinette stitch (St st)
Right side (RS) rows Knit (k) all stitches (sts).
Wrong side (WS) rows Purl (p) all stitches (sts).

Reverse stockinette stitch (RSS)
RS rows P all sts.
WS rows K all sts.

To read these stitch patterns, see pages 64 and 86.

Here's how!

BACK

RSS edging

With smaller needles, cast on 70 (79, 93, 102, 111, 120, 130) sts. Work RSS for 4 (4, 6, 6, 6, 6) rows, beginning with k (WS) row and ending with p (RS) row.

Next (increase) row (WS) With smaller needle, k9 (9, 6, 5, 5, 4, 9), *k into st below plus k into next st (lifted increase, page 67), k9, repeat from * 4 (5, 7, 8, 9, 10, 10) times more, increase 1, k10 (9, 6, 6, 5, 5, 10)—76 (86, 102, 112, 122, 132, 142) sts.

St st body

Change to larger needles and, beginning with RS row, work St st to 15 (19, 25, 25, 26,

26½, 27)" from fold line of edging and ending with WS row.

SHORTEN OR LENGTHEN HERE.

Continue St st through all shaping and bind-offs that follow.

Left neck shaping

Next row (RS) K21 (24, 29, 34, 39, 44, 49), bind off next 34 (38, 44, 44, 44, 44, 44) sts (for neck), k remaining 21 (24, 29, 34, 39, 44, 49) sts.

Next row (WS) P21 (24, 29, 34, 39, 44, 49) sts of left shoulder.

Turn. Work over sts of left shoulder only.

*Bind off 1 st at beginning of next 3 RS rows (at neck edge). Work 2 WS rows straight.

Bind off remaining 18 (21, 26, 31, 36, 41, 46) sts next WS row.

Right neck shaping

Return to 21 (24, 29, 34, 39, 44, 49) sts (of right shoulder), ready to work WS row.

Work as for left neck shaping from * to end but with reverse shaping (page 19).

FRONT

Work as Back to 2 (2, 2½, 2½, 2½, 2½, 2½)" from natural fold line of edging, ending with WS row. Continue St st through remainder of garment.

1 Pocket front

Next row (RS) K58 (63, 76, 86, 91, 96, 101).

Put remaining 18 (23, 26, 26, 31, 36, 41) sts on holder. Turn.

Next row (WS) P40 (40, 50, 60, 60, 60, 60) sts for pocket front. Put remaining 18 (23, 26, 26, 31, 36, 41) sts on holder.

Work center 40 (40, 50, 60, 60, 60, 60) sts for 2 rows, beginning with RS row and ending with WS row.

Next (decrease) row (RS) K1, work left-slanting decrease (SKP or SSK, page 18), k to 3 sts remaining, work right-slanting decrease (k2tog), k1.

Work 7 rows straight.

Repeat these last 8 rows to 30 (30, 38, 44, 44, 44, 44) sts remaining, ending with RS decrease row.

Work 3 more rows—pocket front measures approximately 5½ (5½, 6½, 8½, 8½, 8½, 8½)" in height. Break yarn.

Put pocket front sts on holder.

2 Pocket trim

With RS facing and smaller needles, pick up and k3 sts for each 4 rows (page 45) along one side of pocket front—30 (30, 36, 48, 48, 48, 48) sts. Turn. Continuing on smaller needles, work 3 rows RSS, beginning and ending with k (WS) row. Bind off in purl. Work other side of pocket front in same manner.

3 Body, continued

With larger needles and RS facing, k18 (23, 26, 26, 31, 36, 41) sts from first holder, then pick up and k40 (40, 50, 60, 60, 60, 60) sts from WS purl bumps (page 86) behind first row of pocket front, then k18 (23, 26, 26, 31, 36, 41) sts from second holder—75 (86, 102, 112, 122, 132, 142) sts.

Work straight in St st until body is same height as pocket front, ending with WS row.

4 Joining pocket front to body

Put sts from pocket front on spare needle, ready to work RS row.

Next row (RS) K23 (28, 32, 34, 39, 44, 49). With pocket front sts to front of work, k2tog (1 st from pocket front with 1 st from body) across next 30 (30, 38, 44, 44, 44, 44) sts, then k to end.

St st body (above pocket)

Work straight to 13½ (17½, 23, 23, 24, 24½, 25)" from natural fold line of edging, ending with WS row.

SHORTEN OR LENGTHEN HERE.

Right neck shaping

K28 (32, 38, 43, 48, 53, 58) sts, bind off next 20 (22, 26, 26, 26, 26, 26) sts (for center Front neck), k remaining 28 (32, 38, 43, 48, 53, 58) sts.

Next row (WS) P sts of right shoulder. Turn.

*Bind off 3 sts at beginning of next RS row.

Work all following WS rows straight.

Bind off 2 sts at beginning of next 1 (2, 2, 2, 2, 2, 2) RS rows. Bind off 1 st at beginning of next 5 (4, 5, 5, 5, 5, 5) RS rows—18 (21, 26, 31, 36, 41, 46) sts remain.

Work straight to same length as Back, ending with WS row.

Bind off.

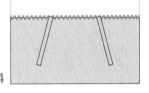

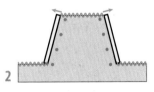

Pick up and k from purl bumps

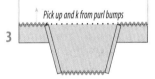

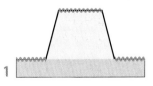

Left neck shaping

Return to 28 (32, 38, 43, 48, 53, 58) sts (of left shoulder), ready to work WS row.

Work as right neck shaping from * to end but with reverse shaping.

SLEEVES
RSS edging

With smaller needles, cast on 33 (40, 44, 44, 50, 55, 55) sts. Work RSS for 4 (4, 6, 6, 6, 6, 6) rows, beginning with k (WS) row and ending with p (RS) rows.

Next (increase) row (WS) With smaller needle, k6 (5, 7, 4, 2, 3, 3), *work lifted increase in next st, k9 (9, 9, 4, 4, 3, 3), repeat from * 2 (3, 3, 7, 9, 12, 12) times, increase 1, k6 (4, 6, 4, 2, 3, 3)—36 (44, 48, 52, 60, 68, 68) sts.

St st body

Change to larger needles and, beginning with RS row, work St st for 4 rows.

Next (increase) row (RS) K1, work lifted increase in next st, k to 2 sts remaining, work lifted increase in next st, k1.

Work 3 rows straight.

Repeat last 4 rows to 80 (90, 106, 112, 112, 120, 120) sts.

Work straight to 15 (16, 22, 22, 22, 22, 22)" from natural fold line of edging, ending with WS row.

SHORTEN OR LENGTHEN HERE.

Bind off.

HOOD
RSS edging

With smaller needles, cast on 99 (108, 117, 117, 117, 117, 117) sts.

  To make hood taller by 1" cast on 9 more sts.

Work RSS for 4 (4, 6, 6, 6, 6, 6) rows, beginning with k (WS) row and ending with p (RS) row.

Next (increase) row (WS) With smaller needles, *k8, work lifted increase in next st, repeat from * 10 (11, 12, 12, 12, 12, 12) times more—110 (120, 130, 130, 130, 130, 130) sts.

St st body

Next row (RS) With larger needles, k55 (60, 65, 65, 65, 65, 65), place marker, k to end.

Beginning with WS row, work St st to 6 (7, 8, 8, 8, 8, 8)" from natural fold line of edging, ending with WS row.

Next (decrease) row (RS) K to 3 sts from marker, SKP (or SSK), k2, k2tog, k to end.

P 1 row.

Repeat these 2 rows to 80 (90, 100, 100, 100, 100, 100) sts remaining, ending with WS row.

Bind off.

FINISHING

Sew shoulder seams.

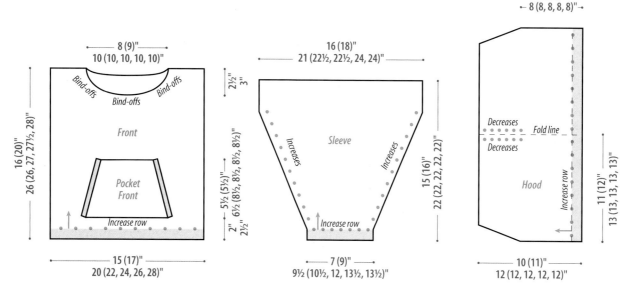

Hood

Fold Hood in half, and sew center back seam. Sew cast-on row of edging to WS of first row of Hood, leaving beginning and end open for elastic cord. Thread elastic cord loosely through edging. Thread both ends of elastic cord through cord lock, then finish with secure knot before trimmings ends of elastic.

With front edgings of Hood meeting at center Front neck, pin Hood to neck opening, easing extra fullness into center Back neck. Sew Hood, evenly, into neck opening, taking 1 selvedge st from Hood and bind-off row or selvedge st from neck opening into seam allowance.

Pockets

Sew bind-off row of edgings to seam allowance of Pocket fronts.

Sew beginning and end of edging to Front of garment, allowing edgings to curl along natural fold lines.

Sew drop-shoulder Sleeves to garment (page 26).

Sew left Sleeve and side seams, including lower edgings (page 22).

Beginning at right side seam, sew cast-on row of edging to WS of first row of Front and Back body, leaving beginning and end open for elastic cord.

Sew right Sleeve and side seams, leaving edging open for elastic cord.

Thread elastic cord loosely through edging. Thread both ends of elastic cord through cord lock, then finish with secure knot before trimming ends of elastic.

Reading reverse stockinette stitch

Reverse stockinette stitch is the wrong side—the bumpy side—of stockinette stitch. In this chapter it is used for edging, to counteract the roll of the stockinette stitch pieces.

How do you know where you are in this stitch pattern?

Oops, I knit when I should have purled! What do I do now? See page 166.

Oops, I dropped a stitch! What do I do now? See page 164.

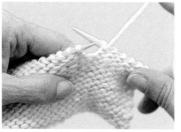

If you are working (or ready to work) a bumpy, right-side row, you will purl.

If you are working (or ready to work) a smooth, wrong-side row, you will knit.

Picking up and knitting from purl bumps

1 Find the row of purl bumps from which you want to pick up and knit. (Here I have folded the piece so that row sits along the top).

2 Insert right-hand needle under first purl bump . . .

3 . . . and draw through a loop.

4 *Insert right-hand needle under next purl bump, and draw through a loop. Repeat from * until entire row of purl bumps has been worked.

Fulling

Pure, non-superwash wool is affected by the following when wet: soap, a sudden change of water temperature, and agitation. This change can be a bad thing; think of shrunken wool garments you've known. Or it can be a good thing; think of beautiful, traditional boiled wool jackets.

Fulling is the term used for the controlled process of deliberately shrinking wool to make a more felt-like fabric. The stitches in the finished piece may be slightly visible or not at all—which makes it a nice project for a beginner whose stockinette stitch has not yet achieved a regular tension.

For minimal fulling, as was done to the vests of this chapter, work as follows.

1 Make a gauge swatch twice the size of the pattern gauge. (In this chapter, the vest requires 19 stitches and 26 rows over stockinette stitch, so you will cast on 38 stitches and work 52 rows.)

2 Mark, with thread, an area that represents the gauge of the pattern. (For example, 19 stitches wide and 26 rows tall.)

3 Wash the swatch as you would a wool sweater that you don't want to shrink, and do not use fabric softener. (I recommend using Eucalan or some other gentle wool wash.) Now put it into a warm dryer with a similar-colored, non-shedding towel. Check it frequently; remove it when you like the fabric.

4 When dry, measure the length of the marked area: it might be 3½". Now measure the width of the marked area: it should be 4". If it does not measure 4" wide, proceed to Step 5; if it does measure 4", proceed to Step 6.

5 If the area did not measure 4" wide, rewet the swatch, and see if you can stretch it to 4". Alternatively, you need to do what you would normally do if you did not match stitch gauge: work another swatch on smaller or larger needles, and repeat Steps 2–4.

6 Now divide 4" by the length of your marked area. The result is your **fulling factor**. (For example, if your length = 3½", your fulling factor = 1.125.)

To full the knit garment, work as Step 3 (above). Do not be discouraged if it doesn't come out to the measurements you expected. (Often enough, I have knit identical pieces from the same yarn but in different colors, and they came out differently!) Try rewetting and stretching to the measurements you wanted. Or see what follows if more drastic measures are required.

If the piece is too large, you have two choices:
• use only the dryer;
• repeat the process of washing and drying.
The most dramatic results come from rewashing! Unless the piece is much too large, I would not recommend doing this. For more controlled shrinkage, use only the dryer. Rewet the piece and put it in the dryer on the warm cycle with a dry towel. Check it frequently, and when it is the desired size, remove it.

If the piece is too small, you have only one option here (other than giving it to a smaller person or cutting it up for oven mitts).
• Fill a tub or sink with the hottest water you can; then pour in as much coarse salt as the water will absorb.
• Let the solution come to room temperature.
• Add the garment, and soak for 3 hours.
• Rinse the garment well.
• Squeeze out as much moisture as you can.
• Stretch the garment to desired shape, and dry flat.

It may seem like a lot of knitting to produce such a large gauge swatch, but small pieces don't give accurate information.

To dramatically shrink a piece of knit fabric, see the first sentence in this section. "Pure, non-superwash wool is affected by the following when wet: soap, a sudden change of water temperature, and agitation." So, for the most shrinkage, wash the piece in a warm or hot wash with soap, and then rinse with cold. (The more extreme the change in water temperature, the more extreme the result.)

Over the required 3 hours, the salt will break down the bonds in the wool, allowing it to be pulled larger. The fabric is weakened by this, but it should hold it to shape well enough to wear.

WHY DON'T MORE GUYS GET THIS?

I am curious as to why more men haven't discovered knitting in the same great and growing numbers that women have. Do they know what they're missing? Consider how knitting could improve their quality of life.

- Knitting (because it is physically repetitive, intellectually undemanding, visually stimulating) puts us into the right brain—a place that is intuitive and optimistic, where time has no meaning and where new possibilities present. Guys *tend* to be left-brain–dominant and so might *really need* knitting in their lives.
- Knitting relieves tedium and makes us patient. We don't mind waiting in a doctor's office or at a child's piano lesson, as long as we have our knitting. Mind you, it takes a strong man to knit in public. (I knew one who entertained his children this way: he'd knit, and they'd watch curious onlookers walk into walls.)
- Knitting helps us to focus and to develop math skills, hand-eye coordination, and spatial relations. The Waldorf Schools introduce knitting to 6-year-olds for these reasons, and the boys take to it every bit as well as girls. (Wouldn't we understand a guy's need to focus and demand, "Wait 'til I finish this row!")
- Knitting calms our nerves and sustains us through difficult times. (How *can* anyone watch a hockey game without knitting?)
- Knitting produces great *stuff*! (Imagine the guy who knits a hat, scarf, or sweater for his girl-friend. How popular would *he* be? But, given the jinx associated with knitting for a current relationship, we'd have to hope that the guys have better luck—that three weeks after the gift there'd still be a girlfriend!)
- For most of knitting's history, men did the knitting—and still do in many parts of the world. It seems that if it's *production* knitting, the men do it. But what about the benefits of the *process*? (See page 51.)
- Indeed, present knitting culture is dominated by women. But—wait a minute—wouldn't that make it a *great* place for a guy if he were inclined to meet women?

So why haven't more men figured this out? What's the roadblock here? Is it that men are still reluctant to engage in activities traditionally viewed as feminine?

Maybe there needs to be another revolution, paralleling the women's from which we all benefited. After the wisdom of feminist thinking, doors were opened to activities previously thought to be exclusively male, so women became doctors, lawyers, airline pilots, members of government. Maybe we now need a men's or even a *humanist* revolution, where all choices are open to everyone—where it really is okay for men to choose activities traditionally female, to stay home with children, to become nurses, to cry in public, to knit.

But wait a minute: didn't that revolution already happen? Men can apply for paternity leave. There *are* male nurses. And we've certainly seen male athletes, politicians, CEOs convicted of tax evasion *crying*!

So where are the great hordes of new male knitters?

Here's another stitch pattern we associate with knitting—the regular interplay of knits and purls that produces ribbing. This interplay is most often seen in 1 × 1 rib (1 knit stitch then 1 purl stitch) or 2 × 2 rib (2 knit stitches then 2 purl stitches).

There are some significant features of this kind of simple ribbing. One is the fact that it sits flat and doesn't roll. Another is its extreme elasticity (its 'grab' factor). A third is its aesthetic appeal (its strong vertical line). These three together mean that ribbing can be used alone to knit a simple, attractive, body-hugging little pullover (like the first piece in this chapter).

But we don't always want quite this much elasticity. If we have more right-side knits, between the purls, then the fabric has less 'grab.' The rest of the chapter explores a less elastic rib—with edgings done in 1 × 1 rib and with the body of each garment done in 3 × 1 rib (3 knit stitches then 1 purl stitch).

Combinations of rib stitch patterns add to the difficulty level of patterns that use them. We need to start off with the correct multiple of stitches, and we need to pay constant attention to our knits and purls so we don't disrupt the stitch pattern (especially through shaping). All of this is helped by an ability to 'read' our knitting, as discussed in the skills section of this chapter.

What's with the title of this chapter? Ribbing is also a stitch pattern with a timeless, classic look, and many of the garments that follow have this designation in their title. These garments are not trendy: they could have been worn 40 years ago. With no overriding revolution in fiber development, they might be worn 40 years from now. And given ribbing's elasticity, they should still fit!

Chapter Four

The Patterns

Additional Skills

Small: 9 balls KOIGU Kersti in color 104, or
MUENCH Verikeri in color 4108 (shown on page 90)

RAGLAN BODY-HUGGER

I am not a huge fan of the raglan style (the name for the sleeve shaping of this garment): it can do nasty things to those of us with a large bust, and it can be difficult to write patterns for many sizes. Having said that, this simple little piece is such a classic that I couldn't not make one for this book. (Actually, I made two: the second is in a glitzy yarn and shown on page 90.)

What makes it simple is its 'non-neck': the garment just ends, without any sort of neck shaping or edging. This makes it simple to knit and easy enough to wear—as long as you don't mind the bareness at the neck, and if you have a bust that you don't mind accentuating!

> *The A measurement (the finished circumference) of this garment is approximate: it depends very much on how much you block the pieces and how permanently the yarn responds to this blocking—by either staying where you put it or springing back.*

> *If you want a smaller garment, see the note in the Finishing section.*

> *The C measurement (the finished length from center back neck to cuff) reflects how the garment will stretch when worn. The schematic shows the measurements as knit.*

STITCH PATTERN
2 × 2 rib (multiple of 2 sts + 2)
Right-side (RS) rows Knit (k) 2, *purl (p) 2, k2, repeat from * to end.
Wrong-side (WS) rows P2, *k2, p2, repeat from * to end.
> *To read this stitch pattern, see page 106.*

Here's how!
BACK/FRONT
Cast on 118 (130, 146, 158, 170) sts.
Work 2 × 2 rib stitch pattern to 9 (9, 10, 9½, 9½)" from beginning, ending with WS row.
SHORTEN OR LENGTHEN HERE.
Armhole shaping
> *Maintain stitch pattern through all shaping.*

Rows 1 & 5 (decrease) K2, p2, k1, work left-slanting decrease (SKP or SSK, page 18), work to 7 sts remaining, work right-slanting decrease (k2tog), k1, p2, k2.

Rows 2 & 4 (decrease) P2, k2, p1, work left-slanting decrease (p2tog, page 110), work to 7 sts remaining, work right-slanting decrease (SSP, page 110), p1, k2, p2.

Row 3 (RS) K2, p2, k2, work to 6 sts remaining, k2, p2, k2.

Row 6 (WS) P2, k2, p2, work to 6 sts remaining, p2, k2, p2.

Repeat last 6 rows to 46 (48, 52, 54, 54) sts remaining, ending with WS row.
Bind off in rib (page 109).

SLEEVES

Cast on 46 (50, 54, 58, 62) sts.
Work 2 × 2 rib stitch pattern for 4 rows.

Maintain stitch pattern through all shaping (page 111).

Next (increase) row (RS) K2, work into st below next st plus into next st (lifted increase, page 67), work to 3 sts remaining, work lifted increase in next st, k2.
Work 5 (5, 3, 3, 3) rows straight.
Repeat last 6 (6, 4, 4, 4) rows to 78 (88, 98, 108, 118) sts.

Work straight to 16½ (16, 15, 14½, 13½)" from beginning, ending with WS row.
SHORTEN OR LENGTHEN HERE.

Armhole shaping

Row 1 (decrease) K2, p2, k1, SKP (or SSK), work to 7 sts remaining, k2tog, k1, p2, k2.

Row 2 (WS) P2, k2, p2, work to 6 sts remaining, p2, k2, p2.

Repeat last 2 rows to 22 (24, 26, 28, 30) sts remaining, ending with WS row.
Bind off in rib.

FINISHING

Block pieces to shape before seaming.

If you want a smaller garment than the A measurement, block very lightly or do not block at all. You may still block it a little larger after seaming.

Sew armhole edges together.

There will be 2 (4, 0, 2, 4) more rows in the Sleeves than in the Back/Front, so begin sewing with Sleeve armhole edges, and ease these in as you go.

Sew Sleeve and side seams.

If garment does not sit on shoulders as tightly as desired, tighten bound-off edge (page 175).

EXPERience

• *easy*
• *repetitive stitch pattern*
• *simple shaping*
• *simple finishing*

STANDARD FIT

S (M, L, 1X, 2X)
A 36 (40, 44, 48, 52)"
B 19 (20½, 21, 21½, 22½)"
C 28 (28½, 29, 29½, 30)"

10cm/4"

32
26
GET GAUGE!

• *over 2 × 2 rib stitch pattern*
• *after blocking*

You'll need

1 2 **3** 4 5 6

• *light weight*
• *1020 (1140, 1300, 1400, 1550) yds*
• *something smooth enough to show stitch pattern*

I used

• *4mm/US 6*

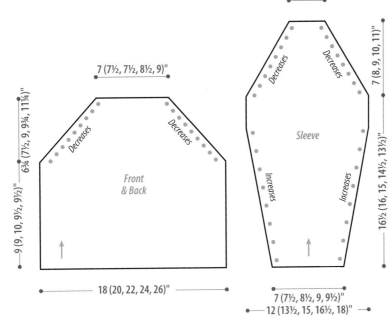

3½ (3¾, 4, 4¼, 4½)"

7 (7½, 7½, 8½, 9)"

9¾ (7½, 9, 9¾, 11¼)"

9 (9, 10, 9½, 9½)"

Decreases

Front & Back

18 (20, 22, 24, 26)"

7 (8, 9, 10, 11)"

Decreases

Sleeve

Increases

16½ (16, 15, 14½, 13½)"

7 (7½, 8½, 9, 9½)"

12 (13½, 15, 16½, 18)"

EXPERIence

- *intermediate*
- *repetitive stitch pattern*
- *mid-level shaping*
- *simple finishing*

LOOSE FIT

S (M, L, 1X, 2X)

A *37/39" (41/44, 46/49, 51/54, 56/59)"*

B (for sleeveless)
19 (19½, 20, 20½, 21)"

B (with sleeves)
22 (23, 23½, 23½, 24)"

C *28 (29, 30, 30½, 31½)"*

10cm/4"

19 | **GET GAUGE!**
13

- *over 3 × 1 rib stitch pattern*
- *using larger needles*
- *after blocking*

You'll need

1 2 3 4 **5** 6

- *bulky weight*
- *480 (525, 610, 660, 710) yds (for sleeveless)*
- *710 (765, 885, 940, 1015) yds (for version with sleeves)*
- *something smooth, to show stitch pattern*

I used

- *5mm/US 8*
- *6mm/US 10*

Cotton Medium: 8 balls GGH Goa in color 29

WITH-A-TWIST TURTLENECK

I first knit this piece with the sleeves. But then I had lunch one day with Bev Nimon, who did some of the styling for this book, and she mentioned how the 'Sharon Stone' turtleneck (big yarn and sleeveless) was ever-popular. So I made the pink and sleeveless version. Both have the möbius strip (a piece that is twisted and attached to itself) as a cool alternative to the standard turtleneck.

Two versions are offered within each size: look at the size you would normally consider (perhaps M); choose the larger of the two if working with wool and the smaller of the two if working with cotton. (This variability is to accommodate the elasticity of the yarns. Yarn that is mostly wool may block out but then spring back; yarn that is mostly cotton may block out and stay there.)
Because of this variability, plus the thickness of the yarn, all sizes are generous.

The sewing in of the collar is the only part of this pattern that's a little challenging. If preferred, a basic turtleneck is an option. You will need a circular needle in the size used for the edgings.

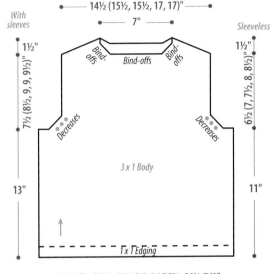

STITCH PATTERNS

1 × 1 rib (multiple of 2 sts + 3)
Right-side (RS) rows Knit (k) 1, *k1, purl (p) 1, repeat from * to 2 stitches (sts) remaining, k2.
Wrong-side (WS) rows P2, *k1, p1, repeat from * to 1 st remaining, p1.

3 × 1 rib (multiple of 4 sts + 5)
RS rows K2, p1, *k3, p1, repeat from * to 2 sts remaining, k2.
WS rows P2, *k1, p3, repeat from * to 3 sts remaining, k1, p2.

To read these stitch patterns, see page 106.

Here's how!
BACK
1 × 1 edging
With smaller needles, cast on 61/65 (69/73, 77/81, 85/89, 93/97) sts.
Work 1 × 1 rib for 6 rows.
3 × 1 body
Change to larger needles, and work 3 × 1 rib to 11" from beginning for sleeveless version, 13" from beginning for version with sleeves. End with WS row.
SHORTEN OR LENGTHEN HERE.
Armhole shaping
For this and all following bind-offs, bind off in rib, page 109.
Bind off 3 (3, 4, 5, 6) sts at beginning of next 2 rows—55/59 (63/67, 69/73, 75/79, 81/85) sts remain.

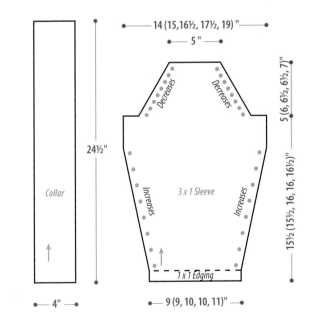

Next (decrease) row (RS) K2, work left-slanting decrease (SKP or SSK, page 18), work in stitch pattern as established to 4 sts remaining, work right-slanting decrease (k2tog), k2.

For sleeveless version, all following WS rows With yarn in front (yf), sl first st purl-wise (sl 1 p-wise), p2, work in stitch pattern as established to 3 sts remaining, p2, yf, sl 1 p-wise.

For version with sleeves, all following WS rows P3, work in stitch pattern as established to 3 sts remaining, P3.

Repeat last 2 rows to 47 (51, 51, 55, 55) sts remaining, then work straight as follows.

For all versions, all RS rows K3, work in stitch pattern as established to 3 sts remaining, k3.

For all versions, all WS rows Work WS rows as established (with sl st and p2 at edges for sleeveless and with p3 at edges for sleeves). Continue to 6½ (7, 7½, 8, 8½)" above armhole bind-off for sleeveless version and 7½ (8½, 9, 9, 9½)" above armhole bind-off for version with sleeves, ending with WS row.

Left shoulder and neck shaping

For turtleneck, knit center sts then put on holder, rather than binding off.

▌ *Maintain stitch pattern as established through all bind-offs.*

Bind off 4 (4, 4, 5, 5) sts at beginning of next RS row, work 10 (12, 12, 13, 13) sts, bind off center 19 sts (for neck), work remaining 14 (16, 16, 18, 18) sts.

Bind off 4 (4, 4, 5, 5) sts at beginning of next WS row (for left shoulder), work to neck edge. Turn.

*Bind off 1 st at beginning of next RS row (at neck edge), work to end.

Bind off 4 (5, 5, 5, 5) sts at beginning of next WS row, work to neck edge.

Bind off 1 st at beginning of next RS row, work to end.

Bind off remaining 4 (5, 5, 6, 6) sts next WS row.

Right shoulder and neck shaping

Return to 10 (12, 12, 14, 14) sts left behind for right shoulder, ready to work WS row. Work as right shoulder and neck from * to end but with reverse shaping (page 19).

FRONT

Work to 4½ (5, 5½, 6, 6½)" above armhole bind-off for sleeveless version and 5½ (6½, 7, 7, 7½)" above armhole bind-off for version with sleeves, ending with WS row.

Right neck shaping

▌ *For turtleneck, knit center sts then put on holder, rather than binding off.*

▌ *Maintain stitch pattern as established through all shaping.*

Work 17 (19, 19, 21, 21) sts, put these sts (for left neck and shoulder) onto holder, bind off center 13 sts, work to end.

Work 1 WS row (over sts of right shoulder).

*Bind off 2 sts at beginning of next RS row (for right Front neck), work to end.

Work 1 WS row.

Bind off 1 st at beginning of next RS row, work to end.

Repeat last 2 rows twice more—12 (14, 14, 16, 16) sts remain.

Right shoulder shaping

Bind off 4 (4, 4, 5, 5) sts at beginning of next WS row.

Work 1 RS row.

Bind off 4 (5, 5, 5, 5) sts at beginning of next WS row.

Work 1 RS row.

Bind off remaining 4 (5, 5, 6, 6) sts at beginning of next WS row.

Left neck and shoulder shaping

Return to sts of left shoulder, ready to work WS row.

Bind off 2 sts at beginning of next WS row (for right Front neck), work to end.

Work 1 RS row.

Work as right neck and shoulder shaping from * to end but with reverse shaping.

SLEEVES

1 × 1 edging

With smaller needles, cast on 29 (29, 33, 33, 37) sts.

Work 1 × 1 rib for 6 rows.

3 × 1 sleeve

Change to larger needles, and work in 3 × 1 rib for 4 rows.

▌ *Maintain stitch pattern through all shaping (page 111).*

Next (increase) row (RS) K2, work into st below next st plus k into next st (lifted increase, page 67), work to 3 sts remaining, work lifted increase in next st, k2.

Work 5 (5, 5, 3, 3) rows straight.

Repeat last 6 (6, 6, 4, 4) rows to 45 (49, 53, 57, 61) sts.

Work straight to 15½ (15½, 16, 16, 16½)" from beginning, ending with WS row.

SHORTEN OR LENGTHEN HERE.

Cap

Bind off 3 (3, 4, 5, 6) sts at beginning of next 2 rows—39 (43, 45, 47, 49) sts remain.

Next (decrease) row (RS) K2, SKP (or SSK), work in stitch pattern as established to 4 sts remaining, k2tog, k2.

Next row (WS) P3, work in stitch pattern as established to 3 sts remaining, p3.

Repeat last 2 rows to 15 sts remaining, ending with WS row.
Bind off 2 sts at beginning of next 2 rows.
Bind off remaining 11 sts.

FINISHING
Sew shoulder seams.

Turtleneck
With smaller circular needle, RS facing, and beginning at left shoulder, pick up and k around curve (page 46)—approximately 80 sts.
Place marker to indicate beginning of round (rnd).

You need a multiple of 2 sts; if you do not have this, k2tog somewhere in the next round as you establish the 1 × 1 rib as follows.

Next 18 rnds *K1, p1; repeat from *.
Bind off in rib.

Möbius collar
With smaller needles, cast on 80 sts.
Work 1 × 1 rib for 18 rows.
Bind off.

1 Hold collar with cast-on edge to bottom, bind-off edge to top, and open edge toward you.

2 Give right edge a half twist (to form a möbius loop).

3 Sew open ends together, taking selvedge st at each end into seam allowance.

4 Attach collar as follows.

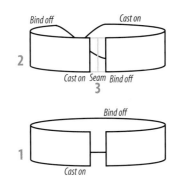

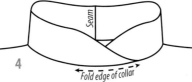

- Pin collar into neck opening, putting seam at center back and matching each st of collar to each bound-off st or to each 2-row jog between bound-off sts or to each row worked straight; fold of collar sits along center front.
- When sewing as follows, take cast-on edge of collar, and selvedge st of neck into seam allowance.
- Starting at center Back, sew across to right shoulder seam; then sew down right Front neck, stopping before 13 bound-off sts at center Front.

- Return to center Back, and sew across to left shoulder; then sew down left Front neck, stopping at 2-row jog just before 2 bound-off sts (of left Front neck shaping).
- Collar should form a V, slightly to left of center.
- Sew fold line of collar into remaining Front neck edge.

For the version with Sleeves, sew set-in Sleeves to armholes (page 27); then sew Sleeve seams.
For all versions, sew side seams.
Block garment to shape.

Wool Medium: 5 balls LION BRAND Wool-Ease Chunky in color 099 (Fisherman)

EXPErience

- *easy*
- *repetitive stitch pattern*
- *simple shaping*
- *simple finishing*

OVERSIZED FIT

Child's 6-8 (10-12, Man's S, M, L, 1X, 2X)

A *34 (39, 41, 46, 51, 56, 61)"*

B *19 (24, 30, 30, 30, 30)"*

C *22½ (25½, 32, 33, 34, 35, 36½)"*

10cm/4"

19 | GET GAUGE!
13

- *over 3 × 1 rib stitch pattern*
- *using larger needles*
- *after blocking*

You'll need

1 2 3 4 **5** 6

- *bulky weight*
- *600 (870, 1200, 1290, 1380, 1480, 1590) yds*
- *something smooth, to show stitch pattern*

I used

- *6mm/US 10*

- *5mm/US 8, 40cm/16" (for collars)*

Man's Large: 21 balls GGH Goa in color 22 (Forest green)

CLASSIC RIBBED PULLOVERS

These are just as suggested—the classics you grab when you want something easy and comfortable to wear. The cross-over V-neck is really neat and very much a guy's neck shaping. The basic turtleneck is a great option for the kids.

And here's a testimonial for this garment. My friend Tricia was searching for a sweater pattern to knit for her two grown sons. I suggested this one, with the cross-over V-neck, hoping it would suit her very tall and very hip boys. When she finished the first, her son Graham put it on, admired it greatly, then picked her up and swung her around the kitchen. It was the perfect choice and produced a perfect mother-son moment. Tristan is apparently delighted with his sweater, too.

The instructions that follow offer both neck shapings for all sizes.

The A measurements are the maximum to which the garment can be blocked; it might fall narrower than this, depending on how your fabric behaves. (Yarn that is mostly wool may block out but then spring back; yarn that is mostly cotton may block out and stay there.) Because of this variability, plus the thickness of the yarn, all sizes are generous.

STITCH PATTERNS
1 × 1 rib (multiple of 2 sts + 3)
Right-side (RS) rows Knit (k) 1, *k1, purl (p) 1, repeat from * to 2 stitches (sts) remaining, k2.
Wrong-side (WS) rows P2, *k1, p1, repeat from * to 1 st remaining, p1.

3 × 1 rib (multiple of 4 sts + 5)
RS rows K1, *k3, p1, repeat from * to 4 sts remaining, k4.
WS rows P4, *k1, p3, repeat from * to 1 st remaining, p1.
To read these stitch patterns, see page 106.

Here's how!
BACK
1 × 1 edging
With smaller needles, cast on 57 (65, 69, 77, 85, 93, 101) sts.
Work 1 × 1 rib for 6 rows.
3 × 1 body
Change to larger needles, and work 3 × 1 rib to 18 (23, 29, 29, 29, 29, 29)" from beginning, ending with WS row.
SHORTEN OR LENGTHEN HERE.
Maintain stitch pattern through all shaping.
Neck shaping
Next row (RS) Work 20 (23, 24, 28, 32, 36, 40) sts, put next 17 (19, 21, 21, 21, 21, 21) sts on holder (for neck), join new yarn, and work remaining 20 (23, 24, 28, 32, 36, 40) sts.
Next row (WS) Work 20 (23, 24, 28, 32, 36, 40) sts (of left shoulder). Turn.
Bind off 1 st at beginning of next 2 RS rows, working 1 WS row straight.
Bind off remaining 18 (21, 22, 26, 30, 34, 38) sts in rib (page 109) at beginning of next WS row.
Return to 20 (23, 24, 28, 32, 36, 40) sts (of right shoulder), ready to work WS row.
Work as left shoulder from * to end but with reverse shaping (page 19).

FRONT
Work as Back to 16½ (21, 27, 27, 27, 27, 27)" from beginning for turtleneck *or* to 13 (18, 22, 22, 22, 22, 22)" from beginning for cross-over V-neck, ending with WS row.
SHORTEN OR LENGTHEN HERE.
Maintain stitch pattern through all shaping.
Turtleneck shaping, right neck
Next row (RS) Work 24 (28, 29, 33, 37, 41, 45) sts, put next 9 (9, 11, 11, 11, 11, 11) sts on holder (for center Front neck), join new yarn and work remaining 24 (28, 29, 33, 37, 41, 45) sts.
Next row (WS) Work 24 (28, 29, 33, 37, 41, 45) sts (of right shoulder). Turn.
Bind off 2 sts at neck edge, work to end.
Work 1 WS row.
Bind off 1 st at beginning of next 4 (5, 5, 5, 5, 5, 5) RS rows, work WS rows straight—18 (21, 22, 26, 30, 34, 38) sts remain.
If not already same length as Back, work straight to same length as Back, then bind off remaining sts in rib at beginning of next RS row.
Turtleneck shaping, left neck
Return to 24 (28, 29, 33, 37, 41, 45) sts (of left shoulder), ready to work WS row.
Work 1 WS row then 1 RS row.
Work as right neck from * to end but with reverse shaping.
V-neck shaping, right neck
Work 25 (28, 30, 34, 38, 42, 46) sts, bind off next 7 (9, 9, 9, 9, 9, 9) sts (for neck), work remaining 25 (28, 30, 34, 38, 42, 46) sts.
Next row (WS) Work 25 (28, 30, 34, 38, 42, 46) sts (of right shoulder). Turn.
*Next (decrease) row (RS) K1, work left-slanting decrease (SKP or SSK, page 18), work to end.

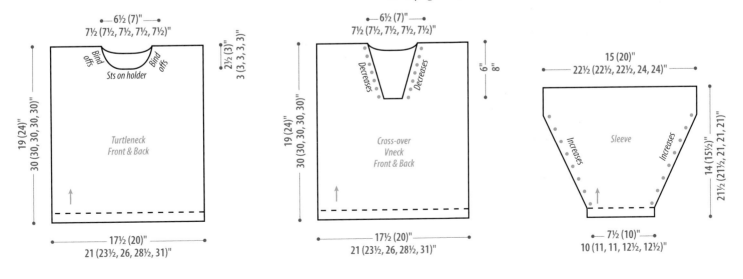

Work 3 rows straight.

Repeat last 4 rows to 7 (7, 8, 8, 8, 8, 8) neck decreases—18 (21, 22, 26, 30, 34, 38) sts remain.

Work straight to same length as Back, then bind off remaining sts at beginning of next RS row.

V-neck shaping, left neck

Return to 25 (28, 30, 34, 38, 42, 46) sts (of left shoulder), ready to work WS row.

Work as right neck from * to end but with reverse shaping.

SLEEVES

1 × 1 rib edging

With smaller needles, cast on 25 (33, 33, 37, 37, 41, 41) sts.

Work 1 × 1 rib for 6 rows.

3 × 1 rib Sleeve

Change to larger needles, and work 3 × 1 rib for 4 rows.

Maintain stitch pattern through all shaping (page 111).

Next (increase) row (RS) K2, work into st below next stitch plus into next st (lifted increase, page 67), work to 3 sts remaining, work lifted increase in next st, k2.

Work 3 rows straight.

Child's 6-8: 4 balls LION BRAND Wool-Ease Chunky in color 141 (Appleton)

Repeat last 4 rows to 49 (65, 73, 73, 73, 79, 79) sts.

Work straight to 14 (15½, 21½, 21½, 21, 21, 21)" from beginning, ending with WS row.

SHORTEN OR LENGTHEN HERE.

Bind off in rib.

FINISHING

Sew shoulder seams.

Use smaller circular needle for all collars.

Turtleneck

With RS facing and beginning at left Front shoulder, pick up and k around curve (page 46)—approximately 66 (70, 72, 72, 72, 72, 72) sts.

Place marker to indicate beginning of round (rnd).

You need a multiple of 2 sts; if you do not have this, k2tog somewhere in the next round as you establish the 1 × 1 rib as follows.

Next 14 (16, 18, 18, 18, 18, 18) rnds *K1, p1; repeat from *.

Bind off in rib.

Cross-over collar

Ignore bound-off sts at center Front opening for now.

1 With RS facing and beginning at corner of right Front neck opening, pick up and k (page 45) 5 sts for every 6 rows (up right Front V-neck shaping), then pick up and k around curve of Back neck (page 46), then work left V-neck as right Front—approximately 75 (75, 99, 99, 99, 99, 99) sts.

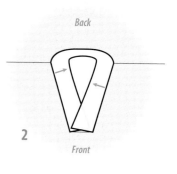

Work 1 × 1 rib for 11 (11, 14, 14, 14, 14, 14) rows.

Bind off in rib.

2 Lap left Front collar over right. Sew lower edge of left Front collar to bound-off sts at center Front opening, taking collar selvedge st and bound-off edge into seam allowance.

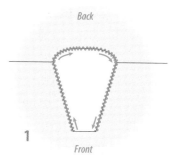

Sew right Front collar edge to WS.

Sew drop-shoulder Sleeves to garment (page 26).

Sew side and Sleeve seams.

Block garment to shape.

EXPERIence
- *intermediate*
- *repetitive stitch pattern*
- *maintenance of stitch pattern through shaping*
- *simple finishing*

OVERSIZED FIT

S (M, L, 1X, 2X)

A 42 (47½, 52, 57½, 62)"

B (for man's) 32"

B (for woman's) 28"

C (for man's)
32 (33, 33½, 34, 35)"

C (for woman's)
28 (29, 30, 31, 32)"

10cm/4"

19 **GET GAUGE!**

13

- *over 3 × 1 rib stitch pattern*
- *using larger needles*
- *after blocking*

You'll need

1 2 3 4 **5** 6

- *bulky weight*
- *for woman's: 830 (910, 1000, 1080, 1180) yds in main color*
- *for man's: 960 (1040, 1140, 1220, 1310) yds in main color*
- *for both: 150 yds in contrast color*
- *something smooth, to show stitch pattern*

☺

- *Five 5/8" buttons (for woman's)*
- *Six 5/8" buttons (for man's)*

I used

- *6mm/US 10*
- *5mm/US 8*

CLASSIC COLLEGE CARDIGANS

One of the wonderful things happening in the knitting world is its growth on college campuses. There are, apparently, groups of young folk balancing the rigors of left-brain study with time spent in the right-brain activity of knitting. Cheers to all of you, and congrats on doing something so very good for yourself.

Here is my gift to you: an oversized cardigan to wrap yourself in, made in a yarn that even a college student can afford. There's a guys' version—so the girls can knit one for 'the boyfriend'—and there's a girls' version—so the guys can return the favor. (We have to believe that the guys are clever enough to have discovered the value of knitting, right? And can you imagine how appreciated the fellow would be who knit his girl a sweater?)

The maintenance of the stitch patterns through all the shaping makes this a more difficult pattern. If you want to lower this garment's difficulty level, don't make the pockets.

The A measurement is the maximum to which the garment can be blocked; it might fall narrower than this, depending upon how your fabric behaves. (Yarn that is mostly wool may block out but then spring back; yarn that is mostly cotton may block out and stay there.) Because of this variability, plus the thickness of the yarn, all sizes are generous. The buttonholes are on the male side, to make the pattern less complex.

The V-neck on the male model garment is low; the pattern is written for it to be shaped higher, as shown on the schematic.

STITCH PATTERNS
1 × 1 rib (multiple of 2 sts + 3)
Right side (RS) rows Knit (k) 1, *k1, purl (p) 1, repeat from * to 2 stitches (sts) remaining, k2.
Wrong side (WS) rows P2, *k1, p1, repeat from * to 1 st remaining, p1.

3 × 1 rib (multiple of 4 sts + 5)
RS rows K2, p1, *k3, p1, repeat from * to 2 sts remaining, k2.
WS rows P2, *k1, p3, repeat from * to 3 sts remaining, k1, p2.

To read these stitch patterns, see page 106.

Here's how!
BACK
1 × 1 edging
With larger needles and main color (MC), cast on 69 (77, 85, 93, 101) sts.
Work 1 × 1 rib for 8 rows.
3 × 1 body
Continuing on larger needles and MC, work 3 × 1 rib, ending with WS row, to 15" from beginning.
SHORTEN OR LENGTHEN HERE.
Color pattern
Continue stitch pattern through color work.
Do not break MC. Introduce contrast color (CC), and work 2 rows.
Do not break CC. With MC, work 2 rows.
Break MC. With CC, work
10 rows for man's S, M, L, 1X,
8 rows for woman's and man's 2X.
Do not break CC. Introduce MC, and work 2 rows.
Do not break MC. With CC, work 2 rows.
Break CC, and continue with MC, ending with WS row, to 27" for woman's, to 31" for man's.
Left neck shaping
For all bind-offs, bind off in rib (page 109).
Next row (RS) Work 23 (27, 31, 35, 39) sts. Bind off center 23 sts (for neck), then work remaining 23 (27, 31, 35, 39) sts.
Work 1 WS row (over sts of left shoulder).
***Next row (RS)** Bind off 1 st at beginning of row (for neck), work to end.
Repeat last 2 rows once.
Bind off next WS row.
Right neck shaping
Return to sts of right shoulder, ready to work WS row.
Work 1 WS row.
Work 1 RS row.
Work as for left neck shaping from * to end but with reverse shaping (page 19).

RIGHT FRONT

1 × 1 edging

With larger needles and MC, cast on 38 (42, 46, 50, 54) sts. Work 1 × 1 rib as follows and for 8 rows.

Row 1 (RS) *K1, p1, repeat from * to 2 sts remaining, k2.

Row 2 (WS) P2, *k1, p1, repeat from * to 2 sts remaining, k1, with yarn in front (yf), slip last st purl-wise (sl 1 p-wise).

1 × 1 edge with 3 x 1 body

Continue on larger needles and MC.

Row 1 (RS) *K1, p1, repeat from * 3 times more (8 sts in 1 × 1 rib), then work 3 × 1 rib stitch pattern (k3, p1) to 2 sts remaining, k2.

Row 2 (WS) P2, *k1, p3, repeat from * to 8 sts remaining, **k1, p1, repeat from ** twice more (6 sts in 1 × 1 rib), then k1, yf, sl 1 p-wise. Repeat last 2 rows to 5" from beginning, ending with WS row.

If you don't want pockets, work to same length as Back, and skip to Color pattern.

1 Pocket edging

Next row (RS) Work 14 (18, 22, 22, 26) sts as established (in 1 × 1 rib then 3 × 1 rib, ending with k2). Place marker. For pocket edging, work 1 × 1 rib (*k1, p1; repeat from *, end k1) over next 15 (15, 15, 19, 19) sts. Place marker. Work 9 remaining sts as established (in 3 × 1 rib, beginning and ending with k2).

Next row (WS) Work as established to marker, work 1 x 1 rib as established over sts between markers (beginning and ending with p1), then work as established to end (with p-wise sl st at end of row). Work RS row once more.

Next row (WS) Work as established to marker, remove marker, bind off 15 (15, 15, 19, 19) sts between markers (in rib), remove marker, work to end.

2 Pocket lining

Use another ball of yarn and smaller needles. Leaving 12" tail, e-wrap cast on 17 (17, 17, 21, 21) sts.
Work 3 × 1 rib to 5", ending with WS row. Leaving 18" tail, break yarn.

3 Pocket lining to Front

Use larger needles, and continue stitch patterns as established.

Next row (RS) Work 13 (17, 21, 21, 25) sts, sl 1 knit-wise (k-wise) (last st from Right Front before pocket edging), k1 (first st from pocket lining), pass slip stitch over, k1, p1, *k3, p1, repeat from * 2 (2, 2, 3, 3) times more (over sts of pocket lining), k1, k2tog (last st from pocket lining together with first st from Right Front after pocket edging), work to end. Beginning with WS row, work as established (in rows 1–2 of 1 × 1 edge with 3 × 1 body, opposite) to same length as Back to Color pattern, ending with RS row.

You will begin the Color pattern on a WS row so you are carrying color changes up the edge to be seamed.

Color pattern

Work Color pattern as Back.
After final 2 rows of CC, break CC, then work 1 WS row in MC.

V shaping

Through shaping that follows, work stitch patterns as established unless directed to do otherwise.

It's especially important that you not forget the p-wise slip at the end of WS rows.

Row 1 (RS) Work 6 sts in 1 × 1 rib, Make 1 in space before next st (M1) and in opposite manner to previous st (if st before space was p, then M1 k-wise; if st before space was k, then M1 p-wise), place marker, work left-slanting decrease (SKP or SSK, page 18), work 3 × 1 rib to end.

Rows 2 & 4 (WS) Work 3 × 1 rib to marker, then work 1 × 1 rib after marker.

Row 3 (RS) Work 1 × 1 rib to marker, then work 3 × 1 rib after marker.

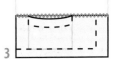

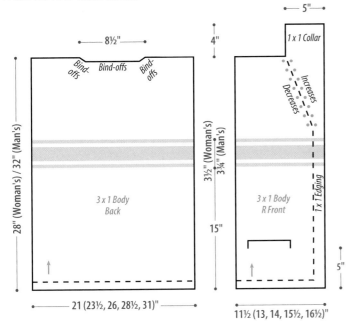

Row 5 (RS) Work 1 × 1 rib to marker, M1 in opposite manner to previous st, SKP (or SSK), work 3 × 1 rib to end.
Repeat rows 2–5 until there are 14 sts before marker on RS row. Work straight as rows 2 and 3 (above) and to same length as Back at final bind-off, ending with row 3.

Collar

Next row (WS) Bind off (in stitch pattern) until 15 sts remain on left-hand needle (1 st before marker), M1 p-wise in space, bind off 1 more st (binding off over M1) on right-hand needle, 15 sts on left-hand needle. Remove marker, then work 1 × 1 rib as established to end—16 sts remain.
Row 1 (RS) *K1, p1, repeat from * to 2 sts remaining, k2.
Row 2 (WS) P2, *k1, p1, repeat from * to 2 sts remaining, k1, yf, sl 1 p-wise.
Repeat last 2 rows to 4", then put sts on holder.

LEFT FRONT

Mark spots on Right Front for buttonholes: 5 for woman's, 6 for man's. Place the first 2" above the lower edge, the last just below the beginning of V-neck shaping, and the others spaced evenly between. While working Left Front, make buttonholes as follows and in corresponding places along length.
Begin buttonholes: RS rows Work to 5 sts remaining, work left-slanting decrease (SKP or SSK, page 18), yarn over (yo), work to end.
End buttonholes: WS row Yf, sl 1 p-wise, yarn back (yb), k1, p1, k1 through yo so as to twist it (page 49), work to end.

1 × 1 edging

With larger needles and MC, cast on 38 (42, 46, 50, 54) sts.

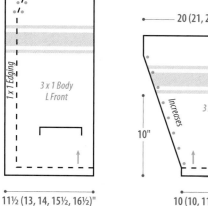

5"
1 x 1 Collar
Increases
Decreases
1 x 1 Edging
3 x 1 Body
L Front
5"
11½ (13, 14, 15½, 16½)"

Work 1 × 1 rib as follows and for 8 rows.
Row 1 (RS) K2, *p1, k1, repeat from * to end.
Row 2 (WS) Yf, sl 1 p-wise, yb, k1, *p1, k1, repeat from * to 2 sts remaining, p2.

1 × 1 edge with 3 × 1 body

Continue on larger needles and MC.
Row 1 (RS) Work 3 × 1 rib until 8 sts remain (ending with k3), then *p1, k1, repeat from * 3 times more (8 sts in 1 × 1 rib).
Row 2 (WS) Yf, sl 1 p-wise, yb, k1, *p1, k1, repeat from * twice more, then work 3 × 1 rib as established to end.
Repeat last 2 rows to 4" above rib, ending with WS row.
If you don't want pockets, work to same length as Right Front to Color pattern.

Pocket edging

Work as Right Front from pocket edging to V-shaping but with reverse shaping and ending with WS row.

Color pattern

Work Color pattern as Back.
After final 2 rows of CC, break CC, then work 1 RS and 1 WS row in MC.

V-neck shaping

Through shaping that follows, work stitch patterns as established unless directed to do otherwise.
It's especially important that you not forget the p-wise slip at the beginning of WS rows.

Row 1 (RS) Work 3 × 1 rib to 8 sts remaining, k2tog, place marker, M1 in space before next st and in opposite manner to next st (if st after space is p, then M1 k-wise; if st after space is k, then M1 p-wise), work 1 × 1 rib to end.
Rows 2 & 4 (WS) Work 1 × 1 rib to marker, then work 3 × 1 rib after marker.
Row 3 (RS) Work 3 × 1 rib to marker, then work 1 × 1 rib after marker.
Row 5 (RS) Work 3 × 1 rib to marker, k2tog, M1 and in opposite manner to next st, work 1 × 1 rib to end.
Repeat rows 2–5 until there are 14 sts after marker on RS row. Work straight as rows 2 and 3 (above), and to same length as Back at final bind-off, ending with row 2.

Collar

Next row (RS) Bind off until 15 sts remain on left-hand needle (1 st before marker), M1 k-wise in space, bind off 1 more st (binding off over M1)—1 st on right-hand needle, 15 sts on left-hand needle. Remove marker, then work 1 × 1 rib as established to end—16 sts remain.

20 (21, 22½, 23½, 25) "
Increases
3 x 1 Sleeve
Increases
10"
17½ (17, 17, 17, 16½)" (Woman's)
21½ (21, 20½, 20, 19½)" (Man's)
10 (10, 11½, 11½, 11½)"

Row 2 (WS) Yf, sl 1 p-wise, yb, *k1, p1, repeat from * to 1 st
remaining, p1.
Row 3 (RS) K2, *p1, k1, repeat from * to end.
Repeat these last 2 rows to 4", then put sts on holder.

SLEEVES
1 × 1 rib edging
With smaller needles, cast on 33 (33, 37, 37, 37) sts.
Work 1 × 1 rib stitch pattern, ending with WS row,
to 10 rows for woman's,
to 12 rows for man's.
3 × 1 rib Sleeve
Change to larger needles, and work 3 × 1 rib stitch pattern for 4 rows.
   Maintain stitch pattern through all shaping that follows.
   Pay attention to length through Sleeve increases: at 10" from
   beginning, Color pattern begins.
Next (increase) row (RS) K2, work into st below plus into next
st (lifted increase, page 67), work to 3 sts remaining, work lifted
increase in next st, k2.
Work 1 WS row.
Repeat last 2 rows
0 (0, 1, 5, 9) times more for man's—33 (33, 41, 49, 57) sts,
5 (7, 7, 11, 15) times more for woman's—45 (49, 53, 61, 69) sts.
Next row (RS) Work increase row (as above).
Work 3 rows straight.
Repeat last 4 rows to 65 (69, 73, 77, 81) sts, AT SAME TIME beginning Color pattern at 10" from beginning.
Color pattern
Work Color pattern as Back, with center CC rows as follows: 6 rows
for woman's, 8 rows for man's.
After final 2 rows in CC, break CC, and continue with MC, ending
with WS row,
to 17½ (17, 17, 17, 16½)" from beginning for woman's,
to 21½ (21, 20½, 20, 19½)" from beginning for man's.
SHORTEN OR LENGTHEN HERE.
Next row (RS) Bind off.

FINISHING
Sew buttons to Right Front to correspond to buttonholes.
Sew shoulder seams.
Sew drop-shoulder Sleeves to garment (page 26).
Sew side and Sleeve seams.
Collar
   Since the collar can be worn straight or rolled over, there really is
   not a right or wrong side. But the 3-needle bind-off will produce
   a ridge on the side of work opposite the sides you put together.

Put sides of collar together. Join yarn, work 3-needle bind-off
(in 1 × 1 rib) to seam collar together (page 174).
Sew collar to neck edge, easing to fit curve and taking bound-off
edge of Back neck and 1 st at edge of collar into seam allowance.
Pockets
Using 12" tails for seaming, sew sides and cast-on edges of pockets
to back of Fronts.
Block garment to shape.

Woman's Medium: LION BRAND Wool-Ease Chunky, 6 balls in color 127
(Walnut) and 1 ball in color 187 (Foliage)
Man's 1X: LION BRAND Wool-Ease Chunky, 8 balls in color 152 (Charcoal)
and 1 ball in color 141 (Appleton)

Ribbing

ABOUT RIBBING

Ribbing is a fabric produced by combining knits and purls in the same row (for example, *knit 1, purl 1, repeat from * across the row). This combination is then repeated in subsequent rows to produce a vertical pattern of ribs. While there are many variations possible, here are the two standard rib stitch patterns.

The result of 1 × 1 or 2 × 2 rib is a flat fabric with lots of elasticity that is commonly used for snug little garments and for cuffs, bottom bands, neck edgings—anywhere you want the knitting to hug a body part or curve.

Sometimes the number of knit stitches is not the same as the number of purl stitches. An example of this is 3 × 1 (knit 3, purl 1) rib, used in this chapter. It's helpful to know that the number of right-side knit stitches is always given first, and the number of right-side purl stitches follows.

1 1 × 1 (knit 1, purl 1) rib.

2 2 × 2 (knit 2, purl 2) rib.

How does this pattern of ribs happen?

There are rib stitch patterns where the rules don't apply—where the ribs are interrupted somehow. (See Elaine's Scarf, page 116, or the Canadian-winter Hat and Mitts, page 124.) But it's best to understand ribbing in its most common and classic execution before considering rib patterns where these rules are broken.

A right-side knit stitch throws its bump to the back; the front is smooth and forms the vertical ribs that you see. They sit forward in the knitting.

A right-side purl stitch throws its bump to the front. These bumps tuck behind the smooth stitches.

What are the rules for maintaining a standard rib pattern?
• Any stitch that is knit on a right-side row is purled on a wrong-side row.
• Any stitch that is purled on a right-side row is knit on a wrong-side row.

Oops, I knit when I should have purled (or vice versa)! What do I do now? See pages 166–167.

Oops, I dropped a stitch! What do I do now? See page 164.

READING RIBBING

It can also help to see that if your next stitch is to be a smooth stitch, you knit it; if your next stitch is to be a bumpy stitch, you purl it. It doesn't matter whether you are on a right-side or a wrong-side row.

Multiples in stitch patterns

Often stitch patterns are given as follows: 3 × 1 rib (multiple of 4 sts + 5). What does this mean? It means that the stitch pattern can be worked over any multiple of 4 stitches (1 × 4, or 4 × 4, or 8 × 4, or 25 × 4) plus 5 extra. (The total number of stitches for the examples would be 9, 21, 37, 105.)

EXECUTING RIBBING

To work ribbing, you must switch from knits to purls in the middle of the row. Here are the rules.

- All knit stitches are worked with yarn in back.
- All purl stitches are worked with yarn in front.
- To switch from one to the other, you must take the yarn to where it is required without producing a yarn over.

Knitters regularly get into discussions regarding the efficiency and speed of any particular method. While you'll hear as many opinions as there are voices, here is one point on which we all generally agree. In the right-hand carry method, it takes almost as much time to move the yarn from front to back as it does to work a stitch. In the left-hand carry methods, this is not the case; it's a relatively minor movement to move the yarn from front to back.

RIGHT-HAND CARRY

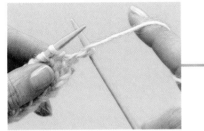 

1 If you have knit and now need to purl, bring yarn between the two needles and to the front. Now put right-hand needle into next stitch on left-hand needle, and purl as usual.

2 If you have purled and now need to knit, take yarn between the two needles and to the back. Now put right-hand needle into next stitch on left-hand needle, and knit as usual.

LEFT-HAND CARRY, WITH YARN IN LEFT HAND

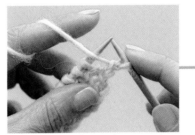 

1 If you have knit and now need to purl, bring yarn between the two needles and to the front. Then put right-hand needle into next stitch on left-hand needle, and purl as usual.

2 If you have purled and now need to knit, take yarn between the two needles and to the back. Then put right-hand needle into next stitch on left-hand needle, and knit as usual.

LEFT-HAND CARRY, WITH YARN AROUND NECK

 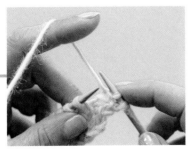

1 To purl, put right-hand needle into next stitch on left-hand needle, and purl as usual.

2 To knit, lift yarn with left index finger and take between the two needles and to the back. Now put right-hand needle into next stitch on left-hand needle, and knit as usual. If next stitch is a purl, remove index finger so yarn returns to front.

For the 'yarn around the neck' method to work, the yarn has to sit on the floor and have enough weight that gravity can exert tension on it.

For clarity, the tails are shown in contrasting-color yarn.

Tails in rib

You may end one ball and begin another by working the two tails together for a few stitches (page 64). But if you find the doubled stitches too visible, or if you're in a situation where it's not possible to secure tails this way, here is a way to sew in tails in rib that's invisible from the right side.

Secure tails with one right-side purl stitch worked with both tails; 4" of each tail remains to be sewn in as follows. With wrong side facing,

1 run threaded tapestry needle down rib for 1".

2 Run it back up for 1".

3 Finish by taking it back down for ½"; then trim close.

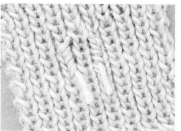

Here are tails sewn into the wrong side of a ribbed fabric. On the right side, the tails are not visible.

Cable cast-on in rib

I like the standard cable cast-on for ribbing. It's strong yet elastic and has a ropey, slightly decorative texture. However, the rib cable cast-on is a wonderful option. (I show this with right-hand carry. It's possible to do it with left-hand carry, but you must bring the yarn to the front of the left-hand needle before working a purl stitch.)

For this sample, I am assuming your 1 × 1 rib begins and ends with a knit stitch.

1 With a slip knot on left-hand needle, insert right-hand needle as if to knit, draw through a loop, put loop onto left-hand needle. (This is a knit cast-on stitch.)

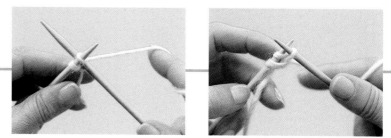

2 Insert right-hand needle as if to knit between 1st and 2nd stitches on left-hand needle, draw through a loop, put loop onto left-hand needle. (This is a standard cable cast-on stitch.)

Seaming in rib

I prefer ribbing to always begin and end with right-side knits and wrong-side purls. Patterns that are set up this way will allow you to produce neat seams (as shown in photos and discussed to right).

When there is only 1 knit stitch at each edge, seam as shown, much as stockinette stitch (page 22), but only take one-half of each knit stitch into the seam allowance.

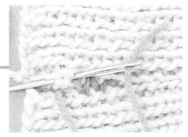

The result of a half-stitch seam allowance shows how the seam runs up the center of the edge knit stitches. If there are 2 knit stitches at each edge, seam as for stockinette stitch (page 22), and take 1 knit stitch from each edge into the seam allowance.

Binding off in rib

When binding off in rib, continue with the stitch pattern through the bind-off row. If you do not (if, for example, you work the bind-off row all in knit stitches rather than knit 2, purl 2), the bind-off row will be quite a bit tighter than the ribbed fabric.

Working a gauge swatch in rib

Work a gauge swatch as you did for stockinette stitch (by casting on more stitches and working more rows over which the gauge is offered). Before measuring, block the swatch—by steam pressing or by washing and pinning to shape. Measure when dry, and be sure to count all purl stitches tucked behind the knit stitches.

Oops, I have an ugly loop at the end of my bind-off! What do I do now? See page 165.

Be careful when blocking ribbing. It's an elastic fabric, and it's easy to over-block it—to press it out too far. (This is especially likely to happen with man-made fibers.) Having said that, you might block a swatch (with lots of wool content) and find that it springs back to a tighter gauge than you want. In this case, redo the swatch on larger needles.

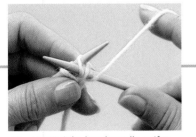

3 Insert right-hand needle as if to purl between 1st and 2nd stitches on left-hand needle . . .

. . . draw through a loop; put loop onto left-hand needle. (This is a purl cast-on stitch.)

4 Repeat Steps 2–3 until 1 stitch remains to be cast on; then repeat Step 2.

Here is the result after some rows of rib.

Remember that to make the neatest seams possible, increases and decreases are never worked in the selvedge stitch. They are always worked at least one stitch into the body of the piece.

Working a decrease in purl

PURL 2 TOGETHER *p2tog*
This maneuver forms a **left-slanting decrease** on the purl side of the fabric, but it will be a right-slanting decrease on the knit side of the fabric.

1 Put right-hand needle into next 2 stitches on left-hand needle, as if to purl.

2 Purl both stitches together, as if they were 1.

SLIP 1, SLIP 1, PURL 2 TOGETHER *SSP*
This maneuver forms a **right-slanting decrease** on the purl side of the fabric, but it will be a left-slanting decrease on the knit side of the fabric.

1 Slip 1 stitch knit-wise from left-hand needle onto right.

2 Slip the next stitch from left-hand needle onto right, also knit-wise.

3 Slip these stitches back onto left-hand needle.

4 Put right-hand needle into back of the 2 stitches on left-hand needle, starting with the 2nd stitch from the end of the left-hand needle.

5 Purl the 2 stitches together.

Maintaining a stitch pattern through increases

My favorite increase in stockinette stitch, in rib, and in stitch patterns that combine knits and purls, is the lifted increase (page 67). But it requires some attention to maintain the stitch pattern through the increases. Here this is demonstrated in 3 × 1 rib and where the stitch pattern dictates that the increases should be purled.

What's tricky is that the beginning of the row is very different from the end of the row. And while the beginning of the row makes perfect sense, the end of the row seems backwards. I promise you it is not! Why? Because the lifted stitch will sit to the right (into the already established stitch pattern), and the stitch from the needle will sit to the left (where the new stitch belongs).

1 Work increases on right-side rows. Work selvedge stitch(es). Here the next stitch should be purled, so bring yarn forward . . .

2 . . . and make a lifted increase in purl.

3 Work the stitch on the needle as established by the stitch pattern. Here it should be knit; so take yarn to back, and knit the stitch on the needle.

4 Work across the row to 1 stitch before the selvedge stitch(es).

5 Work the lifted increase as established by the stitch pattern. Here it should be knit.

6 Work the stitch on the needle as the new stitch in the stitch pattern should be worked. Here it should be purled, so bring yarn forward . . .

7 . . . and purl as usual. Finish by working the selvedge stitch(es).

Here is the result at the beginning of the row.

Here is the result at the end of the row.

Remember that to keep from twisting a yarn over, work through its leading edge (closest to the end of the needle). To twist a yarn over, work through its non-leading edge. (See page 49.)

These buttonholes are shown with an SKP, but an SSK (page 18) would work just as well.

Buttonholes in rib

The best way to make invisible buttonholes in rib is to place them in the purl troughs. Two choices follow.

EYELET BUTTONHOLE IN RIB
The eyelet buttonhole is small but elastic, and here's how to place it in the purl trough of 1 × 1 rib.

1 On a right-side row, work to where you want the buttonhole, ending with a purl stitch. Take yarn to back.

2 Slip the knit stitch, knit the purl stitch, and pass the slip stitch over (SKP).

3 Bring yarn to front, and knit the next stitch as usual, producing a yarn over.

4 On the following wrong-side row, knit the yarn over. (You need to decide whether or not to twist it. This depends upon how small a buttonhole you want: twisting it will produce a smaller, tighter buttonhole than not twisting it.) This photo shows the yarn over not twisted.

Here's the result of an eyelet buttonhole in 1 × 1 rib, after another row and with the yarn over not twisted.

3-ROW BUTTONHOLE IN RIB

The 3-row buttonhole is large and elastic, and here's how to place it in the purl trough of 1 × 1 rib. (It's not used in this book, but it's too wonderful not to offer.) Work Steps 1 and 2 of the Eyelet buttonhole (opposite), and continue as follows.

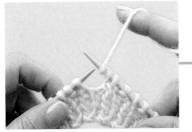

1 Bring yarn to front, wrap it around right-hand needle, and bring it back to the front.

2 Now knit the next stitch as usual. You have produced two yarn overs.

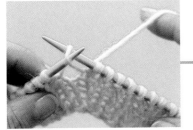

3 On the following wrong-side row, work to the yarn overs . . .

4 . . . drop one yarn over . . .

5 . . . and knit the remaining yarn over so as to twist it.

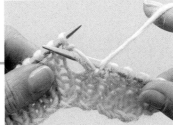

6 On the following right-side row, work to the buttonhole. (You will see a hole, plus two threads.)

7 Bring yarn to front, and purl through the hole.

8 Push the stitch that sits on the left-hand needle off the needle.

9 You will see a bit of a knot; pull it out, and finish the row as usual.

Here's the result of the 3-row buttonhole in 1 × 1 rib.

The title of this chapter has two references. One is that the pieces of this chapter each have a mix of stitch patterns—a little rib, a little stockinette stitch, a little texture, a little plain. The second is that the projects themselves are mostly little— pieces to be carried in a purse or pocket and knit without a huge time commitment.

There is something wonderful about knitting small projects. Their biggest attraction might be other than the small amount of space and yarn and time they take. It might be the immense satisfaction in seeing something grow and take its shape—through increases and other tricks—rather immediately and right in our hands. Or it may be that because they demand less commitment and attention to fit, color, and fabric choices, they are often given as gifts—to loved ones or to charities—and so they give pleasure to many and are the knit pieces with highest visibility in our world.

I didn't want to publish this series of learn-to-knit books without offering patterns for these small but wonderful items. So, in this chapter, you learn to make the basic sock or hat or mitt (plus a few extra items). But please don't assume that 'the basics' is as good as it gets. There are many wonderful books devoted to socks and stockings, to hats and mitts, and to shawls and scarves, and there are patterns for these items that are intricate beyond belief. If you are interested in exploring these items further, you will be amazed at the beauty and variety that await.

Chapter Five

The Patterns

Additional Skills

EXPerience
- very easy
- repetitive stitch pattern

10cm/4"
(for medium version)

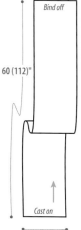

24-28
16-20
- over stitch pattern
- after blocking

(for super-bulky version)

13-15
10-12
- over stitch pattern
- after blocking

You'll need

1 2 3 **4** 5 **6**

- medium (super bulky) weight
- 180 (300) yds
- something soft and fun

I used

- 4.5mm/US 7 (8mm/US 11)

Bind off

60 (112)"

Cast on

4½-5½ (7-8½)"

2 balls TAHKI YARNS Shannon in color 4
3 skeins LION BRAND Thick & Quick Chenille in color 131 (cover scarf)

ELAINE'S SCARF

This is called 'Elaine's scarf' because it was all her doing: she had the idea (that we should always include a large scarf), she found the super-bulky yarn, she picked the color, she chose the stitch pattern (mistake rib; can you see why it's called this?), and she did the knitting. Her result appears on the back cover. I then made the little one, because it has its place, too. But she still gets the credit.

There is no need to make this scarf to the width or length shown. You may cast on 4 or 8 less (or more) stitches and work to the length desired.

STITCH PATTERN
Mistake rib (multiple of 4 sts + 1)
All rows Knit (k) 2, purl (p) 2, repeat from * to 1 stitch (st) remaining, k1.

This stitch pattern forms the following sequence (reading from left to right): 1 garter stitch, 1 reverse stockinette st (RSS), 1 garter st, 1 stockinette st (St st), repeat from *, then end with 1 garter st. If you get lost in the middle of the row, count back to the beginning.

Here's how!
Cast on 21 sts.
Work stitch pattern to 60 (112)" or until no less than 28 (48)" yarn remains.
Bind off in rib (page 109).
Block flat.

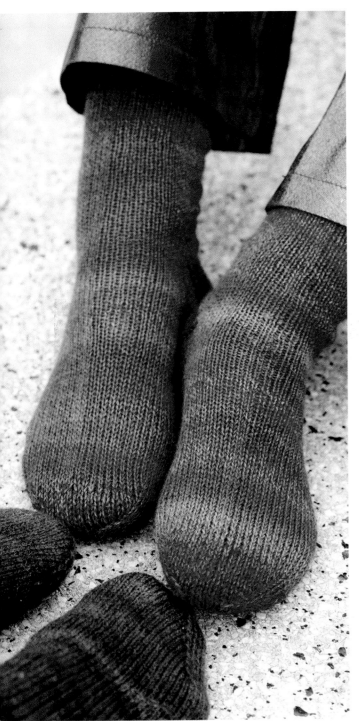

SCHOELLER + STAHL Fortissima Colori Socka:
2 balls in color 2420 + matching reinforcing thread (top),
2 balls in color 2418 + matching reinforcing thread (bottom)

SIMPLE SOCKS

I really did not understand the sock-knitting thing until recently. But when I saw socks in all the new patterned and multicolored yarns, I thought I'd give it a try. Well! Immediately and totally addicted! I think I have knit at least a pair a month for the past 2 years! I never wear anything else, and they are all holding up very well.

There is lots to love about knitting socks: they're little; they're quick; they're relatively inexpensive; and handknit socks feel delicious on the feet. I wish I had a permanent record of my son's expression the day he donned his first pair! He was absolutely stunned at how wonderful they felt!

If you think there are too many exclamation points in this intro, believe me, this is how I feel about the knitting of socks and how my family feels about wearing them. If you are someone who expected to never knit socks, be careful of starting—you might never stop!

Please read all the notes that follow. There is stuff you really need to know before you begin—about sock-knitting and about this pattern. And while the pattern does follow the criteria for a rating of 'intermediate,' my new-knitter daughter made socks as her fourth project. (She gave them to me for Christmas. Isn't that wonderful?)

I used double-pointed needles, and the pattern is written this way. If you wish to use two circulars, see page 128.

This pattern is written to make socks one of four ways:
- *all in one color, with or without reinforcing thread;*
- *with calf and foot in main yarn and with heels and toes in alternate color, with or without reinforcing thread.*

EXPErience
- *easy intermediate*
- *mid-level shaping*
- *mid-level finishing*

It'll fit
Almost everyone
(see chart on next page)

10cm/4"

34-52 **GET CLOSE**
24-36

- *over stockinette stitch (see chart)*

You'll need

1-2 3 4 5 6

- *super fine or fine weight*
- *350 yds main color*
- *1 50g pkg reinforcing thread (optional)*
- *85 yds contrast color (optional)*

I used

set of 5

(see chart for needle sizes)

A standard sizing for socks is difficult to establish: it depends too much on your yarn and your needles and your gauge . . . and your feet! To avoid confusion, I've referred to them only by the number of stitches cast on: 48 (52, 56, 60, 64). To determine the number of stitches you need to cast on, use the following chart. (If a number of stitches is not offered, it's not appropriate at that gauge.)

- Choose one of the needle sizes below; then cast on 4 more stitches than suggested as a stitch gauge over 4".
- Find your stitch gauge in stockinette stitch; working flat (back and forth) is fine. (You want a fabric that feels firmer rather than looser.)
- Row gauge is offered, but it doesn't matter much.
- Measure the circumference of the recipient's foot. (You may measure at more than one place then take an average measurement.)
- Look at the chart. Find the gauge closest to yours (in the far left column); then find the circumference ½–1" less than the actual foot circumference (in the far right column). (Yarn is stretchy, so a circumference up to 1½" less will also work. A circumference greater than the actual foot measurement will not be comfortable.)
- Note the number of stitches to the left of the circumference. This is your best choice. Follow all directions for that number of stitches.
- If your gauge lies between two gauges offered, so will your circumference.

stitch gauge	row gauge	needles I used	circumferences you will achieve
6/inch 24/4"	8½/inch 34/4"	3.25mm/US 3	48 sts = 8" 52 sts = 8½" 56 sts = 9¼" 60 sts = 10"
7/inch 28/4"	9½/inch 38 / 4"	2.75mm/US 2	48 sts = 7" 52 sts = 7½" 56 sts = 8" 60 sts = 8½" 64 sts = 9"
8/inch 32/4"	11/inch 44/4"	2.25mm/US 1	48 sts = 6" 52 sts = 6½" 56 sts = 7" 60 sts = 7½" 64 sts = 8"
9/inch 36/4"	13/inch 52/4"	2mm/US 0	52 sts = 5½" 56 sts = 6¼" 60 sts = 6½" 64 sts = 7"

STITCH PATTERN
1 × 1 rib (multiple of 2 sts)
All rounds (rnds) *Knit (k) 1, purl (p) 1, repeat from * to end.
Read about rib, page 106.

Here's how!
1 1 × 1 edging
With main yarn and long-tail cast-on, cast on 48 (52, 56, 60, 64) stitches (sts), all onto one needle.
Starting at end opposite yarn and tail, slip (sl) 12 (13, 14, 15, 16) sts onto needle (N) 1, then 12 (13, 14, 15, 16) sts onto N2, then 12 (13, 14, 15, 16) sts onto N3—12 (13, 14, 15, 16) sts remain on N4.
Needle with yarn attached is N4; needle with first cast-on st is N1.
Hold 4 needles in circle, being careful not to twist cast-on.
I prefer to leave the 5th needle aside for now and to work as follows.
Rnd 1 With RS facing, work 1 × 1 rib, working sts from N1 onto N4. (Sts are now distributed over 3 needles.)
Continue 1 × 1 rib over sts of N2 and N3.
Continue 1 × 1 rib over first 12 (13, 14, 15, 16) sts of N4. Place safety pin marker onto st at end of N4.
Introduce 5th needle. Work 1 × 1 rib over remaining sts. (This is now N1.)
Sts are now evenly distributed over 4 needles.
Continue 1 × 1 rib to 8 rows, ending at marker.

2 Calf
K all sts, all rnds, to desired height (7–9" is usual) from beginning, ending at marker.
Back of heel
Add reinforcing thread for Back and Turning of heel, if desired.
If using more than one color, introduce contrast color now. If using only one color, introduce new ball of main color now, but do not cut ball you have been using.
New yarn will be called 'heel yarn.'
Even if you are working your sock all in one color, I recommend introducing new yarn for the heel. This leaves a tail to close the hole that often occurs at the corner between the heel and the instep.
Work over sts of N1 and N2 only, with heel yarn and as follows.
RS rows *Slip 1 purl-wise (sl 1 p-wise), k1, repeat from * to 24 (26, 28, 30, 32) sts all on one needle. Put extra needle aside for now.
Turn, so you are working over these 24 (26, 28, 30, 32) sts only.
WS rows Sl 1 p-wise, p remaining 23 (25, 27, 29, 31) sts.

8

7

Heel turn

6

Heel turn

5

4

Sl st edges

Tail

3

1x1 edging

2

1x1 edging

Cast on   Tail

1

3 Repeat last 2 rows to 24 (26, 28, 30, 32) rows—12 (13, 14, 15, 16) sl sts up each side.

Count these sl sts as follows: the lowest one (at the right corner) will be in main color, will not have reinforcing thread, and will be 1 st before the first st worked in heel yarn. The highest sl st will be on N1.

Turning of heel

Short row 1 (RS) Sl 1 p-wise, k15 (16, 18, 19, 20), work left-slanting decrease (SKP or SSK, page 18)—6 (7, 7, 8, 9) sts now on left-hand needle. Turn.

Short row 2 Sl 1 p-wise, p8 (8, 10, 10, 10), work left-slanting decrease (p2tog, page 110)—6 (7, 7, 8, 9) sts now on left-hand needle. Turn.

Short row 3 Sl 1 p-wise, k8 (8, 10, 10, 10), SKP (or SSK). Turn.

Short row 4 Sl 1 p-wise, p8 (8, 10, 10, 10), p2tog. Turn.

At the end of every short row, you will work 2 sts together—one from the center group of sts and one from the sts on the sides.

4 Repeat short rows 3 & 4 until only 10 (10, 12, 12, 12) sts remain, ending with WS row.

Break heel yarn (and reinforcing thread).

Instep

Return to base of heel (end of N4, at marker), and work what follows with main color.

5 **N1** Pick up and k12 (13, 14, 15, 16) from sl sts (up first edge of heel), then k5 (5, 6, 6, 6) (to center of heel).

It doesn't matter if you pick up along the back or the front edge of the sl sts; just be consistent.

N2 K remaining 5 (5, 6, 6, 6) sts (from center to edge of heel), then pick up and k12 (13, 14, 15, 16) from sl sts (down second edge of heel).

N3 & N4 K12 (13, 14, 15, 16) (from each needle across top of foot).

N1 SKP (or SSK), k to end.

N2 K to 2 sts remaining, work right-slanting decrease (k2tog).

K 2 rnds straight.

6 Repeat from * (decreasing each 3rd rnd) until 12 (13, 14, 15, 16) sts remain on N1 and N2.

7 **Foot**

K all sts, all rnds, to 1½ (1¾, 2, 2¼, 2½)" short of actual foot length, ending at marker.

Measure foot of recipient from back of heel to end of longest toe. Measure sock from back of heel to sts on needles.

For tighter gauges, finished sock length may be ¼–½" shorter than foot length, but this is fine: the sock will stretch. (It's better to have the sock a little short than too long.)

8 **Toe**

If changing color for toe (and adding reinforcing thread), cut main color and do so before decreasing to 11 sts on each needle.

***N1** K1, SKP (or SSK), k to end.

N2 K to 3 sts remaining, k2tog, k1.

N3 K1, SKP (or SSK), k to end.

N4 K to 3 sts remaining, k2tog, k1.

K 1 rnd straight.

Repeat from * (decreasing each 2nd rnd) until 7 sts remain on all needles.

Repeat from * but without rnd worked straight (so decreasing every rnd) until 5 sts remain on all needles, ending at marker.

Work 1 more rnd, decreasing as above and, AT SAME TIME, working sts from N2 onto N1 and sts from N4 onto N3—8 sts remain on only 2 needles.

Break yarn, leaving 10" tail.

Graft sts from two needles together (page 130).

Sew in tails, closing any holes at corners of instep and heel.

2 skeins KOIGU Painter's Palette Premium Merino in color 322 + ½ skein in color 2395 + matching reinforcing thread

NOT-KNIT-ROUND SCARF

I really loved the Knit-round Scarf of The Knit Stitch. *I was especially impressed with its possibilities after Elaine Rowley knit one in a very light yarn and wore it with a sleeveless summer suit. Since this is one of the pieces that I had decided should be explored in each book of this series, I decided to do one for this book in a very open knit-and-purl stitch.*

The stitch used is a variation of rib: 2 right-side knit stitches sit on either side of a simple lace panel. This lace panel is just a yarn over, purl 2 together. Why a purl 2 together rather than a knit 2 together? If you try each of them, you'll find that the purl 2 together is an easier movement. You'll appreciate this choice when you do 48 of them in each row.

This piece could have been done in the round (which would have made it another Knit-round Scarf), but it would have made the pattern much more difficult.

This piece is shown in two different yarns. If you want a summery version, use weight 3 yarn and (surprisingly) larger needles to attain gauge.

The circumference of this piece may seem large, but it actually needs to be—for comfort around the shoulders and to not be too warm. And if it's large enough, it can be worn as a skirt!

Scarf: 4 skeins BERROCO Cotton Twist in color 8353 (Organic Teal)

Skirt: 5 skeins HARRISVILLE DESIGNS Jasmine in color 210 (Arabian Tea)

STITCH PATTERNS

2 × 2 rib (multiple of 4 sts + 2)

Right-side (RS) rows *Knit (k) 2, purl (p) 2, repeat from * to 2 stitches (sts) remaining, k2.

Wrong-side (WS) rows P2, *k2, p2, repeat from * to end.

A rib-with-lace (multiple of 4 sts + 2)

RS rows *K2, yarn over (yo before a p st, page 48), purl 2 together (p2tog, page 110), repeat from * to 2 sts remaining, k2.

WS rows P2, *yo, p2tog, p2, repeat from * to end.

B rib-with-lace (multiple of 6 sts + 8)

RS rows *K4, yo, p2tog, repeat from * to 2 sts remaining, k2.

WS rows P2, *yo, p2tog, p4, repeat from * to end.

To read—and correct mistakes in—these lace patterns, here's what you need to see.

- *The patterns are like rib except that instead of 2 p sts, there is a 2-st lace panel.*
- *The 2-st lace panel is a yo followed by p2tog, always in that order. When you see them on the next row, the p2tog will be first on the needle.*
- *If you forgot to make a yo in the previous row, just lift the thread before the p2tog.*
- *If you made an extra yo, just drop it.*

Here's how!

Cast on 194 sts.

For weight 3, go straight to rib-with-lace body.

2 × 2 edging (for weight 4 only)

Work 2 × 2 rib to 1", ending with WS row.

Rib-with-lace body

Work A rib-with-lace to 9" from beginning, ending with WS row.

Next row (decrease) *K1, work left-slanting decrease (SKP or SSK, page 18), work right-slanting decrease (k2tog), k1, yo, p2tog, repeat from * to 2 sts remaining, k2—146 sts on needle.

What you have just done is eliminate every second lace panel.

Work B rib-with-lace, beginning and ending with WS row, to 13" from beginning.

Next row (decrease) *K2tog, SKP (or SSK), yo, p2tog, repeat from * to 2 sts remaining, k2—98 sts remain.

Work A rib-with-lace, beginning and ending with WS row, to 16" (for weight 4) and 17" (for weight 3). For weight 3, bind off loosely in rib (page 109).

2 × 2 edging (for weight 4 only)

Work 2 × 2 rib stitch pattern to 17" from beginning. Bind off loosely in rib (page 109).

FINISHING

Block piece.
Seam.

EXPErience

- *easy*
- *repetitive stitch patterns*
- *minimal shaping*
- *minimal finishing*

It'll fit

One size fits all

10cm/4"

22-26 GET CLOSE

14-16

- *over stitch pattern*
- *after blocking*

You'll need

1 2 **3-4** 5 6

- *light or medium weight*
- *340 yds*
- *wool or cotton, with rayon*

I used

- *5mm/US 8 (for light weight)*
- *4.5mm/US 7 (for medium weight)*

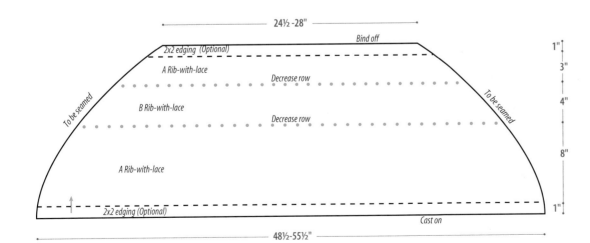

EXPErience
- easy
- simple shaping
- minimal finishing

It'll fit
S-M (L-XL)

10cm/4"
34 (38) ▦ GET CLOSE
24 (28)
- over stockinette stitch

You'll need
 3 4 5 6
- super fine or fine weight
- 350 yds
- tightly spun, soft wool or wool blend

I used
(set of 5)
- 2.75mm/US 2 (for S-M)
- 3.25mm/US 3 (for M-L)

Small–Medium: 2 skeins KOIGU Painter's Palette Premium Merino in color P824 (top) or P326 (bottom)

ELEGANT GAUNTLETS

I first saw a version of these some years ago and thought, "How gorgeous are these?!" I then made a few pair before turning back to the work that still needed to be done on The Knit Stitch. Since then, many versions have appeared in knitting books and magazines, often as learn-to-knit pieces, so I know they are both popular and good beginner projects.

What's different about these is the yarn and the shaping. They're done in a very wonderful but fine yarn that comes in an amazing array of colors and that is quite tightly spun so will hold its shape and wear well. And they're given a most elegant degree of shaping.

I used double-pointed needles, and the pattern is written this way. If you wish to use 2 circulars, see page 128.

Make the shorter-fingered version for 'dress-up' occasions, when you want your jewelry to show.

The yarn used in the model garments straddles the line between super fine (weight 1) and fine (weight 2). The different sizes are achieved by knitting different gauges; otherwise, the patterns for S-M or L-XL are identical.

STITCH PATTERN
1 × 1 rib (multiple of 2 sts)
All rounds (rnds) *Knit (k) 1, purl (p) 1, repeat from * to end.

Read about rib, page 106.

Here's how!
RIGHT/LEFT
Make 2: right and left are identical.

1   1 × 1 edging
With long-tail cast-on, cast on 60 stitches (sts). Starting at end opposite yarn and tail, slip (sl) 15 sts onto needle (N) 1, then 15 sts onto N2, then 15 sts onto N3. 15 sts remain on N4.

Needle with yarn attached is N4; needle with first cast-on st is N1.

Hold 4 needles in circle, being careful not to twist cast-on.

I prefer to leave the 5th needle aside for now and to work as follows.

Rnd 1 With RS facing, work 1 × 1 rib, working sts from N1 onto N4. (Sts are now distributed over 3 needles: 30 on N4, 15 on N2, and 15 on N3.) Continue 1 × 1 rib over sts of N2 and N3. Continue 1 × 1 rib over first 15 sts of N4. Place safety pin marker onto st at end of N4. Introduce 5th needle. Work 1 × 1 rib over remaining 15 sts. (This is now N1.)

Sts are now evenly distributed over 4 needles.
Continue 1 × 1 rib to 8 rows, ending at marker.

2 Arm
K all sts, all rnds, to 6" from beginning, ending at marker.

3 Arm shaping
*N1 K1, work left-slanting decrease (SKP or SSK, page 18), k to end.
N2 K to 3 sts remaining, work right-slanting decrease (k2tog), k1.
N3 K1, SKP (or SSK), k to end.
N4 K to 3 sts remaining, k2tog, k1.
Work 7 rnds straight.
Repeat from * to 40 sts remaining (10 on each needle).

4 Wrist
Work 1½" straight, ending at marker.
Move safety pin marker up the piece as needed.

5 Hand shaping
N1 K1, increase 1 by k into st below next st plus k into next st (lifted increase, page 67), place marker onto needle, k to end.
N2 K to 2 sts remaining, place marker, work lifted increase, k1.
N3 K1, work lifted increase, place marker, k to end.
N4 K to 2 sts remaining, place marker, work lifted increase, k1.
Work 3 rnds straight.
N1 K to 1 st before marker, work lifted increase, k to end.
N2 K to marker, work lifted increase, k to end.
N3 K to 1 st before marker, work lifted increase, k to end.
N4 K to marker, work lifted increase, k to end.
There are now 12 sts on each needle.
Work 3 rnds straight.

Remove markers on N2 and N3: further shaping is for thumb only (on N1 and N4).

6 Thumb shaping
*N1 K to 1 st before marker, work lifted increase, k to end.
N2 & N3 K.
N4 K to marker, work lifted increase, k to end.
Work 3 rnds straight.
Repeat from * twice more, ending with 3 rnds worked straight—15 sts on N1 and N4, 12 sts on N2 and N3.

7 Palm and finger area
Remove markers from needles on this rnd.
Next rnd K all sts on N1, N2, N3, and to 6 sts remaining on N4. Put last 6 sts of N4 and first 6 sts of N1 onto holder or thread. Return to N4. Turn. On end of N4, e-wrap cast on 3 sts, place marker onto needle, e-wrap cast on 3 more sts. Turn. K remaining sts from N1 onto N4—24 sts on N4. Put 5th needle aside for now.
Next rnd K all sts on N1, N2, N3, and to marker at center of N4 (12 sts now on N4). With 5th needle, k next 12 sts. (This becomes N1, and there are now 12 sts on all 4 needles.)
K all sts, in rnds, to 1" (for dressy) or to 2½" (for casual), ending with N4.

8 1 × 1 edging
Work 1 × 1 rib for 4 rows, then bind off in rib (page 109).

9 Thumb
Put 12 thumb sts (from holder or thread) onto 2 needles—N1 is at back of thumb, N2 is at front of thumb.
With N3, pick up and k 8 sts along inside edge of thumb—1 st for each cast-on st plus 1 st at each corner. Work next rnd with 4 needles only and as follows:
N1 K6.
N2 K5, slip last st knit-wise, k1 from N3, pass slip stitch over—6 sts now on N2.
N3 K6, slip last st purl-wise from N3 onto N1.
N1 K2tog, k5.
(There are now 6 sts on all 3 needles.)
K all sts, in rnds, to 1".

1 × 1 edging
Work 1 × 1 rib for 4 rows, then bind off in rib.

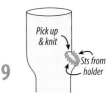

9

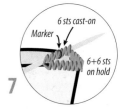

7

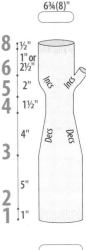

6¾(8)"

8½ (10)"

EXPERIence
- *intermediate*
- *repetitive stitch pattern*
- *mid-level shaping*
- *mid-level finishing*

It'll fit
S (M, L)

10cm/4"
25 (24, 23) GET CLOSE
15 (14, 13)
- *over stitch pattern*

You'll need
1 2 3 4 **5** 6
- **bulky weight or light + medium weight**
- **100 (106, 114) yds of each for hat**
- **100 (111, 114) yds of each for mitts**
- **soft wool or wool blend**

I used

- **4 (4.5, 5)mm/ US 6 (7, 8), 40–60cm/16-24", for hat in single yarn**
- **5 (5.5, 6)mm/ US 8 (9, 10), 40–60cm/16-24", for hat in doubled yarn**

(set of 5)
- **4 (4.5, 5)mm/ US 6 (7, 8) in single yarn**
- **5 (5.5, 6)mm/ US 8 (9, 10) in doubled yarn**

Large, hat or mitts: 1 skein ROSINA Kilim in color 667

CANADIAN-WINTER HAT AND MITTS

These might not be the simplest hats and mitts you've seen, but they might be among the warmest (hence their name). The stitch pattern is what makes them a little more challenging, but I think it adds interest to both the knitting and wearing. The bulky yarn (or doubled lighter yarns)—worked relatively tightly—is what gives the warmth that we appreciate in my part of the world.

Three sizes are offered. They all depend upon gauge. The same number of stitches is used throughout.
Note that the doubled yarn is worked on larger needles than the single yarn.

For the hat, I used a circular needle for the body then changed to double-pointed needles for the crown. For the mitts, I used double-pointed needles throughout. The pattern is written this way. If you wish to use two circulars, see page 128. (Of course, you could use double-pointed needles for everything.)

To make this pattern easier, ignore the garter ridge and the garter rib stitch pattern, and work stockinette stitch throughout.

STITCH PATTERN
Garter rib
Round (rnd) 1 Knit (k) all stitches (sts).
Rnd 2 *K1, purl (p) 1, repeat from * to end.
One round is knit, then one round is 1 × 1 rib. The effect is like rib except that it has garter stitches, rather than purl troughs, between the knit rib stitches.
While working the piece, it should be obvious whether or not the next stitch is a knit or a purl (read about rib, page 106). But it's a little more difficult to sort out whether you are on a knit or a rib round. To determine which round you are on, look at the next purl bump on the left-hand needle. If it sits tight to the left-hand needle, then this is a knit round; if there is a row between the purl bump and the needle, then this is a rib round.

Here's how!
Hat

1 St st edging
With long-tail cast-on and circular needle, cast on 76 sts.
Place marker (safety pin) onto st at end of right-hand needle.
Form circle, being careful not to twist cast-on.
K all sts, all rnds, to 1", ending at marker.
Garter ridge
Next rnd P, ending at marker.

2 Garter Rib
Beginning with rnd 1, work garter rib stitch pattern to 4½ (5, 5½)" from beginning, ending with rnd 1 and at marker.
Garter ridge
Next rnd P, ending at marker.

3 Crown
Change to double-pointed needles (dpns) and work as follows.
Next rnds Onto dpn, *k10, place marker onto needle, k9, introduce new dpn, repeat from * until all sts are on 4 dpns—19 sts on each needle.

*If using 2 circulars, put 38 sts on each of 2 circulars, as follows: *K10, place marker, k9, place marker, k10, place marker, k9, change needle, repeat from * for second needle.*

Rnd 1 (decrease), all needles K to 2 sts before all markers, work right-slanting decrease (k2tog), k to 2 sts from end of needle, k2tog.
Rnd 2 K.
Repeat last 2 rnds to 5 sts remaining on all dpns (10 sts on each circular), ending with rnd 2. Remove markers on next rnd.
Next rnd, all needles *K1, k2tog, k2, repeat from * —4 sts on each dpn (8 sts on each circular).
Next rnd K all sts.
Next rnd, all needles K2tog—2 sts on each dpn (4 sts on each circular).

If you do not wish to add the cords and tassels (or don't have enough yarn remaining), cut yarn and thread onto tapestry needle. Draw through all sts, and pull tight to close.

4 Cords and tassels (optional)
Slip sts onto 2 dpns—4 on each.

With RS facing, and over 4 sts of one needle, work I-cord (page 128) to 6".
Do not cut yarn, and put this I-cord aside for now. Introduce yarn from end of ball, then with RS facing and over 4 sts of other needle, work I-cord to 8".

These I-cords can be any length. But you must stop when you have 36" yarn remaining for each.
Finish each I-cord as follows.
Cut yarn so each cord has a 36" tail. Thread tail onto tapestry needle, then draw through 4 sts (to close).

5 Holding end of I-cord, *wrap yarn around 2 fingers (so loop is about 1½" tall) 6 times and then take tapestry needle through bottom of loops and top of I-cord a few times to secure. (About 10" of yarn remains.)

6 Wrap remaining tail tightly around join between I-cord and loops, 4 times.

7 With remaining tail on tapestry needle, go through wraps 3 times, to secure them, then take remaining tail through to join loops. Cut and trim loops to suit. Tie I-cords in single, tight knot at crown; use remaining tail to secure knot to crown and to direct I-cords toward back of hat.

Mitts
RIGHT MITT

1 St st edging
With long-tail cast-on, cast on 24 sts, all onto one needle.

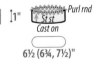

Starting at end opposite yarn and tail, slip (sl) 7 sts onto N1, then 6 sts onto N2, then 6 sts onto N3—5 sts remain on N4.

Needle with yarn attached is N4; needle with first cast-on st is N1.
Hold needles in circle, being careful not to twist cast-on.

I prefer to leave the 5th needle aside for now and work as follows.
Rnd 1 K sts from N1 onto N4. (Sts are now distributed over 3 needles: 12 on N4, 6 on N2, and 6 on N3.)
K sts of N2 and N3. K first 5 sts of N4. Place safety pin marker onto st at end of N4. Introduce 5th needle. K all sts, all rnds, to 1", ending at marker.
Garter ridge
Next rnd P.

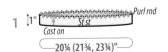

2 Cuff

Beginning with rnd 1, work garter rib stitch pattern over sts of N1 and N2, then k all sts of N3 and N4.
Continue with garter rib over N1 and N2 and St st over N3 and N4 to 2 (2, 3)" from fold line of rolled edge, ending at marker.

3 Palm and thumb shaping
Next (increase) rnd
N1 & N2 Continue garter rib.
N3 Increase 1 by k into st below next st plus k into next st (lifted increase, page 67), k to end—7 sts.
N4 K to 1 st remaining, work lifted increase in last st—6 sts.
Work 3 rnds straight.
***Next (increase) rnd*
N1 & N2 Continue garter rib.
N3 Work lifted increase in first st, k to end.
N4 K.
Work 3 rnds straight.
Repeat from * once more—7 sts on N1, 6 sts on N2, 9 sts on N3, 6 sts on N4.
Next (increase) rnd
N1 & N2 Continue garter rib.
N3 Work lifted increase in first st, k2, work lifted increase in next st, k to end—11 sts on N3.
N4 K.
Work 3 rnds straight.

4 Hand only
Next rnd
N1 & N2 Continue garter rib.
N3 K2, put next 5 sts onto holder (for thumb), turn, e-wrap cast on 3 sts, turn, k to end—9 sts on N3.
N4 K.
Next rnd Continue garter rib over 7 sts of N1 and 6 sts of N2. K to 1 st remaining on N3. Sl this last st onto N4—8 sts on N3, 7 sts on N4.
Work stitch patterns as established (with garter rib on N1 & N2 and St st on N3 & N4) to 1" above thumb opening.

5 Hand shaping
Next (decrease) rnd
N1 & N2 Continue garter rib.

N3 Work left-slanting decrease (SKP or SSK, page 18), k to end.
N4 K to 2 sts remaining, work right-slanting decrease (k2tog).
There are now 7 sts on N1 & N3 and 6 sts on N2 & N4.
Work stitch patterns as established (with garter rib on N1 & N2 and St st on N3 & N4) to 3 (3½, 4)" above thumb opening (approximately 1½" short of desired length), ending with rnd 2 of garter rib.
***Next (decrease) rnd*
N1 SKP (or SSK), k to end.
N2 K to 2 sts remaining, k2tog.
N3 SKP, k to end.
N4 K to 2 sts remaining, k2tog.
Next rnd: Work stitch patterns as established.
After the first and every alternative decrease, there will be a k2 at the beginning of N1 and end of N2.
Repeat from * until 3 sts remain on N1 & N3 and 2 sts remain on N2 & N4, ending with decrease rnd.
Sl sts from N2 onto N1 and sts from N4 onto N3.
Graft sts from 2 needles together (page 130).
If you choose not to graft, you could cut yarn and thread onto tapestry needle then draw through all sts, pulling tight to close.

6 Thumb
Return to base of thumb. Sl sts from holder onto needle.
Leaving 8" tail, introduce yarn.
For all picking up and knitting that follows, go under 2 threads. This will produce a firmer join.
Next rnd
N1 K3 (of the 5 sts).
N2 Introduce N2 and k2 (the remaining sts), then pick up and k 1 along edge before e-wrap cast-on.
N3 Pick up and k 1 for each of 3 e-wrap cast-ons, then pick up and k 1 along edge after e-wrap cast-on and before sts of N1.
Thumb has 10 sts: 3 on N1, 3 on N2, 4 on N3.
K all sts, all rnds, to 1¼ (1½, 2)" from base of thumb (just short of desired height).
Next rnd K2tog around—5 sts remain.
Cut yarn and thread onto tapestry needle. Draw through all sts and pull tight to close.
Use tail at base of thumb to close any holes.

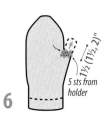

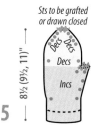

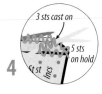

5 sts from holder

Sts to be grafted or drawn closed

Decs Decs
Decs
Incs

8½ (9½, 11)"

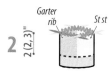

3 sts cast on
5 sts on hold
St st   Incs

St st
Inc

Garter rib   St st

2 (2, 3)"

6

5

4

3

2

LEFT MITT
Work as Right mitt to palm and thumb shaping.
Palm and thumb shaping
Next (increase) rnd
N1 & N2 Continue garter rib.
N3 Work lifted increase, k to end—7 sts.
N4 K to 1 st remaining, work lifted increase in last st—6 sts.
Work 3 rnds straight.
*Next (increase) rnd
N1 & N2 Continue garter rib.
N3 K.
N4 K to 1 st remaining, work lifted increase in last st—7 sts.
Work 3 rnds straight.
Repeat from * once more—7 sts on N1, 6 sts on N2, 7 sts on N3, 8 sts on N4.
Next (increase) rnd
N1 & N2 Continue garter rib.
N3 K.
N4 K to 4 sts remaining, work lifted increase in next st, k2, work lifted increase in last st—10 sts on N4.
Work 3 rnds straight.
Hand only
Next rnd
N1 & N2 Continue garter rib.
N3 K.
N4 K to 7 sts remaining. Put next 5 sts onto holder (for thumb), turn, e-wrap cast-on 3 sts, turn, k2—8 sts on N4.
Next rnd Continue stitch patterns as established to end of N3. K1 from N4 onto N3. K sts of N4.
There are 7 sts on N1, 6 sts on N2, 8 sts on N3, 7 sts on N4.
Work stitch patterns as established (with garter rib on N1 & N2 and St st on N3 & N4) to 1" above thumb opening.
Work as Right mitt from hand shaping to end.

Middle photo:
Medium, hat or mitts: 1 skein KOIGU Kersti Merino Crepe in color K104 + 1/2 skein CASCADE YARNS Cascade 220 in color 9412

To help you see what's going on, Needle 1 is silver and Needle 2 is green.

Using two circulars

I personally love the rhythm of working in the round over double-pointed needles, and I love that they tuck into a purse or pocket. But some knitters don't like them and prefer to work with two circular needles. Here's how to do this when a pattern has been written for five double-pointed needles.

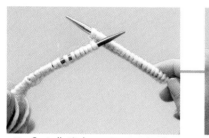

1 Cast all stitches onto one circular.

2 Leave stitches for Needles 1 and 2 on one circular; slip stitches for Needles 3 and 4 onto a second circular.

3 Push the stitches on the first circular to the right end of that needle (above).

4 Knit these stitches onto the other end of the same needle.

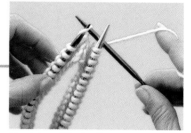

5 Repeat Steps 3–4 with the second circular needle.

Here's how it looks after some rows have been knit.

I-cord

This is really just the old 'spool knitting' but done with knitting needles. Use it whenever you need a knitted cord.

This I-cord is shown in stockinette stitch, knitting all stitches. You could also work I-cord in reverse stockinette stitch, purling all stitches.

Use one short circular needle or two double-pointed needles.

1 Begin with the number of stitches directed in the pattern (usually 3–4).

2 *Knit these stitches as usual.

3 At the end of the row, do not turn work.

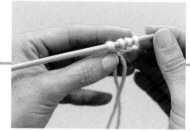

4 Instead, just slip the stitches to the other end of the same needle.

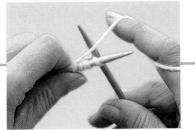

5 Draw yarn from behind, pulling tightly, and repeat from *.

Here is the result, from the back, after a few rounds have been knit.

Here's the result after tugging on the tail.

Oops, I dropped a stitch! What do I do now? See page 164.

Oops, I knit when I should have purled (or vice versa)! What do I do now? See page 166.

Grafting the toes of socks

Grafting is a method of joining live stitches to live stitches, without a seam. This is particularly useful for the toes of socks where the seam would irritate a sensitive part of the body.

Grafting live stitches to live stitches can happen anywhere in knitting, and it's a useful skill to know. But it's quite possible that you may have a full life of knitting and never use it or need it except for the toes of socks!

I sure wish you were not seeing it for the first time over the toes of socks, 'cause grafting from small needles is not the easiest learning environment. However, there just isn't room in this book for a Grafting 101, and besides, you might never use grafting anywhere else!

For clarity, grafting is shown in contrasting-color yarn.

Here's what you need to know to understand what follows.
- *Knit-wise* means to insert the tapestry needle into the stitch as if to knit.
- *Purl-wise* means to insert the tapestry needle into the stitch as if to purl.
- Once a stitch is removed from a knitting needle, it is not touched again. The leading stitch then becomes the next stitch on that knitting needle.
- Do not try to pull tight as you are working. It is easier to go back and do this later.
- Be very careful not to split stitches or yarn as you work. This will make it impossible to go back and tighten.

Move slowly through the steps that follow. It may be helpful to use paper to cover all but the step you are working on and to complete the process in one sitting.

Begin with stitches distributed evenly on two sock needles. Through what follows, I'll call these *back needle* and *front needle*. The tail is hanging from leading stitch on back needle and threaded onto blunt tapestry needle.

1 Insert tapestry needle into leading stitch on front needle purl-wise. Draw tail through, but leave stitch on front needle.

2 Insert tapestry needle into leading stitch on back needle purl-wise. Remove stitch from back needle.

3 Insert tapestry needle into leading stitch on back needle knit-wise. Draw tail through, but leave stitch on back needle.

If you really dislike grafting your sock toes, you could use the 3-needle bind-off. It will leave a ridge along the outside of the toe of your sock, but you might not mind that. Here's how it's done: when you have your final 16 stitches distributed on two needles, take a third needle, and knit-2-together (1 stitch from each needle) across the row, binding off as you go.

What you have does not look very neat and finished.

It can help to put your hand inside the sock and push your fingers against the grafting, so you can see the grafted stitches more clearly, because . . .

4 Insert tapestry needle into leading stitch on front needle, knit-wise. Remove stitch from front needle.

Repeat Steps 1–4, ending with Step 2. 1 stitch remains on back needle, and 2 stitches remain on front needle. Work Step 3, and then remove final stitch from back needle. Draw tail through. Work Steps 4 and 1, and then remove final stitch from front needle. Draw tail through.

As you tighten your grafting, it can help to remember that a stitch looks like V.

. . . you need to go back to the beginning of the row and tug on the grafted stitches until . . .

. . . they are the same size as the knit stitches.

Here is the result in the yarn of the piece and with tails sewn.

The stitch pattern upon which all the garments in this chapter are based is actually a combination of three now-familiar stitch patterns: garter stitch, stockinette stitch, and reverse stockinette stitch. And while this stitch-pattern-that-is-actually-three-stitch-patterns can be written out, row by row, it should be easier and quicker to process this material graphically, by reading a chart.

Some folks are wary of charts, and I can certainly understand how charts can make the eyes glaze! But if you take the time to decipher the chart, with either written directions or a photo of the fabric in hand, then the chart should make wonderful sense. And I certainly did not want to finish a book on knits and purls in combination without giving you the opportunity to explore the use of charts.

If you do learn to read charts, I suspect you will become someone who easily 'reads' your knitting. And reading your knitting is something that can only serve to make you a better, more intuitive, more competent knitter.

Chapter Six

The Patterns

Additional Skills

COLLARED WRAP

EXPerience
- *easy*
- *repetitive stitch pattern*
- *some finishing*

It'll fit
One size fits all

10cm/4"
25-27
15-17
- *over 3-Block stitch pattern*
- *after blocking*

You'll need
1 2 3 **4** 5 6
- *medium weight*
- *900 yds*
- *something soft*

I used
- *5mm/US 7*

7 balls NATURALLY Merino & Fur in color 05

I'm not sure what makes this a 'wrap' rather than a 'shawl.' My take on it is that the former is a rectangle, the latter a triangle. But the only thing that I know for sure is that when a triangular 'shawl' wraps around the neck, it produces a 'shawl collar' (hence the name). Here, the shawl collar was added after knitting the main piece.

STITCH PATTERN
2 × 2 rib (multiple of 4 sts + 2)
Right-side (RS) rows K2, *p2, k2, repeat from * to end.
Wrong-side (WS) rows P2, *k2, p2, repeat from * to end.
To read this stitch pattern, see page 106.

Here's how!
BODY
Cast on 50 stitches (sts).
Row 1 (RS) Knit (k) 1, work Row 1 of 3-Block stitch pattern, reading chart (see page 148), from right to left, beginning at A and ending at B, to 1 st remaining, k1.
Row 2 (WS) Purl (p) 1, work Row 2 of 3-Block stitch pattern, reading from left to right, beginning at B and ending at A, to 1 st remaining, p1.
Continue to work from chart and with 1 stockinette st at beginning and end of all rows to 320 rows—approximately 50".
The piece will stretch at least 10% when blocked.
SHORTEN OR LENGTHEN HERE.

Approximate measurements, after blocking

FINISHING

2 **Short ends edging**
On edge with live stitches, k 1 RS row.
*K 1 WS row, then p 2 rows.
Next (RS) row Work 2 × 2 rib
stitch pattern.
Continue with 2 × 2 rib for 2", then
3 bind off in rib (page 109).
Along cast-on edge and with RS
facing, pick up and k 50 sts, then
4 finish as from * to bind-off.
Lower edging
Along one long edge and with RS
facing, pick up and k 3 sts for every 4
rows.

> *Do what you need—working one or
> more k2tog on the next row—to have
> a multiple of 4 sts + 2 (page 106).*

5 Work as from * to bind-off of Short
ends edging.
Collar edging
Along remaining edge and with RS
facing, pick up and k 3 sts for every 4
rows. K 1 WS row, then p 2 rows.
Next (increase) row *K2, p in front and
back of next st, repeat from * across.

> *Do what you need to do to have a
> multiple of 4 sts + 2.*

Work 2 × 2 rib for 4½–5".
Bind off loosely and in rib.
Block, spreading collar out.

5½"
5
12"
2½"
4
62"

20"

2
20"
1
3

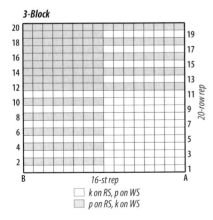

3-Block

20
19
18
17
16
15
14
13
12
11 20-row rep
10
9
8
7
6
5
4
3
2
1
B   16-st rep   A

☐ k on RS, p on WS
▨ p on RS, k on WS

7 balls NATURALLY Merino & Fur in color 02

size 7
needles 2 → 17/4"

EXPERIence

- *intermediate*
- *repetitive stitch pattern*
- *mid-level shaping*
- *mid-level finishing*

LOOSE FIT

Child's 6-8 (10-12, Woman's S, M, L, 1X, 2X, 3X)

A 31 (35, 39, 42, 46, 50, 54, 57)"

B 23 (25, 28, 28½, 28½, 29, 29½, 30)"

C 21 (25, 28, 28½, 28½, 29, 29½, 30)"

10cm/4"

28 **GET GAUGE!**

17

- *over 3-Block stitch pattern*
- *after blocking*

You'll need

1 2 3 **4** 5 6

- *medium weight*
- *650 (860, 1090, 1220, 1300, 1380, 1470, 1550) yds*
- *anything*

☺

Two ¾" buttons

I used

- *4.5mm/US 7 (for wool)*
- *4mm/US 6 (for cotton)*

- *3.75mm/US 5, 40-60cm/16-24"*

Large: 16 balls MISSION FALLS 1824 Cotton in color 305

TO-THE-COTTAGE PULLOVERS

I see these as garments the family dons for a weekend at the cottage. That a wool one is offered speaks to the fact that cottage country, in my part of the world, can be cold!

To keep the directions cleaner, I've only offered children's and women's sizes. Read the notes below to make this garment for a man.

Here's how to make this into a loose fitting garment for a man.
- *Man's S = woman's M; man's M = woman's L; man's L = woman's 1X; man's 1X = woman's 2X; man's 2X = woman's 3X.*
- *The woman's lengths are for a 5'4"–5'6" standard. For every 2" taller the recipient is, add 1" wherever the pattern says SHORTEN OR LENGTHEN HERE. You will, of course, need more yarn—perhaps 6–7% for every inch of length added.*

Here's how!
BACK
Edging
With smaller needle, cast on 68 (76, 84, 92, 100, 108, 116, 124) stitches (sts).
Work 5 rows stockinette stitch (St st, knit RS rows, purl WS rows), beginning and ending with knit (k) row.
Body
Change to larger needles.
Row 1 (RS) K2, work Row 1 of 3-Block stitch pattern as follows: reading chart from right to left, work 0 (8, 0, 8, 0, 8, 0, 8) sts as from D to A, work 16-st repeat from A to B (see page 148), to 2 sts remaining, k2.
Row 2 (WS) Purl (p) 1, k1, work Row 2 of 3-Block stitch pattern as follows: reading from left to right, work 16-st repeat from B to A to 2 (10, 2, 10, 2, 10, 2, 10) sts remaining, work 0 (8, 0, 8, 0, 8, 0, 8) sts as from A to D, k1, p1.
Continue to work from chart, beginning all rows with 1 St st then 1 k st and ending all rows with

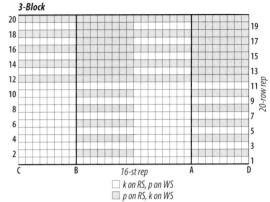

3-Block

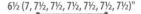

16-st rep

☐ k on RS, p on WS
▨ p on RS, k on WS

20-row rep

6½ (7, 7½, 7½, 7½, 7½, 7½, 7½)"

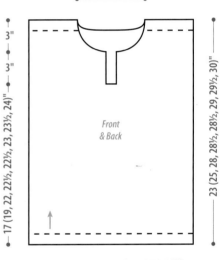

Front & Back

23 (25, 28, 28½, 28½, 29, 29½, 30)"

17 (19, 22, 22½, 22½, 23, 23½, 24)"

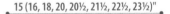

16 (18, 20, 21½, 23½, 25½, 27½, 29)"

15 (16, 18, 20, 20½, 21½, 22½, 23½)"

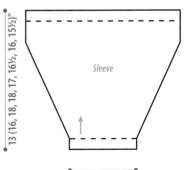

Sleeve

13 (16, 18, 18, 17, 16½, 16, 15½)"

6½ (8½, 8½, 8½, 10½, 10½, 10½, 10½)"

---

1 k st then 1 St st, to 22½ (24½, 27½, 28, 28, 28½, 29, 29½)" from beginning, ending with WS row.
SHORTEN OR LENGTHEN HERE.

Right neck and shoulder

You really do discontinue stitch pattern and k all remaining rows.

Next row (RS) K21 (24, 27, 31, 35, 39, 43,

FR

E

W

Ch

Ro
patt
work
2, 1(
8, 0,

Row 2
stitch p
right,
to B, work 16-st repeat from B to A to 2 sts remaining, k1, p1.
Continue to work from chart, beginning all rows with 1 St st then 1 k st and ending all rows with 1 k st then 1 St st, to 6" short of Back length, ending with WS row.

Right neck

Maintain stitch pattern through all shaping.
Work 32 (36, 40, 44, 48, 52, 56, 60) sts, then put on holder for Left neck. Bind off next 4 sts. Continue over remaining 32 (36, 40, 44, 48, 52, 56, 60) sts, and work to 3" from bind-off, ending with WS row.
Bind off 5 (5, 7, 7, 7, 7, 7, 7) sts at

beginning of next RS row, then 3 sts at beginning of next RS row, then 2 sts at beginning of next RS row, then 1 st at beginning of next 2 (3, 2, 2, 2, 2, 2, 2) RS rows—20 (23, 26, 30, 34, 38, 42, 46) sts remain.
Work straight to same length as Back, ending with 4 k rows, then bind off.

Left neck

Maintain stitch pattern through all shaping.
Return to 32 (36, 40, 44, 48, 52, 56, 60) sts left behind, ready to work WS row.
Work 1 WS row then 1 RS row.
Work as for Right neck but with reverse shaping.

SLEEVES

Edging
With smaller needle, cast on 28 (36, 36, 36, 44, 44, 44, 44) sts.
Work 4 rows St st, beginning and ending with k row.

2X and 3X only K 1 more row, increasing 8 sts evenly across row—52 sts.

All other sizes K 1 more row.

Body
Change to larger needles.

Row 1 (RS) K2, work Row 1 of 3-Block stitch pattern as follows: reading from right to left, work 16-st repeat from A to B to 10 (2, 2, 2, 10, 10, 2, 2) sts remaining, work 8 (0, 0, 0, 8, 8, 0, 0,) sts as from B to C, k2.

Row 2 (WS) P1, k1, work Row 2 of 3-Block stitch pattern as follows: reading from left to right, work 8 (0, 0, 0, 8, 8, 0, 0) sts as from C to B, work 16-st repeat from B to A to 2 sts remaining, k1, p1.
Continue to work from chart, beginning all rows with 1 St st then 1 k st and ending all rows with 1 k st then 1 St st, to 1" from beginning, ending with WS row.

Maintain stitch pattern through all increases that follow (page 111).

Next (increase) row K1, work into st below next st then work next st (lifted increase, page 67), work to 2 sts remaining, work lifted increase, k1.

3

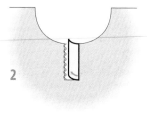

2

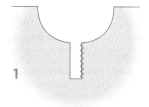

1

Child's 6–8: 6 balls Lite-Lopi (REYNOLDS in color 418, ALAFOSS in color 9418)

Work 3 rows in stitch pattern.
Repeat last 4 rows to 64 (68, 76, 84, 88, 92, 96, 100) sts.
SHORTEN OR LENGTHEN HERE.
Work straight to 12½ (15½, 17½, 17½, 16½, 16, 15½, 15)" from beginning, ending with WS row.
K 4 rows, then bind off.

FINISHING
Use smaller needles for all edgings.
Buttonholes are on female side. For buttonholes on male side, work as follows but in reverse (working Right placket edging first without buttonholes, then working Left placket edging with buttonholes spaced evenly).

1 Left placket edging
Beginning at Left Front neck opening, pick up and k 2 sts for every 3 rows along placket opening.
K 11 rows.
***Next (RS) row** P.*
K 1 row, then p 1 row, then bind off in k.

2 Right placket edging
Beginning at base of Right placket opening, pick up and k as Left placket opening, then k 5 rows.
***Work buttonholes (RS)** K3, work 1-row buttonhole as follows.*
Yarn forward, slip next st purl-wise (sl1 p-wise), yarn back, sl1 p-wise, pass sl st over (psso), sl1 p-wise, psso (2 sts bound off). Return remaining sl st to left-hand needle. Turn work (to WS). Yarn back, cable cast on 1 st. Begin to cable cast on next st but before putting new st onto left-hand needle, bring yarn between needles and to front, then place new st onto left-hand needle. Turn work (to RS), k to 5 sts from end of row, work second 1-row buttonhole as above, k to end.
K 5 more rows.
Work as Left placket edging from * to end.
For male garments, Left placket edging overlaps right, so work what follows in reverse.
Sew lower edge of Right placket edging to bound-off sts.
Sew lower edge of Left placket edging behind right.
Sew buttons to left placket to match placement of buttonholes.

3 Neck edging
Sew shoulder seams.
Beginning at fold of Right placket edging, pick up and k around curve (page 46), ending at fold of Left placket edging.
Work 4 rows RSS, then bind off.
Sew drop-shoulder Sleeves to garment (page 26).
Sew side and Sleeve seams.

Large: 12 balls Lite-Lopi (REYNOLDS in color 426, ALAFOSS in color 9426)

Medium: 13 skeins BERROCO Cotton Twist in color 8353, 2 skeins in color 8323

ANOTHER COCO JACKET

Coco Chanel sure got it right when she designed her trademark jacket, because it never goes out of style. For my first attempt at this classic, I had lots of fun constructing it but also choosing somewhat unusual colors. If you don't like them, it's difficult not to be distracted by them, isn't it? Try taking a black-and-white photocopy and then 'seeing' it in other colors.

Because of the nature and weight of cotton, and with the addition of the front edging, the finished neck width will be approximately 8" when worn.

Here's how!
BACK
Edging
With smaller needle and main color (MC), e-wrap cast on 98 (106, 114, 122, 130) stitches (sts).

Next right-side (RS) row Knit (k) 1, *k2, purl (p) 2, repeat from * to 1 st remaining, k1.

Next wrong-side (WS) row P1, *k2, p2, repeat from * to 1 st remaining, p1.

Repeat last 2 rows once more. Leave MC attached.

Continuing with smaller needle but with contrast color (CC), k 2 rows, then p 1 row, k 1 row. Cut CC.

Body
Change to larger needles and MC.

Row 1 (RS) K1, work Row 1 of 3-Block stitch pattern as follows: reading chart from right to left (page 149), work 16-st repeat from D to E to 1 (9, 1, 9, 1) sts remaining, work 0 (8, 0, 8, 0) sts from E to B, k1.

Row 2 (WS) P1, work Row 2 of 3-Block stitch pattern as follows: reading from left to right, work 0 (8, 0, 8, 0) sts from B to E, work 16-st repeat from E to D to 1 st remaining, p1.

Continue to work from chart, beginning and ending all rows with 1 stockinette (St) st, to 11½ (11½, 11, 11, 11)" from beginning, ending with WS row.

SHORTEN OR LENGTHEN HERE.

Armhole shaping
Maintain stitch pattern (with 1 St st at beginning and end of all rows) through all shaping.

Bind off 5 (5, 7, 9, 11) sts at beginning of next 2 rows—88 (96, 100, 104, 108) sts remain.

Next (decrease) row (RS) K1, work left-slanting decrease (SKP or SSK, page 18), work to 3 sts remaining, work right-slanting decrease (k2tog), k1.
Next row (WS) Work straight.
Repeat last 2 rows to 70 (74, 78, 82, 86) sts remaining. Work straight to 7 (7½, 8½, 9, 10)" from beginning, ending with WS row.
Shoulder shaping
Bind off 5 (5, 6, 6, 7) sts at beginning of next 2 rows.
Right shoulder and neck shaping
Next row (RS) Bind off 5 (6, 6, 7, 7) sts, work 12 (13, 14, 15, 16) sts. Put center 26 sts on holder for center Back neck. Turn.
*__Next row (WS)__ Bind off 1 st at neck edge, work to end.
Next row (RS) Bind off 5 (5, 6, 6, 7) sts at shoulder edge, work to end.
Next row (WS) Bind off 1 st at neck edge, work to end.
Next row (RS) Bind off remaining 5 (6, 6, 7, 7) sts.
Left shoulder and neck shaping
Return to 17 (19, 20, 22, 23) sts for left shoulder. Work 1 RS row.
Next row (WS) Bind off 5 (6, 6, 7, 7) sts at shoulder, work to end.
Work as right shoulder and neck from * to end but with reverse shaping (page 19).

RIGHT FRONT
Edging
With smaller needle and main color (MC), cast on 50 (50, 58, 58, 66) sts.
Work as Back edging from * to end.
Body
Change to larger needles and MC.
Row 1 (RS) K1, work Row 1 of 3-Block stitch pattern as follows: reading from right to left, work 0 (0, 8, 8, 0) sts from A to E, work 16-st repeat from E to C to 1 st remaining, k1.
Row 2 (WS) P1, work Row 2 of 3-Block stitch pattern as follows: reading from left to right, work 16-st repeat from C to E to 1 (1, 9, 9, 1) sts remaining, work 0 (0, 8, 8, 0) sts from E to A, p1.

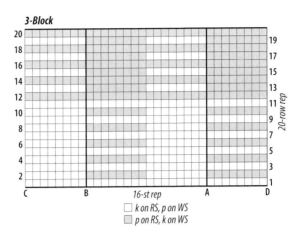

Continue to work from chart, beginning and ending all rows with 1 St st, to same length as Back to armhole, ending with RS row.
Armhole shaping
Maintain stitch pattern through all shaping.
Bind off 5 (5, 7, 9, 11) sts at beginning of next WS row—45 (45, 51, 49, 55) sts remain.
Next (decrease) row (RS) Work to 3 sts remaining, work right-slanting decrease (k2tog), k1.
Next row (WS) Work straight.
Repeat last 2 rows to 32 (34, 36, 38, 40) sts remaining.
Work straight to 2" short of Back length to shoulder shaping, ending with WS row.
Neck shaping
Bind off 5 sts at beginning of next neck edge, then 3 sts at next neck edge, then 1 st at next 4 neck edges—20 (22, 24, 26, 28) sts remain.
Shoulder shaping
Bind off 5 (5, 6, 6, 7) sts at beginning of next WS row.
Bind off 5 (6, 6, 7, 7) sts at beginning of next WS row.
Bind off 5 (5, 6, 6, 7) sts at beginning of next WS row.
Bind off 5 (6, 6, 7, 7) sts at beginning of next WS row.

EXPERIEnce
• advanced intermediate
• repetitive stitch patterns
• mid-level shaping
• mid-level finishing

LOOSE FIT
S (M, L, 1X, 2X)
A 40 (41½, 46½, 48, 52½)"
B 19½ (20, 20½, 21, 22)"
C 28 (29, 29½, 30½, 32)"

10cm/4"

28 / 20
• over 3-Block stitch pattern
• after blocking

You'll need
1 2 3 **4** 5 6
• medium weight
• 1020 (1100, 1240, 1320, 1420) yds in MC
• 155 (170, 190, 205, 220) yds in CC
• cotton or cotton blend

Eleven 5/8" buttons

I used

• 4mm/US 6
• 3.75mm/US 5

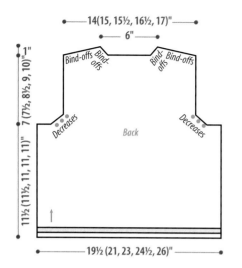

14(15, 15½, 16½, 17)"

6"

1"

Bind-offs Bind-offs Bind-offs Bind-offs

7 (7½, 8½, 9, 10)"

Decreases Decreases

Back

11½ (11½, 11, 11, 11)"

19½ (21, 23, 24½, 26)"

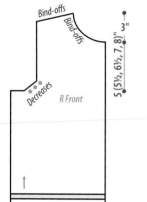

Bind-offs Bind-offs

3"

Decreases

R Front

5 (5½, 6½, 7, 8)"

10 (10, 11½, 11½, 13)"

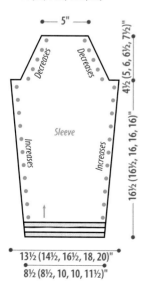

5"

Decreases Decreases

Sleeve

Increases Increases

4½ (5, 6, 6½, 7½)"

16½ (16½, 16, 16, 16)"

13½ (14½, 16½, 18, 20)"

8½ (8½, 10, 10, 11½)"

LEFT FRONT

Edging
Work as Right Front.

Body
Change to larger needles and MC.

Row 1 (RS) K1, work Row 1 of 3-Block stitch pattern as follows: reading from right to left, work 8 (0, 8, 0, 8) sts from D to A, work 16-st repeat from A to B to 9 (1, 1, 9, 9) sts remaining, work 8 (0, 0, 8, 8) sts from B to C, k1.

Row 2 (WS) P1, work Row 2 of 3-Block stitch pattern as follows: reading from left to right, work 8 (0, 0, 8, 8) sts from C to B, work 16-st repeat from B to A to 9 (1, 9, 1, 9) sts remaining, work 8 (0, 8, 0, 8) sts from A to D, p1.

Continue to work from chart, beginning and ending all rows with 1 St st, to same length as Right Front to neck shaping, ending with WS row.

Armhole, neck, shoulder shaping
Work as Right Front but with reverse shaping.

SLEEVES

Edging
With smaller needle and CC, cast on 42 (42, 50, 50, 58) sts.

K 1 row, p 1 row, k 1 row, p 1 row. Leave CC attached. Introduce MC and work as for Back edging from * to end.

Body
Change to larger needles and MC.

Row 1 (RS) K1, work Row 1 of 3-Block stitch pattern as follows: reading from right to left, work 8 (8, 0, 0, 0) sts from D to A, work 16-st repeat from A to B to 1 st remaining, k1.

Row 2 (WS) P1, work Row 2 of 3-Block stitch pattern as follows: reading from left to right, work 16-st repeat from B to A to 9 (9, 1, 1, 1) sts remaining, work 8 (8, 0, 0, 0) sts from A to D, p1.

Continue to work from chart, beginning and ending all rows with 1 St st, to 4 rows above edging.

Maintain stitch pattern through all increases (page 111).

Next (increase) row (RS) K1, work into st below next st then work next st (lifted increase, page 67), work to 2 sts remaining, work lifted increase, k1.

Work 5 (5, 3, 3, 3) rows straight.

Repeat last 6 (6, 4, 4, 4) rows to 68 (72, 82, 90, 100) sts.

Work straight to 16½ (16½, 16, 16, 16)" from beginning, ending with WS row.

SHORTEN OR LENGTHEN HERE.

Cap
Bind off 5 (5, 7, 9, 11) sts at beginning of next 2 rows—58 (62, 68, 72, 78) sts remain.

Next (decrease) row (RS) K1, SKP (or SSK), work to 3 sts remaining, k2tog, k1.

Next row (WS) Work straight.

Repeat last 2 rows to 26 sts remaining.

Bind off 2 sts at beginning of next 2 rows, then bind off remaining 22 sts.

FINISHING
Use smaller needles for all edgings.

1 Button band
Beginning at Left Front neck edge, use CC and pick up and k 3 sts for every 4 rows along Left Front edge.

If you did not end with a multiple of 4 sts + 2 (page 106), k2tog 1–3 times evenly across next row to do so.

K 1 (WS) row, p 1 row, k 1 row. Leave CC attached.

Work next 4 rows in MC.

Next row (RS) K all sts.

Next row (WS) P1, *k2, p2, repeat from * to 1 st remaining, p1.

Next (RS) row K1, *k2, p2, repeat from * to 1 st remaining, k1.

Repeat WS row once more. Cut MC.

With CC, k 1 (RS) row, k 1 row, p 1 row, k 1 row, then bind off in p.

2 Buttonhole band
Beginning at lower Right Front edge, work as for button band to first row in MC. Mark spots for 7 buttons as follows: first approximately

½" from neck edge, last approximately 2" from lower edge, 5 spaced evenly between.

Begin buttonholes (RS/MC) *K to 2 sts before buttonhole, SKP (or SSK), yarn over (yo), repeat from * to final buttonhole, SKP (or SSK), yo, k to end.

End buttonholes (WS/MC) P1, *k2, p2, repeat from * to 1 st remaining, p1 AT SAME TIME working yo's as directed by stitch pattern and so as not to twist (page 49).

Next (RS/MC) row K1, *k2, p2, repeat from * to 1 st remaining, k1.

Next row (WS/MC) P1, *k2, p2, repeat from * to 1 st remaining, p1. Cut MC.

With CC, k 1 (RS) row, k 1 row, p 1 row, k 1 row, then bind off in p.

3 Neck edging

Sew shoulder seams.

With CC and beginning at fold line of Right Front CC edging, pick up and k 2 sts from CC edgings, 3 sts from 2 x 2 MC edgings, plus pick up and k around curve of neck (page 46).

K 1 (WS) row, p 1 row, k 1 row, then bind off in p.

4 Lower edging

Sew side seams.

With CC and beginning and ending at fold line of CC edgings, begin at lower Left Front edge and work as follows: pick up and k 2 sts from CC edgings, pick up and k 3 sts from 2 x 2 MC edgings, plus pick up and k 1 st in each cast-on st of Fronts and Back.

K 1 (WS) row, p 1 row, k 1 row, then bind off in p.

5 Right faux pocket edgings

Try jacket on. Mark lower edge of garter and reverse stockinette st (RSS) squares that best suits placement: upper pocket should be approximately 8" below shoulder, and lower pocket should be approximately 5" from lower edge of garment.

Upper pocket edging

With RS facing and beginning 8 sts from buttonhole band, slip smaller needle through bumps of next 16 (garter or RSS) sts.

Row 1 (RS) With CC, k each st.

K 1 (WS) row, p 1 row, k 1 row, then bind off in p.

Lower pocket edging

Work as for upper pocket edging, slipping needle through 24 sts.

Left faux pocket edgings

Mark spots on Left Front that correspond to Right faux pocket edgings. Work as for Right faux pocket edgings, but with reverse shaping (pick up row will end 8 sts from button band).

Tack any CC edgings down at corners if needed.

Sew buttons to match placement of buttonholes.

Sew buttons to ½" below center of each faux pocket edging.

Sew set-in Sleeves to garment (page 27).

Sew Sleeve seams.

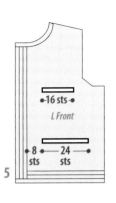

5

4

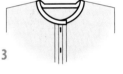

3

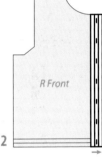

2

1

EXPERience

- *easy intermediate*
- *repetitive stitch patterns*
- *mid-level shaping*
- *simple finishing*

LOOSE FIT

S (M, L, 1X, 2X)

A *39 (42, 46, 50, 54)"*

B *19½ (20, 20½, 21, 21½)"*

C *28 (28½, 29, 29½, 30)"*

10cm/4"

28   *GET GAUGE!*

17

- *over 3-Block stitch pattern*
- *('Touch Me' only) after washing and drying*

You'll need

1 2 3 **4** 5 6

- *medium weight*
- *910 (975, 1090, 1180, 1300) yds (fulled Touch Me)*
- *1120 (1200, 1340, 1450, 1600) yds (non-fulled yarn)*
- *something yummy*

I used

- *4.5mm/US 7*
- *4mm/US 6*

Off-white, non-fulled—Medium: 8 balls PATONS Katrina in color 10010; Smoke, fulled—Medium: 16 balls MUENCH Touch Me in color 3640; Blue, fulled (shown in Wardrobe) in color 3603

LUSCIOUS PULLOVER

I first made this pullover in Muench 'Touch Me,' a luscious chenille that worms (but that is remedied by fulling; see notes below). The fulling obscures the stitch pattern but also skews it: the garter stitch areas sit straight and balance the stockinette stitch areas (which slant to the right) and the reverse stockinette areas (which slant to the left). The result is the most beautiful fabric— the lower edge waves slightly, you can't quite tell what you are seeing, what the stitch pattern is, or even if it is knit!

Of course you may knit this piece in other yarns—without the fulling, without the skewing, with the stitch pattern quite visible. I've done it in Patons 'Katrina.'

SPECIAL NOTES FOR 'TOUCH ME'
'Touch Me' gauge before fulling should be 15 sts × 26–28 rows. This pre-fulling, looser gauge requires less yarn. (The slipperiness of the yarn made it possible to achieve this looser gauge on the same size needles I used when knitting to gauge with a less slippery yarn.)
Post-fulling stitch gauge should be 17; post-fulling row gauge may be tighter (closer to 30), but the garment will be heavy and should fall to row gauge of 28. This means that you should knit the pieces to the measurements suggested and know that the finished garment will hang to these measurements.
As you knit, occasional loops (called 'worms') may appear. They disappear with fulling. However, if a ball worms excessively (every 4th stitch), it has been improperly spun and should not be used.
To full 'Touch Me,' wash and rinse the knitted garment in warm water and in the washing machine. It will come out of the washer small and hard. Dry in a warm dryer with a similar colored, non-shedding towel, and it will soften to something extraordinarily beautiful. For further washing, repeat the process. The measurements will not change.

Here's how!
BACK
Edging
With smaller needle, cast on 84 (92, 100, 108, 116) stitches (sts).
Knit (k) 1 row, purl (p) 1 row, k 1 row.
Body
Change to larger needles.
Row 1 (right side, RS) K2, work Row 1 of 3-Block stitch pattern as follows: reading chart from right to left (page 149), work 0 (8, 0,8, 0) sts from D to A, work 16-st repeat from A to B to 2 sts remaining, k2.
Row 2 (wrong side, WS) P1, k1, work Row 2 of 3-Block stitch pattern as follows: reading chart from left to right, work 16-st repeat from B to A to 2 (10, 2, 10, 2) sts remaining, work 0 (8, 0, 8, 0) sts from A to D, k1, p1.
Continue to work from chart, beginning all rows with 1 stockinette stitch (St st) then 1 k st and ending all rows with 1 k st then 1 St st, to 11" from beginning, ending with WS row.
SHORTEN OR LENGTHEN HERE.
Maintain stitch pattern (including 1 St st and 1 garter st at beginning and end of all rows) through all shaping.

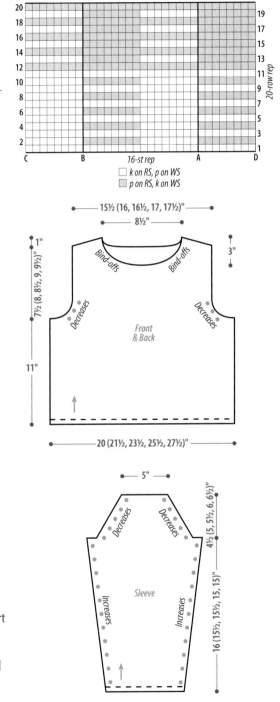

3-Block

□ k on RS, p on WS
▨ p on RS, k on WS

Eggplant, fulled—Medium: 16 balls MUENCH Touch Me in color 3628

Armhole shaping

Bind off 5 (5, 7, 9, 11) sts at beginning of next 2 rows—74 (82, 86, 90, 94) sts remain.

Next (decrease) row (RS) K1, work left-slanting decrease (SKP or SSK, page 18), work to 3 sts remaining, work right-slanting decrease (k2tog), k1.

Work 1 WS row.

Repeat last 2 rows to 66 (68, 70, 72, 74) sts remaining. Work straight to 7½ (8, 8½, 9, 9½)" above armhole shaping, ending with WS row.

Shoulder shaping

Bind off 4 sts at beginning of next 2 rows.

Next (RS) row Bind off 4 (4, 4, 4, 5) sts at beginning of row, work 9 (10, 11, 12, 12) sts.

Put next 32 sts on holder (for center Back neck). Turn, leaving 13 (14, 15, 16, 17) sts behind for left shoulder.

Right shoulder and Back neck shaping

Next (WS) row* Bind off 1 st at neck edge, work to end.

Next (RS) row Bind off 4 (4, 4, 5, 5) sts at shoulder edge, work to end.

Next (WS) row Bind off 1 st at neck edge, work to end.

Next (RS) row Bind off remaining 3 (4, 5, 5, 5) sts.

Left shoulder and Back neck shaping

Return to 13 (14, 15, 16, 17) sts of left shoulder, ready to work RS row.

Work 1 RS row.

Bind off 4 (4, 4, 4, 5) sts at beginning of next WS row.

Work as Right shoulder and Back neck shaping from * to end but with reverse shaping (page 19).

FRONT

Edging

Work as Back.

Body

Change to larger needles.

Row 1 (RS) K2, work Row 1 of 3-Block stitch pattern as follows: reading from right to left, work 16-st repeat from A to B to 2 (10, 2, 10, 2) sts remaining, work 0 (8, 0, 8, 0) sts from B to C, k2.

Row 2 (WS) P1, k1, work Row 2 of 3-Block stitch pattern as follows: reading from left to right, work 0 (8, 0, 8, 0) sts from C to B, work 16 st repeat from B to A to 2 sts remaining, k1, p1.

Work to 3" short of Back length, ending with WS row.

Maintain stitch pattern through all shaping.

Left Front neck and shoulder shaping

Work 24 (25, 26, 27, 28) sts. Put next 18 sts on holder (for center Front neck). Turn, leaving 24 (25, 26, 27, 28) sts behind for right shoulder.

***Next (WS) row** Bind off 3 sts at neck edge, work to end.
Work 1 RS row.

Next (WS) row Bind off 2 sts at neck edge, work to end.
Work 1 RS row.
Repeat last 2 rows once.

Next (WS) row Bind off 1 st at neck edge, work to end.
Work 1 RS row.
Repeat last WS row once—15 (16, 17, 18, 19) sts remain.
Work WS rows straight over shoulder shaping.

Next RS row Bind off 4 sts at shoulder edge, work to end.
Next RS row Bind off 4 (4, 4, 4, 5) sts at shoulder edge, work to end.
Next RS row Bind off 4 (4, 4, 5, 5) sts at shoulder edge, work to end.
Next RS row Bind off remaining 3 (4, 5, 5, 5) sts.

Right Front neck and shoulder shaping

Return to 24 (25, 26, 27, 28) sts of right shoulder, ready to work RS row.
Work 1 RS and then 1 WS row.
Work as Left Front neck and shoulder shaping from * to end but with reverse shaping.

SLEEVES

Edging

With smaller needle, cast on 36 (36, 44, 52, 52) sts.
K 1 row, p 1 row, k 1 row.

Body

Change to larger needles.

***Row 1 (RS)** K2, work Row 1 of 3-Block stitch pattern as follows: reading from right to left, work 16-st repeat from A to B to 2 (2, 10, 2, 2) sts remaining, work 0 (0, 8, 0, 0) sts from B to C, k2.

Row 2 (WS) P1, k1, work Row 2 of 3-Block stitch pattern follows: reading from left to right, work 0 (0, 8, 0, 0) sts from C to B, work 16-st repeat from B to A to 2 sts remaining, k1, p1.
Continue to work from chart, beginning all rows with 1 St st then 1 k st and ending all rows with 1 k st then 1 St st, to 2" from beginning, ending with WS row.

Maintain stitch pattern through all increases that follow (page 111).

Next (increase) row (RS) K2, work into st below next st then work next st (lifted increase, page 67), work to 3 sts remaining, work lifted increase, k2.
Work 5 (5, 7, 9, 11) rows straight.

Repeat last 6 (6, 6, 6, 4) rows—62 (66, 74, 82, 90) sts.
Work straight to 16 (15½, 15½, 15, 15)" from beginning.
SHORTEN OR LENGTHEN HERE.

Maintain stitch pattern through all shaping that follows.

Cap

Bind off 5 (5, 7, 9, 11) sts at beginning of next 2 rows—52 (56, 60, 64, 68) sts remain.

Next (decrease) row (RS) K1, SKP (or SSK), work to 3 sts remaining, k2tog, k1.
Work 1 WS row.
Repeat these last 2 rows to 22 sts remaining.
Bind off 2 sts at beginning of next 2 rows.
Bind off remaining 18 sts.

FINISHING

Do not use 'Touch Me' for seaming; use strong, smooth, similar-colored cotton or acrylic or non-wool blend.
Sew right shoulder seam.

Neck edging

With smaller needle and RS facing, pick up and k 1 st for every 2 rows along straight edge to curve of Front neck, pick up and k around curve of Front neck (page 46), pick up and k 1 st for every 2 rows along straight edge between curve of Front neck and right shoulder seam, pick up and k around curve of Back neck—approximately 96 sts.

Next (decrease) row (RS) *K7, k2tog, repeat from * around neck edge—approximately 86 sts.
P 1 row, then k 1 row, then bind off in p.
Sew left shoulder seam.
Sew set-in Sleeves into armholes (page 27).
Sew Sleeve and side seams.

There are factors that might make written-out stitch patterns tiresome: the jam-packed abbreviations make it difficult to find your place in the row; they may take more space on the page (especially true with cable or lace patterns); different sizes may complicate them. But the overriding disadvantage to written patterns is that it is difficult to 'see' the stitch pattern by just reading them.

Charts

THE THEORETICAL/ WHY WE USE THEM

The major advantage to a chart is that it helps us see what's going on in the stitch pattern, something written directions often cannot do.

Consider the following example, one of our simplest stitch patterns, 2 × 2 rib.

2 × 2 rib
Row 1 and all right-side (RS) rows K1, *k2, p2, repeat from * to 3 sts remaining, k3.
Row 2 and all wrong-side (WS) rows P3, *k2, p2, repeat from * to 1 sts remaining, p1.

2 x 2 rib

□ *k on RS, p on WS*
▨ *p on RS, k on WS*

4-st rep

Not much may be gained—in terms of seeing the stitch pattern, or in ease of reading, or saving of space—from the 2 × 2 rib chart versus its written form. But now consider the following example, the 3-Block pattern used throughout this chapter.

3-Block pattern
Rows 1, 3, 5, 7, 9, 11, 12 (RS) K all sts.
Rows 2, 4, 6, 8, 10 (WS) P8, *k8, p8, repeat from * to 8 sts remaining, k8.
Rows 13, 15, 17, 19 (RS) P8, *k8, p8, repeat from * to 8 sts remaining, k8.
Rows 14, 16, 18, 20 (WS) K all sts.

While the 3-Block pattern may look simple in written form, I defy anyone to know what's going on without studying it, because the pattern is set on wrong-side rows for the first 10 rows then on right-side rows for the next 10 rows. You'll have to work at least 12 rows before you see this happening. But here's a helpful drawing to show what the 16-stitch pattern produces. Can you see how it's reflected in the chart?

Reverse Stockinette	Garter
Garter	Stockinette

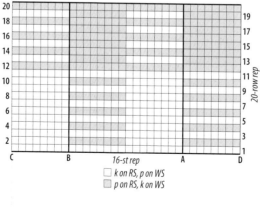

3-Block

16-st rep

20-row rep

□ *k on RS, p on WS*
▨ *p on RS, k on WS*

4-st rep

THE PRACTICAL/HOW TO READ THEM

Reading a chart is quite easy. Here are the rules.

- 1 square = 1 stitch.
- 1 line = 1 row.
- Charts are usually shown with right side facing (but see note to right).
- Read RS rows from right to left; the row number is at the right of the chart.
- Read WS rows from left to right; the row number is at the left of the chart.
- Begin where indicated in the pattern. (You might be told to begin reading at D or A, depending upon the size you are working.)
- Repeat as indicated by the pattern and where shown by the repeat lines in the chart. (In this sample, A to B is the 16-stitch repeat; you will repeat these 16 stitches until you have fewer than 16 stitches remaining in the row.)
- End where indicated in the pattern. (You might be told to end at B.)

My Slovenian friend tells me that the charts she grew up reading showed right-side rows with right side facing but wrong-side rows with wrong-side facing. In other words, in stockinette stitch, every second row would be a row of purls = ▢. When reading charts, always check the key so you will know how to read the row.

Whether using a chart or a written pattern, it can be easy to lose your place. If following a complex chart, use a magnetic board. Slip the board under your page (or photocopy), then place the accompanying magnetic strip below the row you are working (in written instructions) or above the row you are working (in charts). They really will save tons of aggravation! One knitting student of mine said it changed her life! Can't find a magnetic board? Try a sticky note.

Reading the stitch pattern of this chapter

I think the stitch pattern of this chapter is amazing: every second row is knit, so it's not very hard, but the effect is unexpectedly complex. Being able to understand this stitch pattern could be a real gift. Without too much effort, you'll feel like quite the accomplished knitter. And if you like this, a world of knitting texture awaits you!

But with many knitters and most stitch patterns, after knitting a few repeats of a stitch pattern, the knitting becomes your reference. As you become intuitive, you'll know when to knit, when to purl, and you'll rarely need to refer to either a chart or written instructions.

Here's a basic understanding of the 3-Block pattern chart. (It can help if you look at the chart through this discussion.)

- The pattern begins with 8-stitch squares of garter and 8-stitch squares of stockinette.
- To accomplish this, all right-side rows (here 1, 3, 5, 7, 9, 11, 13, 15, 17, 19) are knit.
- Wrong-side rows (here 2, 4, 6, 8, 10, 12, 14, 16, 18, 20) are a combination of knit and purl.
- This part of the pattern is 10 rows = 5 garter ridges.
- The pattern continues with 8-stitch squares of reverse stockinette and 8-stitch squares of garter.
- To accomplish this, all wrong-side rows are knit.
- Right-side rows are a combination of knit and purl.
- This part of the pattern is 10 rows = 5 garter ridges.

If you return to your knitting and need to know where you are, do the following. (Again, it can help to look at the chart through this discussion.)

- Figure out if you are on a right-side or a wrong-side row.
- Determine whether you are in rows 1–10 (garter/stockinette) or rows 11–20 (reverse stockinette/garter).
- If you are in rows 1–10, all right-side rows are knit: if you are in the middle, knit to the end.
- If you are in rows 1–10, the texture is on wrong-side rows: if you are in the middle, the garter squares are knit and the stockinette squares are purled.
- If you are in rows 11–20, all wrong-side rows are knit: if you are in the middle, knit to the end.
- If you are in rows 11–20, the texture is on right-side rows: if you are in the middle, the garter squares are knit and the reverse stockinette squares are purled.

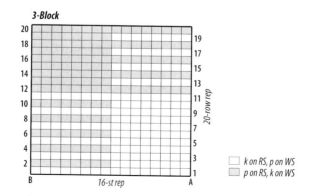

3-Block

k on RS, p on WS
p on RS, k on WS

EXPERIENCE THE KNITTING

TEACHING AN OLD DOG NEW TRICKS

(*Or*, the top 10 things I wish I'd learned earlier, but *better late than never*)

10 How to drink a Cosmopolitan. (This should be done with the girlfriends, while knitting and watching *Sex and the City*!)

9 To say, "I don't know." (Sometimes we are expected to know the answer, so it takes a moment to realize that we don't. It's *very* liberating to say, "I don't know." But then again, it's even *more* freeing to be *wrong* and allowed to apologize!)

8 The crochet cast-on. (For at least 10 years of my knitting life, I had been looking for a cast-on that matched the bind-off. This was it— taught in *The Knit Stitch* and shown here, page 172.)

7 That for every good thing, there's a down side; and for every bad thing, there is a lesson to be learned. (This helps me stay balanced . . . through knitting and through life.)

6 The around-the-neck purl. (I only learned this a few years ago, while teaching in Rochester. I then had to ask myself what I thought all those knitters—in Peru and Portugal and Greece—were *doing* with the yarn around their necks. Why didn't I wonder enough to find out? And how much of life is like this: we notice something but just don't *see* it.)

5 That if it seems too good to be true, it probably is. (We all *know* this, but how we wish to believe otherwise! Those big, thick yarns are *so* seductive and will knit up *so* quickly. But unless used very carefully— with lots of ease—they rarely look good on the body.)

4 To slow down and breathe. (Even when knitting, we can move too quickly, spin our wheels, try to do too many things at once. For most of my life, I did all of these things. But I'm not the same person since I learned to slow down and breathe.)

3 What Maya Angelou says: "People tell you who they are within the first 15 minutes of meeting them." (If we listen, we hear it. If we're strong enough, we do what we should.)

2 To play the drums. (Failure to do 3 led me to 2. What a blast . . . and *great* therapy!)

1 That we are never too old or too experienced or too established to wonder, to learn, to enthuse, to reinvent ourselves.

This chapter has been repeated from *The Knit Stitch*—with some edits and with notable changes in the section on Getting Gauge because we are now working over stockinette stitch rather than garter.

Why repeat this material? Because it is too important to leave out. So, if you didn't need it for *The Knit Stitch* (because you only knit a scarf), or you didn't read it (because you were too anxious to start knitting), perhaps you will now? If you did read it in *The Knit Stitch*, take note of any blue-colored text here—it's new material.

Price does not always correspond to quality. But natural fibers do tend to be more expensive than synthetics, and they do tend to wear better.

Yarns that do not wear well get scruffy-looking. They pill, they stretch, and they don't keep their shape. Ask the yarn shop owner if the yarn you're considering will wear well. Or buy one ball with which to knit a test piece. Treat it, torture it, and see if it holds up through what you would normally subject it to.

For the garments shown, the brand and the name by which the yarn is known is in the caption.

The choices we make

Consider the choices you make in the first hour of a project: color, yarn, needles, garment size. These decisions have everything to do with the successful outcome of the hours of knitting that follow. This chapter is about these decisions.

Choosing a color

The pattern you choose to knit will be shown in a particular color. **This is not necessarily the color you ought to buy.**

If you don't like—and are distracted by—the color of the model garment, make a black-and-white photocopy of the model garment. If you like it, then knit it—in a color you adore!

Choosing a yarn

The pattern you choose to knit will be shown in a particular yarn. **This is not necessarily the yarn you ought to buy.** Yarn substitution is part of knitting. And if you attend to what follows, you'll have fun with it and make the best substitutions possible.

HOW TO KNOW WHAT TYPE OF YARN TO CONSIDER
Every pattern in this book tells you what type of yarn you should use: the vitals column will say *cotton blend,* or *soft wool,* or *novelty yarn.* You will learn easily enough how to find the type of yarn suggested—by asking, by touching, and by checking labels for fiber content.

HOW TO KNOW WHAT WEIGHT OF YARN TO CONSIDER
Every pattern in this book tells you what weight of yarn you should use: the vitals column will give both a number and a word (for example, 4/medium weight). These numbers and terms are part of a new standardized system for classifying yarn weights, and here is what they mean:

1 2 3 4 **5** 6

• *bulky weight*

1 super fine (sometimes known as sock, fingering, or baby)
2 fine (sometimes known as sport or baby)
3 light (sometimes known as DK/double knitting or light worsted)
4 medium (sometimes known as worsted, afghan, or aran)
5 bulky (sometimes known as chunky, craft, or rug)
6 super bulky (sometimes known as bulky or roving)

For the weight of yarn you need, look for the words by which it is sometimes known. Then look at your pattern for the following additional information: the stitch gauge over 4" and the needle size I used.

You now have three pieces of information with which to work: a name by which the yarn is sometimes known, a stitch gauge that is usual for that yarn, and a needle size that is usual for that yarn. Look at the label of the yarn you are considering. In some form or other, some or all of this information will be there. When you find matching information, you've found a yarn to consider.

WHAT IF THE RELEVANT INFORMATION ISN'T ON THE LABEL?
Here is a neat test you can use to compare yarns.

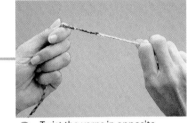

1 Find a sample of the correct weight of yarn and a sample of the yarn of unknown weight.

2 Loop the two yarns through each other.

3 Twist the yarns in opposite directions. Run your hand over the join. If you feel no change in bulk, the test yarn is the same weight.

The stitch gauge you see on the yarn label is over stockinette stitch. Sometimes the stitch gauge for a piece in this book is over stockinette stitch, sometimes over the stitch pattern of the garment. These other stitch patterns will not produce a gauge very different from a typical stockinette stitch gauge, with the exception of rib. Its stitch gauge might be as much as 2 stitches higher over 4" than for stockinette stitch.

Even when you find a yarn whose label gives you the same name or stitch gauge or needle size as your pattern, you don't have to trust this information.

Here's how to ensure perfect results.
1 Find the yarn that was used in the model garment.
2 Employ the substitution test (to left), comparing the yarn used to the yarn you are considering.
3 If the yarn you are considering passes this test, then you've found a yarn the same weight as the one used in the model garment.

Choosing needles

WHAT KIND OF NEEDLES?
There are three kinds of needles: straight, circular, and double-pointed (dpn). Here is how they are most commonly used.

Straight needles are only used for flat knitting, in which you work a right-side row, turn your piece, then work a wrong-side row; the garment pieces are worked back and forth and are usually seamed.

Circular needles can be used for flat knitting (working as you do on straight needles), or they can be used for tubular knitting in which you work continuously around the piece; the garment pieces are worked in rounds and may not require seaming.

Double-pointed needles are most often used for small tubular knitting (working as you do on circular needles) in which you work continuously around small projects like socks, gloves, mitts, and hats. These needles can come in sets of four or five: we recommend sets of five. (See page 128 for a discussion of substituting two circulars.)

Circular needles are not just for circular knitting. I work flat (back and forth) on them. The advantage is that you can't lose your needle (and your stitches) as easily as you might on double-pointed or straight needles. The disadvantage is that the cable—the length that joins the points—can be kinked. (To unkink the cable, soak it in the hottest water you can; then pull straight.)

WHAT KIND OF NEEDLES FOR WHICH PROJECT?

In most of the patterns that follow, you can use straights or circulars. When it doesn't matter, you will see the straight needle icon. When you need to use circular or double-pointed needles, you will see the icons for these needles.

WHAT NEEDLE SIZE?

The pattern you choose to knit will tell you the needle size I used. **This size is not necessarily the size you ought to use.** It is only appropriate if you knit to the same gauge as I do.

In my classes, I have met knitters who swear they never knit a gauge swatch. And I laughingly respond, "But then you give away garments, don't you—to whomever they fit." They laugh in return, and say, "Yup!"

If these are the rules by which you are willing to abide, fine. But if you are not willing to take these risks, if you want no surprises, then make a gauge swatch.

Getting gauge

WHAT IS GAUGE, AND WHY DOES IT MATTER?

Gauge is the relationship of stitches and rows to a standard measure recommended by the pattern. If you knit the piece to that gauge, your garment will work up to the measurements of the pattern; if you knit to a different gauge, your garment will not.

In this book's patterns, you are given gauge information in the vitals column. Here's how to interpret that information.

10cm/4"

24 **GET GAUGE!**

18

• over stockinette stitch
• after blocking

- Gauge is measured over 10cm/4": gauge is almost always measured this way.
- The first bullet tells the stitch pattern you should be working: here, the gauge is measured over stockinette stitch.
- The number at the bottom of the grid is the number of stitches you should have over 4": here, it's 18.
- The number at the left of the grid is the number of rows you should have over 4": here, it's 24.
- Additional bullets tell you how to treat your piece before measuring: here, it says 'after blocking' (see page 157 for a discussion of blocking).

How do you know that you are getting this right? You make a gauge swatch.

WHAT IS A GAUGE SWATCH?

A gauge swatch is a trial piece of knitting. To make sure you can match the gauge of the pattern, make a gauge swatch before you begin your garment.

In this book, you will see three different gauge icons. Here's how to interpret them.

 GET GAUGE! Make a gauge swatch and match the pattern gauge; otherwise, your piece won't fit in the way you expect.

 GET CLOSE Make a gauge swatch and get close to the pattern gauge; the piece is such that exact fit is not terribly important.

 Make a gauge swatch just to make sure you're close to the pattern gauge range; if you fall within this range, you'll get the measurements we offer, but this is a piece for which final measurements don't much matter.

HOW DO YOU MAKE A STANDARD GAUGE SWATCH?

Before you begin your garment, take one ball of yarn to work this trial piece.

What needle size do you use for your gauge swatch? As a starting point, try the needles I used (as shown in the vitals column) or those shown on the yarn label.

Now proceed as follows.

1 Cast on 4 more stitches than the number of stitches given in the gauge information. (If it says 18 stitches, cast on 22 stitches.)

2 Work the square in the stitch pattern directed under the gauge icon and to 4½–5". (Here we show the standard, stockinette stitch).

3 Before measuring, treat the piece as directed in the pattern. (If it says nothing, do nothing. If it says **after blocking**, see note to upper right.)

4 Count number of stitches in 4". Here, stitch gauge is 18.

5 Count number of rows in 4". Here, row gauge is 24.

BLOCKING

This is a process to which we submit our knitting that
- sets the stitches,
- smooths out imperfections,
- shows what measurements we achieved,
- relaxes the fabric so it can be somewhat manipulated, if necessary, to achieve the measurements we really wanted,
- makes the pieces easier to seam.

Sounds great, we usually want to do it, and we usually want to do it before we sew the pieces together.

If the directions say after blocking, here's what you do.
- Treat the piece as you would when you wash it.
- Or, if you are in a hurry, give it a careful pressing on the wrong side of the fabric, using a steam iron set on wool with a wet cloth between the iron and the knitting.

Did you not get the measurements you needed? Do not despair! There is nothing wrong with your knitting! It's okay to knit differently than the designer. Also, the yarn can make a difference. You could knit to the suggested gauge just fine with wool but have a difficult time with more slippery yarns.

And some of us are just loose knitters. It doesn't mean that we don't achieve an even tension; it just means that we achieve the garment gauge on smaller needles than the pattern-writer might use. You will soon enough know if this is who you are, and you will learn to always approach a swatch with smaller needles. If you are a tight knitter, you'll know to go the other way—to always use larger needles.

Needle sizes

Metric (mm)	US
10	15
9	13
8	11
7.5	
7	
6.5	10½
6	10
5.5	9
5	8
4.5	7
4	6
3.75	5
3.5	4
3.25	3
3	
2.75	2
2.25	1
2	0

DID YOU GET GAUGE?

- If you need to GET GAUGE, you should get the required number of stitches and rows in 4".
- If you need to GET CLOSE, you should get the required number of stitches in 4" (± 1 stitch) or the required number of rows (± 2 rows).
- If you were given a range, you should get within 1 or 2 stitches or rows of this range.

If any of the above is the case, your work is done. This is the needle size you use. Proceed to Choosing a garment size, page 159.

Did you get fewer stitches and rows than required? If so, then your knitting is tight, and you need to work another swatch on larger needles.

Did you get more stitches and rows than required? If so, then your knitting is loose, and you need to work another swatch on smaller needles.

WHAT IS MEANT BY SMALLER OR LARGER NEEDLES?

If you are working with US or metric sizes, then the larger the number, the larger the size. (In these systems, US 11 or 8mm are large needles.) To the left is a conversion chart for metric and US sizes. If there is no number on your needle, you may use a needle gauge (usually a small ruler with graduated holes) to determine its size.

IF YOUR GAUGE WAS OFF, HOW MUCH SMALLER OR LARGER DO THE NEEDLES NEED TO BE?

When you need to use smaller or larger needles, you'll have to decide how much smaller or larger, and this is mostly a matter of experience. If your gauge is only slightly off, then go to the very next size. If your gauge is wildly off, then try two or even three sizes up or down.

But be careful here. One size smaller than an US 8 is indeed a 7, but one size larger than an US 10 is a 10½! One size smaller than a metric 9 is an 8, but one size larger than a metric 4 is a 4.5. The conversion chart is a necessary piece of equipment, and it offers both the relationship between the different systems and a list of all sizes readily available.

WHEN IS YOUR GAUGE SWATCH DONE?

When you achieve the required number of stitches and rows in 4" (or close enough, as discussed on the previous page), your gauge swatch is done, and you know the needle size you should use.

If, after a couple of tries, you get the recommended number of stitches but a slightly different number of rows, use the needle size that gives you the recommended number of stitches, and don't worry about the rows. Most knitting patterns determine length by a number of inches, not by a number of rows. Get as close as you can to the row gauge, but remember more rows may require more yarn.

Choosing a garment size

You won't know how much yarn to buy until you determine which garment size you ought to make. The garments that follow are offered in a range of sizes and with their familiar designations: XS, S, M, L, 1X, 2X, 3X. These size designations refer to girth. For now, ignore all measurements for length.

STANDARD SIZES
The sizes XS–3X are based on standard bust/chest measurements, as shown here. This information helps you know what size you really are. But we don't usually wear garments that are our actual bust/chest measurement, do we? What is the relationship between the body measurement and the finished garment measurement?

STANDARDS OF FIT
There are three 'fit' possibilities that appear in this book. Here is an explanation of their icons which appear in the vitals column of each pattern.

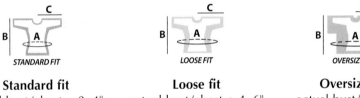

Standard fit
actual bust/chest + 2–4"

Loose fit
actual bust/chest + 4–6"

Oversized fit
actual bust/chest + 6"
or more

HOW DO YOU PUT ALL THIS SIZE INFORMATION TOGETHER?
Look at the sample to the right. The XS–3X sizes in which the patterns are offered appear under the fit icon. The smallest size is given first, and the larger sizes follow in order and in parentheses. If there is only one number, it applies to all sizes. Choose a size based on standard bust/chest measurement (see the chart at upper right).

Look at the fit icon. This tells you how much 'ease' is offered. So now look at the measurements of the finished garment that appear below the icon and that correspond to your size. (A = chest measurement, B = back length, C = measurement from center back to wrist/lowest point of sleeve.) If you knit to gauge, and you do not SHORTEN OR LENGTHEN, you will achieve the measurements given for your size.

WHAT ABOUT HEIGHT?
The garments in this book are made to fit the standard heights of 5'4"–5'6" for a woman or 5'10"–6' for a man. If you are 2" shorter than standard, subtract 1" in length where the pattern says SHORTEN OR LENGTHEN HERE. If you are 4" shorter, subtract 2". If you are 2" taller than standard, add 1" in length wherever the pattern says SHORTEN OR LENGTHEN HERE. If you are 4" taller, add 2".

Standard bust/chest measurements

Size	Women	Men
XS	28–30"	
S	32–34"	34–36"
M	36–38"	38–40"
L	40–42"	42–44"
1X	44–46"	46–48"
2X	48–50"	50–52"
3X	52–54"	

Children

0–3 mos	16"
6 mos	17"
12 mos	18"
2–4	21–23"
6–8	25–27"
10–12	28–30"

XS (S, M, L, 1X, 2X, 3X)
A *32 (36, 40, 44, 48, 52, 56)"*
B *17 (17, 17, 17, 18, 18, 18)"*
C *28 (28, 29, 29, 30, 30, 31)"*

The fact that these garments are made to standard height explains why the back length is pretty much the same for all sizes. If you're 5'4" it doesn't matter if you're an XS or a 3X; your shoulders are still the same distance from the floor.

And what about that back neck-to-wrist measurement? Do you remember the Leonardo da Vinci drawing of the man with his arms extended, standing within a square? Da Vinci illustrated that your 'wingspan' is usually the same as your height. So, if you are 5'4", regardless of garment size, you will still measure pretty much the same from your back neck to wrist.

Having said all that, in these patterns you might notice a slight increase in B and C measurements with each larger size. This is for better overall proportion and to accommodate the extra angles of larger sizes. Isn't geometry fun?

When we refer to a ball of yarn, this isn't necessarily how it is packaged. Yarn can come in a ball, on a cone, or in a skein. For the first two, nothing need be done—although if you pull the yarn from the center of the ball rather than the outside, you will have less tangling. For the skein, you will need to wind the skein into a ball before working with it—by hanging the skein over the back of a chair, over your knees, or over the hands of someone who loves you.

Yes, you need a calculator to figure how much yarn to buy. The yarn shop will have one, because they do these calculations all the time, but you'll probably want one for when you find wonderful yarn in out-of-the-way places.

Every knitter has failed to check dye lots or been tempted to buy unmatched dye lots. (The latter is usually accompanied by, "It shouldn't matter; I could just work two rows in each dye lot for an inch, and maybe I won't see the switch.") It does matter. Don't buy unmatched dye lots.

If you run out of a dye lot before finishing, I suggest the following.
• Cut off all edgings (bands and cuffs); see Shortening a garment, page 168.
• Unravel and straighten the yarn; see margin note, page 168.
• Finish the garment in the recovered yarn.
• Knit new edgings down and in the new dye lot; see Lengthening a garment, page 169.

Buying yarn

The pattern you choose will suggest a particular quantity of yarn for the size you choose to knit. **This is not necessarily the quantity of yarn you ought to buy.**

HOW MUCH YARN DO YOU BUY?

In the vitals column, you are told a quantity of yarn to buy. For example, for a sweater with five sizes, S (M, L, 1X 2X), it may read 1000 (1200, 1400, 1600, 1800) yds. You need to translate this information to determine the number of balls you need. Here are the steps to follow.

• First, choose your size; let's say L— the third size.
• Now find the yardage recommended for the third size; in the sample above, L = 1400 yds.
• Look at the label for the yarn you are considering, and find its yardage; let's say it reads 98 yds.
• Divide the yardage you need by the yarn's yardage; in this sample, 1400 ÷ 98 = 14.28. (Use a calculator for this.)
• Round up to the nearest whole number, and this indicates the number of balls you should buy; in this sample, it would be 15.

Is this really and truly the number of balls you need to buy? Perhaps. But what if the result had been 15.05? Would you have bought 15 or 16 balls? And what if you intend to SHORTEN OR LENGTHEN? And what if your row gauge is a little different? And what if our estimates are a little off? (They are only estimates, and we are only human.)

Once you do the math to determine how many balls you need, buy that amount, but ask if the yarn shop owner will hold an extra ball or two until you finish. Alternatively, buy an extra ball or two, and ask if you can return what you don't use. As you buy this yarn, be sure it is all of the same dye lot.

WHAT IS A DYE LOT?

A dye lot is a batch of yarn dyed at the same time: the batch is designated by a number, found on the yarn label. Different dye lots in the same color can have slight variations in color, and this will show in the garment. You don't want this. Check all dye lot numbers on all the yarn you wish to buy to be sure they match.

Collecting supplies

Besides yarn and needles, there are other standard tools all knitters should carry.
- a flexible tape measure (to measure gauge and your knitting in progress)
- a blunt-tipped tapestry needle (to sew with)
- small scissors (to cut yarn and trim tails)
- stitch holders (to hold live stitches that will be worked later, although a piece of yarn threaded onto a tapestry needle and run through these stitches will work fine)
- markers (to hang on your needle or knitting, designating something that matters; sometimes a paper clip or some yarn will work fine)
- a row counter (if you have days like I do when you can't count to 4!)
- point protectors (to keep your stitches from falling off your needle when you put your knitting down, although a rubber band or elastic hair band wrapped around the end of the needle works)
- a calculator (for when you need to 'do the math')
- a needle gauge (to identify all your unmarked needles)
- non-rusting pins

The other thing you might treat yourself to—once you're truly committed—is a decent knitting bag. So many of us carry our knitting around in grocery bags!

I carried my yarn in grocery bags until my dear friend, Nancy Bush, talked me into a beautiful Klimt-inspired fabric bag. And then my darling daughter gave me a knitting bag for Christmas. I now have two beautiful bags for my knitting. Does this seem excessive? Not really, since I usually have more than one project on the go. (See Process versus Product, page 51.)

Photocopying your pattern

It is perfectly reasonable to photocopy a pattern you have purchased—along with its abbreviations plus any required skills—for your own use. There are things you can do with a photocopy that you might not choose to do with an original: enlarge it, circle the numbers corresponding to the size you are making, write notes in the margins.

Keeping a knitting journal

It's a good idea to keep a record of your knitting experiences. You might address any or all of the following.
- What yarn did you use? (Keep your swatch, and attach the label and a few yards of yarn to it.)
- What needle size did you use to get gauge?
- What size did you make? (Perhaps make a copy of the schematics, noting changes that you made.)
- How many balls did it take?
- How did you launder it?
- Did the measurements change after laundering?
- How much time did it take to finish it?

HONORING YOUR CRAFT

A survey done on Canadian radio posed the question, "What is the most-dreaded Christmas present?"

The answer was NOT the heavy-as-a-brick *fruit cake*. And it wasn't the silly-but-trendy, sold-a-bazillion *pet rock*. It was a *handknit sweater*!

I'm not sure what this says about our craft. Perhaps it harkens back to a childhood in which one desperately wanted a Red Ryder BB gun but was given a brown and orange, ill-fitting but practical handknit sweater.

Whatever this was about, we can all make it our personal mission to override such a dreadful stereotype . . . by learning all that we can to be the best knitters we can and by raising public consciousness about the knitting community. Here are my suggestions.

- Knit in public. (You'll answer questions, meet other knitters, learn a trick or two, and perhaps even teach a new knitter.)
- Be willing to learn anything that will make you a better knitter. (The result will be that you knit stuff that is noticed and admired and even coveted.)
- Access your knitting community. (There are knitting shops and bookstores and Web sites and even a knitters' guild in your area to which you can connect and from which you can learn.)
- If there is no knitting guild in your area, start one. (It's not difficult. Just put the word out that a group is meeting, and be prepared for the enthusiasm!)
- When you knit for others, make sure it works for *them*. (This may mean knitting something you don't like—in a style you don't like, in a stitch pattern you don't like, in a color you don't like. It may also mean ripping and re-knitting to make it fit. But they get what they want—which does much for knitting—and you'll learn from the experience.)
- When you find yourself excusing a mistake ("a blind man on a galloping horse will never see it"), you need to fix it . . . *or* repeat it. If done three or more times, it becomes a design feature.
- Notice—and compliment—the knitting you see. (If I see someone wearing what I think is a handknit sweater, I ask, "Is that a handknit sweater?" If the answer is "Yes," I then ask, "Did you make it yourself?" If the answer is again "Yes," we start a conversation and perhaps bond for life. If the answer is "No," I then say, "Someone loves you very much.")
- Get the guys knitting. (At least 50% of the people who answer surveys or write TV ads are men. If they truly 'got it,' the results might be different.)

Oops!

If you drop a purl stitch/Stitch orientation

Dropping a stitch is not a problem, but if you recover it and then work it improperly, you'll produce a twisted stitch. Here's how to properly recover a purl stitch. (And it's the same maneuver, whether the stitch is a knit or a purl.)

1 If a purl stitch falls off your needle,
2 put it back onto the left-hand needle.

The proper orientation of a stitch (knit or purl) is that the side of the stitch nearest to you is closer to the tip of the left-hand needle than the side of the stitch farthest away from you (see above). If so, work it as usual.

If it looks like this, it is oriented improperly and is 'backwards.'

To remedy a backwards stitch, work through the back of it. (This is how to also purl through the back of a stitch.)

If you notice that you split the yarn of a stitch earlier in your knitting, you can work to that stitch on the needle, take it off the needle, ladder down to and including the split-yarn stitch, then re-work it as shown.

If you dropped a stockinette stitch and have ladders

If you dropped a stitch, often it can come undone (unraveled) for one or more rows. What you then have is a stitch with 'ladders' above it. Here's how to re-knit the stitch.

1 With knit side facing, put the dropped stitch onto a crochet hook.

2 Put crochet hook behind the lowest ladder.

3 Draw the lowest ladder through this stitch.

4 Repeat Steps 2–3 until all ladders have been reworked.
5 Put the stitch back onto the left-hand needle, being sure to work it properly oriented (above).

Tightening the ugly loop at the end of a bind-off

If you look at the end of your bind-off, you may see a large loopy stitch that you'd like to tighten.

1 Stop binding off when you have 1 stitch on each needle.

2 Slip stitch from left-hand needle onto right-hand needle.

3 Find the knot that sits toward the back and just under that last stitch.

4 Pick it up with left-hand needle.

5 Return last stitch to left-hand needle.

6 Knit both knot and stitch together.

7 Bind last stitch off as usual. The result should be neater than when you started.

If a stitch was knit when it should have been purled, discovered on the next row

There will be no purl bump where one should be.

1 Insert right-hand needle purl-wise into stitch below last stitch on left-hand needle.

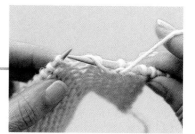

2 Take stitch off left-hand needle, and pull yarn of last stitch loose so it sits in front of stitch on right-hand needle.

3 With left-hand needle behind right-hand needle, use left-hand needle to pass the stitch over the loose yarn—to form a new stitch.

4 Slip stitch from right-hand needle onto left; then work it properly oriented (page 164).

If a stitch was knit when it should have been purled, discovered many rows later

There will be no bump where there should be one.
Turn the work around, and work as if the stitch was purled when it should have been knit (opposite page).

If a stitch was purled when it should have been knit, discovered on the next row

There will be a purl bump where there should not be one.

1 Insert right-hand needle knitwise into stitch below last stitch on left-hand needle.

2 Take stitch off left-hand needle, and pull yarn of last stitch loose so it sits in front of stitch on right-hand needle.

3 With left-hand needle in front of right-hand needle, use left-hand needle to pass the stitch over the loose yarn—to form a new stitch.

4 Slip stitch from right-hand needle onto left; then work it properly oriented (page 164).

If a stitch was purled when it should have been knit, discovered many rows later

There will be a bump where there should not be one.

1 Unknit, or 'ladder' all stitches down to and including this wrongly worked stitch.

2 Rework all ladders as knit stitches (page 164).

If any of these reworked stitches needed to be purled instead of knit, then turn the work to the opposite side. Rework the ladder as a knit stitch.

Truth be told, we don't always end up with the length we wanted. It's comforting to know how easily a piece can be shortened. And while this maneuver is shown in stockinette stitch, you will do as directed no matter in what stitch pattern the garment was knit.

Shortening a garment

Decide how much shorter your piece needs to be. (Through what follows, I will assume you want the piece 2" shorter.)

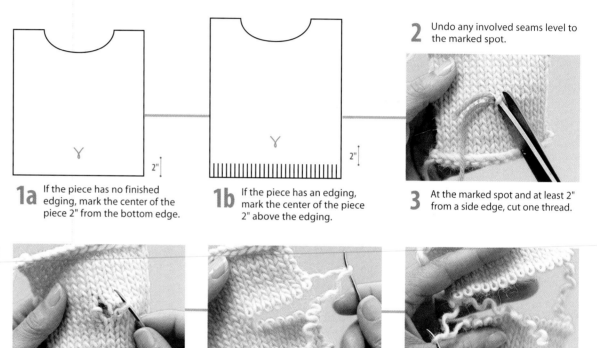

1a If the piece has no finished edging, mark the center of the piece 2" from the bottom edge.

1b If the piece has an edging, mark the center of the piece 2" above the edging.

2 Undo any involved seams level to the marked spot.

3 At the marked spot and at least 2" from a side edge, cut one thread.

If you shorten a piece of knitting, you'll recover yarn, won't you? But it will be very kinky. Can you use it again? Sure enough. What I do is skein it (using a swift or my hand and elbow to make loops of 24" or more), tie it in four places, wash it (in Eucalan), then dry it flat. This should straighten out the kinks enough that you can use it again.

4 Gently unpick—with your fingers or with a knitting needle—the course of this thread, in each direction, until the bottom falls off.

5 You will see loops going down from the remaining piece.

If you put all of these loops onto your needle, you'll have 1 less than your original stitch count. If you put the partial loops (half stitches) that appear at each side edge onto your needle, you'll have 1 more stitch than your original stitch count. Either is correct. (See drawing on next page to see why these half stitches appear.)

6 Finish the piece as it was finished before. (If there was no edging, then simply bind off. If there was an edging, work this edging down from here.)

7 Re-seam, sewing down from the previous seam and maintaining the same vertical line.

Lengthening a garment

1a If the piece has no finished edging, remove the entire cast-on edge; then skip to Step 4.

1b If the piece has an edging, undo any involved seams to just above the edging. Continue with Steps 2–3.

2 Cut one thread, in the middle of the last row of the edging.

3 Work Steps 4–5 of *Shortening a garment;* then go to Step 4 (below).

4 Work new length down, knitting all right-side rows and purling all wrong-side rows; then work Steps 6–7 of *Shortening a garment.*

This shows new length of 4 rows added (4th row is on needle).

The discussion of shortening begs the question of whether or not a piece can be similarly lengthened. Can you cut off the cast-on edge, or the edging, and knit new length down? Yes, in stockinette stitch, you can.

Lengthening a garment in a stitch pattern other than stockinette stitch

Garter stitch is similar to stockinette stitch, because you work all knit stitches across the row, so knitting new length down in garter stitch is almost as simple as knitting new length in stockinette stitch. You just have to make sure that you put the stitches onto the needle with the bumps up close to the needle so that the next row is a knit row.

Here is what happens when you cut a piece of stockinette stitch. The arrows represent the stitches that you pick up and then knit new length down from.

Here is what happens when knits and purls are combined in the same row. Assume the piece is worked in 1 × 1 rib and that the blue stitches represent knits, and the green stitches represent purls.

Do you notice anything unusual about the stitches from which you would knit new length down? They're half blue and half green, aren't they? This means that they're neither knits nor purls, so you cannot knit new length down. This is true of all stitch patterns that combine stitches or colors across a row.

While you cannot knit new length down in the same stitch pattern, you can knit new length down in a different stitch pattern. Just be sure to pick up everything that represents a stitch—a knot that is a switch from a knit to a purl, a pair of crossed threads in two-color work—before knitting new length down.

When picking up things that are to represent stitches but don't look quite like stitches, it can help to remember that your stitch count will be either 1 more or 1 less than your original stitch count, depending upon whether or not you picked up the 2 half stitches at the side edges.

TABLE OF COMPARATIVE RATIOS

This table is useful whenever you are seaming stitches to rows
and facing something other than a 1-to-1 ratio. Here's how it works:
- divide the smaller number (the number of stitches) by the larger number (the number of rows);
- find the closest fraction (in the column at left);
- seam as directed (in the column at right);
- in garter stitch, replace 'rows' with 'garter ridges' (remembering that every garter ridge = 2 rows).

To convert inches measurement to centimeters:

*Simply multiply the inches by 2.5
For example:
4" × 2.5 = 10cm*

The fraction	What it means	How to seam
.5 = 1/2	1 st / 2 rows	Seam 1 st to 2 rows
.6 = 3/5	3 sts / 5 rows	(Seam 1 st to 2 rows) twice, then seam 1 st to 1 row once
.6667 = 2/3	2 sts / 3 rows	Seam 1 st to 2 rows, then seam 1 st to 1 row
.714 = 5/7	5 sts / 7 rows	(Seam 1 st to 2 rows) twice, then (seam 1 st to 1 row) three times
.75 = 3/4	3 sts / 4 rows	(Seam 1 st to 1 row) twice, then seam 1 st to 2 rows once
.8 = 4/5	4 sts / 5 rows	(Seam 1 st to 1 row) 3 times, then seam 1 st to 2 rows once
.85 = 6/7	6 sts / 7 rows	(Seam 1 st to 1 row) 5 times, then seam 1 st to 2 rows once
.9 = 9/10	9 sts / 10 rows	(Seam 1 st to 1 row) 8 times, then seam 1 st to 2 rows once

SUPPLIERS

Aurora Yarns
Distributes Garnstudio
850 Airport Street Unit 3A
Moss Beach, CA 94038

Berroco, Inc.
PO Box 367
Uxbridge, MA 01569
www.berroco.com

Cascade Yarns
1224 Andover Park E
Tukwila, WA 98188
www.cascadeyarns.com

Cherry Tree Hill
PO Box 659
Barton, VT 05822

Classic Elite Yarns
300A Jackson Street
Lowell, MA 01852

Harbinger
(Silver clasps on page 78)
22 Dupont St E
Waterloo, ON N2J 2G9
Canada
(519) 747-4644
harbinger@
harbingergallery.com

Harrisville Designs
41 Main St
Harrisville, NH 03450

JCA Fashion Yarns
Distributes Reynolds
35 Scales Lane
Townsend, MA 01469-1094

Koigu Wool Designs
RR 1
Williamsford, ON N0H 2V0
Canada
www.koigu.com

Lion Brand
34 W 15th Street
New York, NY 10011
www.lionbrand.com

Mountain Colors
PO Box 156
Corvallis, MT 59828

Muench Yarns Inc
Distributes GGH
285 Bel Marin Keys Blvd, #J
Novato, CA 94949
www.muenchyarns.com

Needful Yarns
Distributes Rosina
4476 Chesswood Dr
Toronto, ON M3J 2B9
Canada

Patons Yarns
PO Box 40
Listowel, ON N4W 3H3
Canada
www.patonsyarns.com

Skacel Collection, Inc.
Distributes Schoeller + Stahl
11612 SE 196th St
Renton, WA 98058
www.skacelknitting.com

SR Kertzer LTD
*Distributes Alafoss,
Naturally, and Stylecraft*
105A Winges Road
Woodbridge, ON L4L 6C2
Canada
www.kertzer.com

Swedish Yarn Imports
Distributes Almedahls
PO Box 2069
Jamestown, NC 27282

Tahki/Stacy Charles Inc
8000 Cooper Avenue
Bldg 1
Glendale, NY 11385
www.tahkistacycharles.com

**Trendsetter Yarns/
Lane Borgosesia**
16745 Saticoy St #101
Van Nuys, CA 91406

Unique Kolours, LTD
Distributes Mission Falls
28 North Bacton Hill Road
Malvern, PA 19355
www.uniquekolours.com

Westminster Fibers
*Distributes Jaeger
and Rowan*
4 Townsend West, Unit 8
Nashua, NH 03063

YARN WEIGHTS

Yarn Weight	**1** Super Fine	**2** Fine	**3** Light	**4** Medium	**5** Bulky	**6** Super Bulky
Also called	Sock Fingering Baby	Sport Baby	DK Light Worsted	Worsted Afghan	Chunky Craft Aran	Bulky Roving Rug
Knit Gauge Range in Stockinette Stitch to 10cm/4 inches	27 to 32 sts	23 to 26 sts	21 to 24 sts	16 to 20 sts	12 to 15 sts	6 to 11 sts
Recommended Needle (metric)	2mm to 3.25mm	3.25 to 3.75mm	3.75mm to 4.50mm	4.5mm to 5.5mm	5.5mm to 8mm	9mm to 16mm
Recommended Needle (US)	1 to 3	3 to 5	5 to 7	7 to 9	9 to 11	13 to 19

Every pattern in this book tells you what weight yarn to use. To find an appropriate yarn, look at the name by which it is also called (above); then look at your pattern for the gauge over 10cm/4" and the needle size used. Look on the label of the yarn you are considering for matching information.

Slip knot

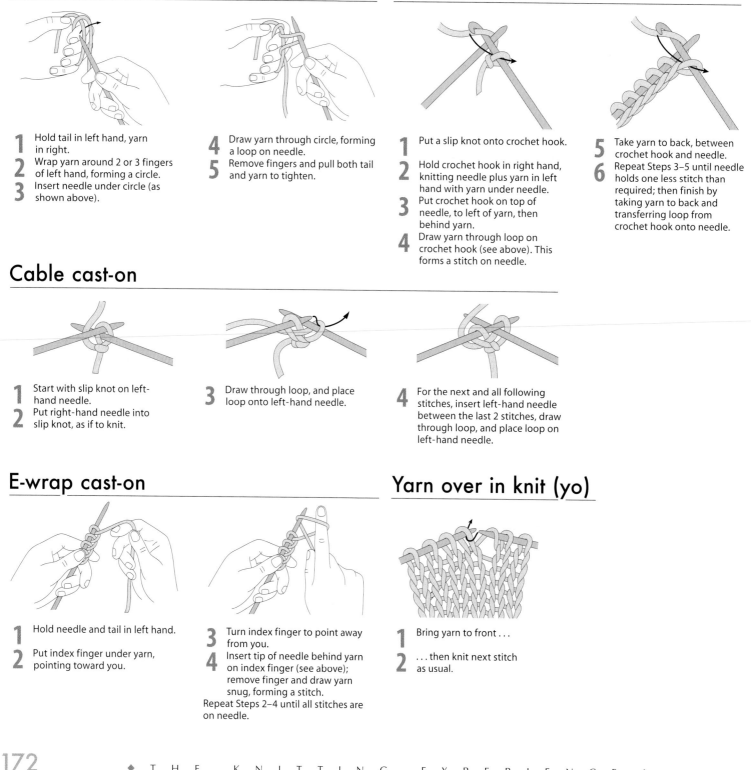

1 Hold tail in left hand, yarn in right.
2 Wrap yarn around 2 or 3 fingers of left hand, forming a circle.
3 Insert needle under circle (as shown above).

4 Draw yarn through circle, forming a loop on needle.
5 Remove fingers and pull both tail and yarn to tighten.

Crochet cast-on

1 Put a slip knot onto crochet hook.
2 Hold crochet hook in right hand, knitting needle plus yarn in left hand with yarn under needle.
3 Put crochet hook on top of needle, to left of yarn, then behind yarn.
4 Draw yarn through loop on crochet hook (see above). This forms a stitch on needle.

5 Take yarn to back, between crochet hook and needle.
6 Repeat Steps 3–5 until needle holds one less stitch than required; then finish by taking yarn to back and transferring loop from crochet hook onto needle.

Cable cast-on

1 Start with slip knot on left-hand needle.
2 Put right-hand needle into slip knot, as if to knit.

3 Draw through loop, and place loop onto left-hand needle.

4 For the next and all following stitches, insert left-hand needle between the last 2 stitches, draw through loop, and place loop on left-hand needle.

E-wrap cast-on

1 Hold needle and tail in left hand.
2 Put index finger under yarn, pointing toward you.

3 Turn index finger to point away from you.
4 Insert tip of needle behind yarn on index finger (see above); remove finger and draw yarn snug, forming a stitch.
Repeat Steps 2–4 until all stitches are on needle.

Yarn over in knit (yo)

1 Bring yarn to front . . .
2 . . . then knit next stitch as usual.

Long-tail cast-on

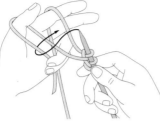

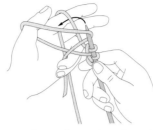

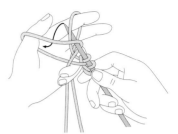

1 Leave a tail 2.5 times the width of the piece for which you are casting on. Holding tail to front and yarn to back, put right-hand needle under yarn at this point.

2 Put left thumb under tail.

3 Put left index under yarn.

4 Hold both tail and index in left palm.

5 Insert tip of needle into front of tail (on thumb).

6 Take needle over top of yarn (on index finger) then around the back and under.

7 Draw yarn through the loop on the thumb (as shown above).

8 Pull both tail and yarn to tighten cast-on stitch.

Repeat Steps 5–8.

Knit stitch

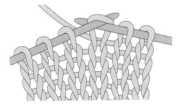

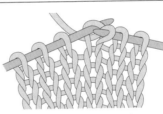

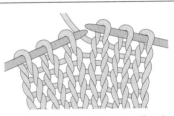

1 With yarn in back, insert right-hand needle into first stitch on left-hand needle so right-hand needle sits behind left-hand needle.

2 Take yarn under right-hand needle and between two needles.

3 Draw right-hand needle from behind left-hand needle to front of left-hand needle.

4 Push right-hand needle off end of left-hand needle so new stitch is on right-hand needle.

Repeat Steps 1–4 until all stitches are on right-hand needle; then transfer needle with stitches into left hand for next row.

K into front and back (kf&b)

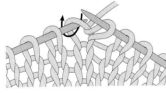

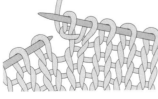

1 Knit into the front of next stitch on left-hand needle, but do not pull the stitch off the needle.

2 Take right-hand needle to back; then knit through the back of the same stitch (as shown above).

3 Now take both stitches off left-hand needle.

Make 1 (M1)

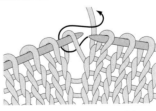

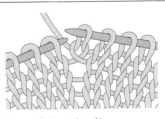

1 With right-hand needle, lift yarn that sits between two needles; then transfer it to left-hand needle.

2 Knit through the back of it (as shown above).

The result is a twisted increase.

Knitting in rounds, on double-pointed needles (dpns)

1 Find the beginning of the round. (It might be designated by the tail of the cast-on or a marker.) The needle to the left is Needle 1, and the needle to the right is Needle 4.

2 As you begin the round, Needle 1 is your left-hand needle, and you will knit stitches from Needle 1 onto your 'free' needle.

3 When stitches are knit onto the free needle, it becomes Needle 1 (because it is the first needle to the left of the marker that designates the beginning of the round). Now you have a new free needle, and the left-hand needle is Needle 2 (because it is the second needle to the left of the marker that designates the beginning of the round).

4 Continue knitting clockwise, knitting the old stitches onto the free needle and always numbering needles by their position relative to the beginning of the round.

Slip stitch knit-wise (sl1 k-wise)

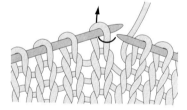

1 Put right-hand needle into next stitch on left-hand needle as if to knit.

2 Slide stitch off left- and onto right-hand needle. Stitch will be oriented as shown.

Slip stitch purl-wise (sl1 p-wise)

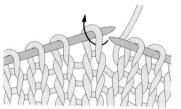

1 Put right-hand needle into next stitch on left-hand as if to purl.

2 Slide stitch off left- and onto right-hand needle. Stitch will be oriented as shown.

Knit 2 together (k2tog)

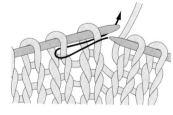 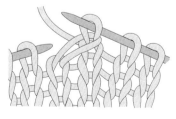

1 Insert right-hand needle into first 2 stitches on left-hand needle, beginning with second stitch from end of left-hand needle.

2 Knit both stitches together, as if they were one. The result is a right-slanting decrease.

3-needle bind-off

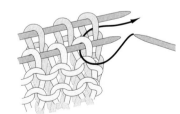

If you want the ridge on the wrong side, hold right sides together. If you want the ridge on the right side, hold wrong sides together.

1 Leave stitches of both pieces on needles, and hold both needles in left hand.

2 With a third needle, knit 2 together, one from each needle (see left).

3 Repeat Step 2.

4 Pass first stitch over second. Repeat Steps 2 and 4 until all stitches have been bound off.

Slip 1, knit 1, pass slip stitch over (SKP)

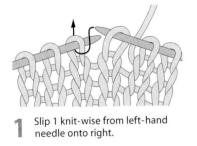
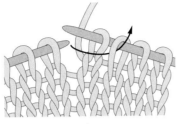
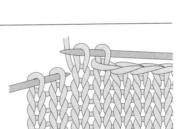

1 Slip 1 knit-wise from left-hand needle onto right.

2 Knit 1 as usual.

3 Pass slip stitch over knit stitch (as shown above).

The result is a left-slanting decrease.

Binding off in knit

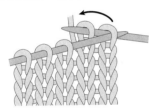
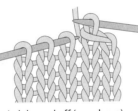

1 Knit 2 stitches as usual.

2 With left-hand needle, pass first stitch on right-hand needle over second stitch on right-hand needle.

3 1 stitch bound off (see above).
Knit 1 more stitch.

4 Pass first stitch over second.

5 Repeat Steps 3–4 until only 1 stitch remains on right-hand needle. Cut yarn to a minimum of 4", take stitch off needle, draw yarn through this stitch, and pull to close.

Ripping back

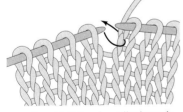
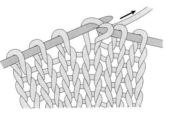

1 Insert left-hand needle through stitch below first stitch on right-hand needle as shown above.

2 Pull right-hand needle out of stitch, and pull working yarn free.

Tightening the bind-off

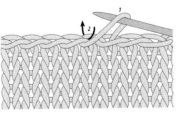
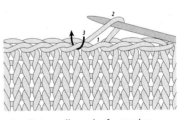

1 Put needle (knitting or tapestry) under front edge of first loop of bind-off. Pull thread toward you; then remove needle.

2 Find the back edge of this same loop (see above), put needle under it, pull excess thread through; then remove needle.

3 Put needle under front edge of next loop of bind-off (as shown by arrow). Pull excess thread toward you, then remove needle.
Repeat Steps 2–3, pulling excess across row.
At end of row, draw excess through final stitch.

b

Back The part of the garment worn to the back of the body

back The side of the knitting not facing while working a row or round

beginning with What you will do next

binding off Closing off stitches

blocking A finishing procedure to which you submit your pieces

casting on Creating a number of stitches, usually by adding them onto the left-hand needle

cm **centimeter** Measure of length equaling .4 of 1"

chart A graphical representation of a knit fabric (with symbols indicating how the fabric is produced)

decreasing Removing a stitch by making two stitches into one

dpn(s) **double-pointed needle(s)** Needle(s) with points at both ends

ending with What you have just finished doing

f

Front The part of the garment worn to the front of the body

front The side of the knitting facing while working a row or round

fulling A controlled process of deliberately shrinking wool to a more felt-like fabric

fulling factor A number by which you multiply (and then work to) all pattern lengths so your piece will measure as directed after fulling

garter stitch The fabric produced by knitting all stitches, all rows

garter ridge A horizontal line of bumps produced by knitting two rows

gauge The number of stitches and rows measured over a specific distance (usually 4"/10cm)

grafting A method of sewing live stitches together that looks like a row of knitting

I-cord A small knit tube produced by working stitches on double-pointed needles without turning at ends of rows

increasing Adding a stitch by making one stitch into two

k **knit** Produce a knit stitch (a stitch with its 'bump' to the back)

k2tog **knit two together** Knit two stitches as if they were one (a right-slanting decrease)

kb **knit into the back of a stitch** Knit into the part of the stitch on the back of the needle

kf **knit into the front of a stitch** Knit into the part of the stitch on the front of the needle

kf&b **knit into the front and back of a stitch** Knit into the front and then the back of the same stitch (a form of increasing)

knit stitch A stitch with its 'bump' to the back

k-wise **knit-wise** As if to knit

Left (Front or Back) The part of the garment worn on the left of the body

leading edge The part of the stitch closest to the tip of the needle

lengthwise edging An edging worked back and forth over a few stitches and usually joined to the piece at the end of alternate rows

lifted increase Knitting into the stitch below the next stitch on the left-hand needle and then working the next stitch on the left-hand needle (a form of increasing)

live stitches Stitches that are ready to be worked into (not bound off)

M1 **Make 1** Picking up the thread between the needles and working into the back of it (a form of increasing)

m **meter** Measure of length equaling 39½" or 100 centimeters (cm)

non-leading edge The part of the stitch farthest from the tip of the needle

picking up Forming stitches by inserting left-hand needle, from left to right, along a finished edge, without using yarn and without knitting a new row

picking up and knitting Forming stitches by inserting right-hand needle into a finished edge, from right to left, using yarn and knitting a new row

p **purl** Produce a purl stitch (a stitch with its 'bump' to the front)

p2tog **purl 2 together** Purl two stitches together as if they were one (a left-slanting decrease on purl side of fabric, a right-slanting decrease on knit side of fabric)

p-wise **purl-wise** As if to purl

reverse shaping Shaping one piece in mirror image of another piece

rib A fabric produced by combining knits and purls in the same row

Right (Front or Back) The part of the garment worn on the right of the body

RS   **right side** The 'public' side of the garment

RSS   **reverse stockinette stitch** The bumpy side of the fabric that is the wrong side of knitting in rounds or that is produced by purling all stitches in rounds or by purling all stitches on wrong-side rows and knitting all stitches on right-side rows when working flat

rnd   **round** A row worked circularly, with no turning at the end

row A row worked flat, turning at the end

selvedge stitches Stitches at the edge of the piece, often taken into seam allowances

short row A row with stitches left behind, by turning before the end of a row

sl   **slip** Transfer a stitch from left- to right-hand needle without working it

SKP   **slip one, knit 1, pass slip stitch over** Slip first stitch from left-hand needle knit-wise, knit the next stitch on left-hand needle, then pass the slip stitch over the stitch just knit (a left-slanting decrease)

sl 1 k-wise   **slip 1 knit-wise** Slip the next stitch from the left-hand needle, as if to knit

sl 1 p-wise   **slip 1 purl-wise** Slip the next stitch from the left-hand needle, as if to purl

sl st   **slip stitch** A stitch transferred from left-hand needle to right-hand needle without working it

SSK   **slip, slip, knit** Slip first stitch from left-hand needle knit-wise, slip next stitch from left-hand needle knit-wise, insert left-hand needle through front of both stitches from left to right, then knit two together as one (a left-slanting decrease)

SSP   **slip, slip, purl** Slip first stitch from left-hand needle knit-wise, slip next stitch from left-hand needle knit-wise, slip both stitches back onto left-hand needle, insert right-hand needle through back of both stitches from left to right, then purl two together as one (a right-slanting decrease on purl side of fabric, a left-slanting decrease on knit side of fabric)

st(s)   **stitch(es)** Loop(s) formed with yarn on the knitting needles

St st   **stockinette stitch** The smooth side of the fabric that is produced by knitting all stitches in rounds or by knitting all stitches on right-side rows and purling all stitches on wrong-side rows when working flat

tail The 'thread' at the beginning or end of a ball or piece

turn Turn work to opposite side, even if in the middle of a row

yb   **with yarn in back** With yarn on the side of your knitting not facing you

yf   **with yarn in front** With yarn on the side of your knitting facing you

working flat Working a row, turning the piece, then working the next row

working in rounds Working a row, then working the next row without turning the piece (also known as *working circularly*)

working straight Continuing without any shaping (increasing, decreasing, etc.)

WS   **Wrong side** The 'non-public' side of the garment

yd   **yard** Measure of length equaling 36" or .9144 meter (m)

yarn The 'thread' with which you form stitches

yo   **yarn over** A stitch produced by laying or wrapping yarn over the right-hand needle

PROJECT INDEX

MEDITATION INDEX

ACKNOWLEDGEMENTS

This series would have pleased my father and his insistence upon striving for excellence. *The Purl Stitch* is dedicated to his memory.

There would not be such beautiful knitting books in the world without the vision and leadership at XRX: Alexis (whose photos make grown women weep), David (who has all the answers), and Elaine (in whom I place absolute trust). And then there's the production crew who do great work in a spirited environment: Bob, Carol, Denny, Ev, Gail, Holly, Jason, Jay, Nancy, Natalie, Rick, and Sue. I am grateful to have found my place amongst you.

Thanks to the yarn companies who responded so generously. Special thanks to the talented (for her styling) and wily (because she made me look) Bev Nimon.

Thanks to the knitters who worked from less-than-perfect directions to test knit or produce the garments of this book: Norma Hounsell, Karen Ireland, Caddy Ledbetter, Lynn Philips, Elaine Rowley, Tricia Siemens, and most especially Stasia Bania (plus her son Conrad, who probably helped some).

I wish to express sincere gratitude to all who responded so positively to *The Knit Stitch*. Your enthusiasm sustains and inspires me. Special thanks to Michele Landsberg who isn't a knitter but is still one of us.

Things happen—bad or good—and isn't it wonderful to have open-hearted friends who talk and listen, who put the ground beneath us, who remind us who (and how lucky) we are. Students, family, friends, co-workers: you helped more than you know with every kind word. And I must say that over this past year I have been especially reliant upon and grateful for Victoria Calhoun, Heather Daymond, Barbara Lamb, and Tricia Siemens.

I am truly supported and blessed by my very grown-up children—my most wise and beautiful daughter Caddy, my most bright and fearless son Jeremy. Be safe.

Finally, and from the cells of my heart, thanks to Laurel Thom, who gave me life and taught me to breathe.

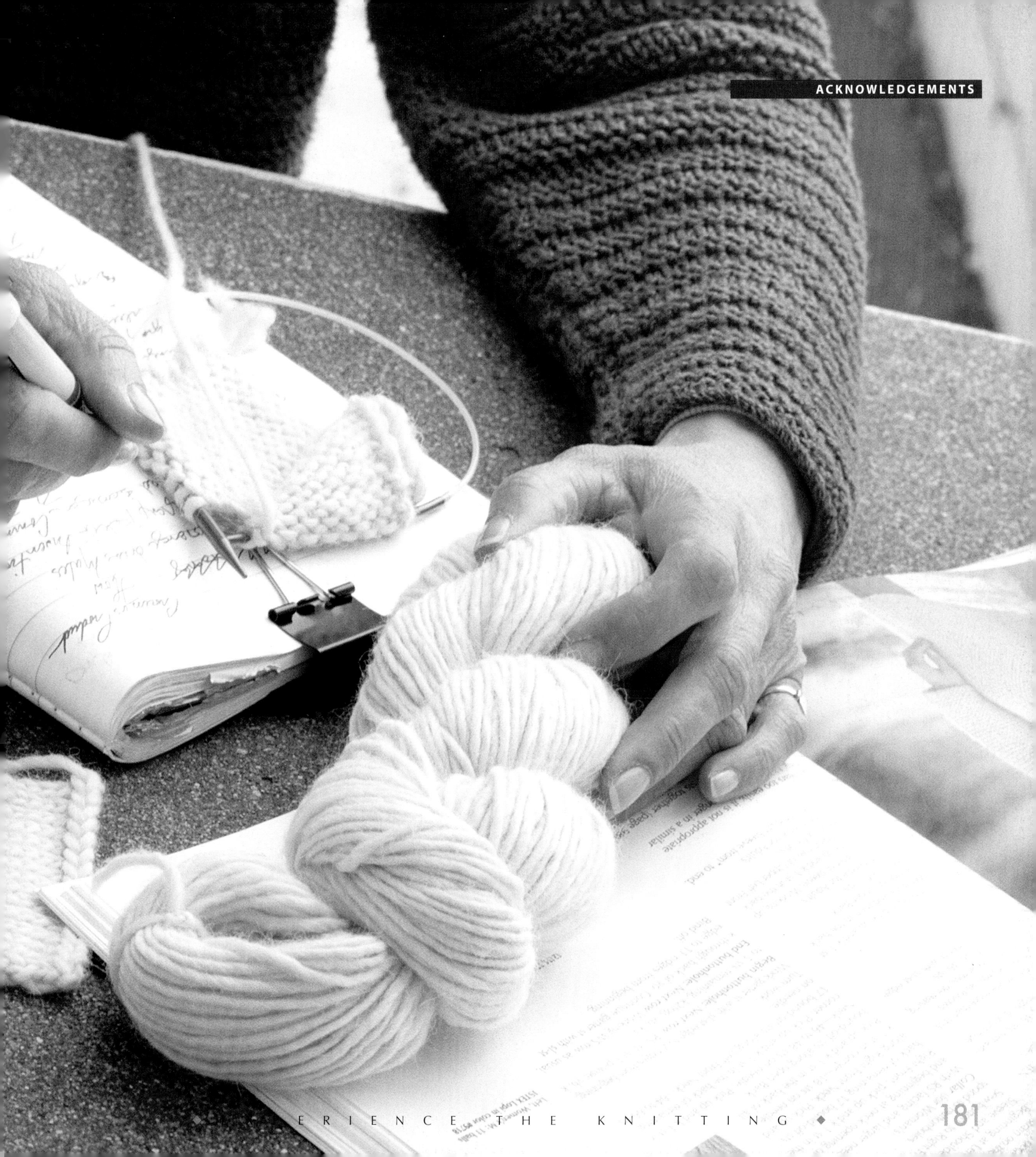

AN ACCIDENTAL KNITTER

"All my life I've wanted to be a writer," Sally Melville says. "I just found an unusual way to become one. And when you connect what you love—knitting—with what you're trained to do—teaching how to learn—then you're doing your life's work.

"I didn't spend my childhood thinking I would become a professional knitter. And why not? Activities like knitting have sustained human beings for thousands of years. And isn't it nice to think about them in ways other than just producing a garment? They do so much more for the heart, the mind, the spirit.

"Don't get me wrong; I love the patterns of the book, but I also love its voice. The Meditations are the most fun part of the book to read—and the part I'm most proud of. It's wonderful that people are willing to listen to someone speak seriously, honorably about knitting."

It's one thing for a favorite author to meditate. But picturing those meditations for the printed page? Would a piano, a flute, a synthesizer do? No, Sally had to have drums. So off we went, driving around Sioux Falls in search of a set.

At Schmidt Music on 41st Street we found not just the perfect red drums but nice people who handed Sally those little sticks. Who knew Sally could flood a store with sound? All I could see through the lens was a blur of motion.

"Alexis gets me bubbling away about what's important in my life," Sally says, "and the next thing I know we're in a music store and I'm playing the drums! Or in the bathtub, for heaven's sake!"

What better place to meditate than a hot bath? And, after stylist Natalie Sorenson's magic touch—silver candlesticks, floating candles, color-coordinated towels, a glass of wine, and, oh, yes, Sally's knitting—how could that shot *not* make it into the book? And what better way to illustrate the Flow Experience than the mighty, roaring falls of the Big Sioux?

(Clockwise from top) Sporting a new look for *Book 3*; served by Mr. Gyros; music shopping at Barnes & Noble; teaching Violetta and Leonora to walk on a leash; at our favorite diner.

The Knit Stitch.

"There has been a heartwarming response to *The Knit Stitch*," Sally says. "I've taught learning skills, and I know how difficult it is to learn from a book, how hard it can be to read instructions. I know the reluctance and frustration you can encounter as you puzzle through drawings and arrows. We did the skills with hands, in incremental movements, so that people could learn in a 'real' environment. It worked. We've had amazing responses from people who learned to knit with the book. Two of my favorites are from Jim Kalbfleisch, former vice president of the University of Waterloo, who knitted over five feet on a scarf—while his wife was out of town—by just looking at the book. A woman who teaches disadvantaged people in Seattle emailed me to say that one of her students, who cannot read or process verbal instructions, learned to knit from the photos.

"Remember how many photos you took the first time to get the hands right? But after we got our system in place, the second book was more like filling in the blanks. We knew what we were doing, and it went so smoothly, listening to Edith Piaf all the while." I smile thinking of the long hours Sally spent caged in reflectors, under my hot tungsten lights. If she ever tires of being an author, she just might have a career as a hand model.

Models were the problem while shooting in the Windy City—they wanted to keep Sally's garments. "I love it when people say to me, 'I knit this from your book,'" Sally says. "I know I've got to figure out designs that are going to work for 25-year-olds like my daughter, and for women my age. Some of the designs are pretty sexy, some are classic, some ethereal; many of the garments feature something odd, exceptional, even funky. I want you to love knitting them because of all the attention to detail, so you can get it right. Bands that work well, pieces that seam together properly, buttonholes that are just right so they will fit you, so you're going to love wearing them. I'm also thrilled when people tell me that they like reading the book and that some have bought it for non-knitters. On to the next one! But what are we going to do to top the cover of the second book?"

Shot against a luminous Chicago mosaic of Marc Chagall, Art Director Bob Natz's design for *The Purl Stitch* called for the orange dress to be painstakingly separated from all those colorful, tiny tesserae (see page 60). It took many, many hours, but David Xenakis, Dennis Pearson, and our production team professionals did just that—over and over again, seven over cover dresses in all.

But it wasn't all cataracts, music stores, and bathtubs. *The Purl Stitch* needed a couple more locations. So off we went to our favorite studio—Chicago! Leafy, expansive Michigan Avenue provided just the right background of cityscape and woods, and continuity with Sally's first book in *The Knitting Experience* series,

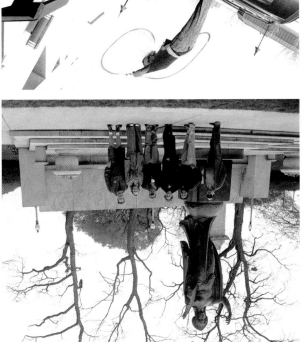

—Alexis Xenakis
Sioux Falls, South Dakota

The Greek Islands that will provide the whitewashed background for the cover?" Sally says. "Off to Greece," Sally says. "We'll just have to take our favorite model with us."

"I'm already working on the cover garment for the third book, *Color*," Sally says. "Do you have any background ideas?"

Shooting in Chicago (top) and Sioux Falls (bottom).